# Borderline Personality Disorder

A Medical Dictionary, Bibliography, and Annotated Research Guide to Internet References

James N. Parker, M.D.
and Philip M. Parker, Ph.D., Editors

ICON Health Publications
ICON Group International, Inc.
4370 La Jolla Village Drive, 4th Floor
San Diego, CA 92122 USA



Printed in the United States of America.

Last digit indicates print number: 10 9 8 7 6 4 5 3 2 1

Publisher, Health Care: Philip Parker, Ph.D.
Editor(s): James Parker, M.D., Philip Parker, Ph.D.

**Publisher's note: The ideas, procedures, and suggestions contained in this book are not intended for the diagnosis or treatment of a health problem.** As new medical or scientific information becomes available from academic and clinical research, recommended treatments and drug therapies may undergo changes. The authors, editors, and publisher have attempted to make the information in this book up to date and accurate in accord with accepted standards at the time of publication. The authors, editors, and publisher are not responsible for errors or omissions or for consequences from application of the book, and make no warranty, expressed or implied, in regard to the contents of this book. Any practice described in this book should be applied by the reader in accordance with professional standards of care used in regard to the unique circumstances that may apply in each situation. The reader is advised to always check product information (package inserts) for changes and new information regarding dosage and contraindications before prescribing any drug or pharmacological product. Caution is especially urged when using new or infrequently ordered drugs, herbal remedies, vitamins and supplements, alternative therapies, complementary therapies and medicines, and integrative medical treatments.

**Cataloging-in-Publication Data**

Parker, James N., 1961-
Parker, Philip M., 1960-

Borderline Personality Disorder: A Medical Dictionary, Bibliography, and Annotated Research Guide to Internet References / James N. Parker and Philip M. Parker, editors
p. cm.
Includes bibliographical references, glossary, and index.
ISBN: 0-597-83769-4
1. Borderline Personality Disorder-Popular works. I. Title.

# Disclaimer

This publication is not intended to be used for the diagnosis or treatment of a health problem. It is sold with the understanding that the publisher, editors, and authors are not engaging in the rendering of medical, psychological, financial, legal, or other professional services.

References to any entity, product, service, or source of information that may be contained in this publication should not be considered an endorsement, either direct or implied, by the publisher, editors, or authors. ICON Group International, Inc., the editors, and the authors are not responsible for the content of any Web pages or publications referenced in this publication.

# Copyright Notice

# Acknowledgements

The collective knowledge generated from academic and applied research summarized in various references has been critical in the creation of this book which is best viewed as a comprehensive compilation and collection of information prepared by various official agencies which produce publications on borderline personality disorder. Books in this series draw from various agencies and institutions associated with the United States Department of Health and Human Services, and in particular, the Office of the Secretary of Health and Human Services (OS), the Administration for Children and Families (ACF), the Administration on Aging (AOA), the Agency for Healthcare Research and Quality (AHRQ), the Agency for Toxic Substances and Disease Registry (ATSDR), the Centers for Disease Control and Prevention (CDC), the Food and Drug Administration (FDA), the Healthcare Financing Administration (HCFA), the Health Resources and Services Administration (HRSA), the Indian Health Service (IHS), the institutions of the National Institutes of Health (NIH), the Program Support Center (PSC), and the Substance Abuse and Mental Health Services Administration (SAMHSA). In addition to these sources, information gathered from the National Library of Medicine, the United States Patent Office, the European Union, and their related organizations has been invaluable in the creation of this book. Some of the work represented was financially supported by the Research and Development Committee at INSEAD. This support is gratefully acknowledged. Finally, special thanks are owed to Tiffany Freeman for her excellent editorial support.

# About the Editors

**James N. Parker, M.D.**

Dr. James N. Parker received his Bachelor of Science degree in Psychobiology from the University of California, Riverside and his M.D. from the University of California, San Diego. In addition to authoring numerous research publications, he has lectured at various academic institutions. Dr. Parker is the medical editor for health books by ICON Health Publications.

**Philip M. Parker, Ph.D.**

Philip M. Parker is the Eli Lilly Chair Professor of Innovation, Business and Society at INSEAD (Fontainebleau, France and Singapore). Dr. Parker has also been Professor at the University of California, San Diego and has taught courses at Harvard University, the Hong Kong University of Science and Technology, the Massachusetts Institute of Technology, Stanford University, and UCLA. Dr. Parker is the associate editor for ICON Health Publications.

# About ICON Health Publications

To discover more about ICON Health Publications, simply check with your preferred online booksellers, including Barnes & Noble.com and Amazon.com which currently carry all of our titles. Or, feel free to contact us directly for bulk purchases or institutional discounts:

ICON Group International, Inc.
4370 La Jolla Village Drive, Fourth Floor
San Diego, CA 92122 USA
Fax: 858-546-4341
Web site: **www.icongrouponline.com/health**

# Table of Contents

FORWARD ... 1
CHAPTER 1. STUDIES ON BORDERLINE PERSONALITY DISORDER ... 3
*Overview* ... 3
*Federally Funded Research on Borderline Personality Disorder* ... 3
*The National Library of Medicine: PubMed* ... 21
CHAPTER 2. NUTRITION AND BORDERLINE PERSONALITY DISORDER ... 65
*Overview* ... 65
*Finding Nutrition Studies on Borderline Personality Disorder* ... 65
*Federal Resources on Nutrition* ... 67
*Additional Web Resources* ... 67
CHAPTER 3. ALTERNATIVE MEDICINE AND BORDERLINE PERSONALITY DISORDER ... 69
*Overview* ... 69
*National Center for Complementary and Alternative Medicine* ... 69
*Additional Web Resources* ... 74
*General References* ... 75
CHAPTER 4. DISSERTATIONS ON BORDERLINE PERSONALITY DISORDER ... 77
*Overview* ... 77
*Dissertations on Borderline Personality Disorder* ... 77
*Keeping Current* ... 80
CHAPTER 5. CLINICAL TRIALS AND BORDERLINE PERSONALITY DISORDER ... 81
*Overview* ... 81
*Recent Trials on Borderline Personality Disorder* ... 81
*Keeping Current on Clinical Trials* ... 81
CHAPTER 6. PATENTS ON BORDERLINE PERSONALITY DISORDER ... 83
*Overview* ... 83
*Patents on Borderline Personality Disorder* ... 83
*Patent Applications on Borderline Personality Disorder* ... 85
*Keeping Current* ... 86
CHAPTER 7. BOOKS ON BORDERLINE PERSONALITY DISORDER ... 87
*Overview* ... 87
*Book Summaries: Online Booksellers* ... 87
*Chapters on Borderline Personality Disorder* ... 90
CHAPTER 8. MULTIMEDIA ON BORDERLINE PERSONALITY DISORDER ... 91
*Overview* ... 91
*Bibliography: Multimedia on Borderline Personality Disorder* ... 91
CHAPTER 9. PERIODICALS AND NEWS ON BORDERLINE PERSONALITY DISORDER ... 93
*Overview* ... 93
*News Services and Press Releases* ... 93
*Newsletter Articles* ... 95
*Academic Periodicals covering Borderline Personality Disorder* ... 95
CHAPTER 10. RESEARCHING MEDICATIONS ... 97
*Overview* ... 97
*U.S. Pharmacopeia* ... 97
*Commercial Databases* ... 98
APPENDIX A. PHYSICIAN RESOURCES ... 101
*Overview* ... 101
*NIH Guidelines* ... 101
*NIH Databases* ... 103
*Other Commercial Databases* ... 105
APPENDIX B. PATIENT RESOURCES ... 107
*Overview* ... 107

*Patient Guideline Sources* ........ *107*
*Finding Associations* ........ *109*
APPENDIX C. FINDING MEDICAL LIBRARIES ........ 111
*Overview* ........ *111*
*Preparation* ........ *111*
*Finding a Local Medical Library* ........ *111*
*Medical Libraries in the U.S. and Canada* ........ *111*

**ONLINE GLOSSARIES ........ 117**

*Online Dictionary Directories* ........ *118*

**BORDERLINE PERSONALITY DISORDER DICTIONARY ........ 119**

**INDEX ........ 147**

# FORWARD

In March 2001, the National Institutes of Health issued the following warning: "The number of Web sites offering health-related resources grows every day. Many sites provide valuable information, while others may have information that is unreliable or misleading."[1] Furthermore, because of the rapid increase in Internet-based information, many hours can be wasted searching, selecting, and printing. Since only the smallest fraction of information dealing with borderline personality disorder is indexed in search engines, such as **www.google.com** or others, a non-systematic approach to Internet research can be not only time consuming, but also incomplete. This book was created for medical professionals, students, and members of the general public who want to know as much as possible about borderline personality disorder, using the most advanced research tools available and spending the least amount of time doing so.

In addition to offering a structured and comprehensive bibliography, the pages that follow will tell you where and how to find reliable information covering virtually all topics related to borderline personality disorder, from the essentials to the most advanced areas of research. Public, academic, government, and peer-reviewed research studies are emphasized. Various abstracts are reproduced to give you some of the latest official information available to date on borderline personality disorder. Abundant guidance is given on how to obtain free-of-charge primary research results via the Internet. **While this book focuses on the field of medicine, when some sources provide access to non-medical information relating to borderline personality disorder, these are noted in the text.**

E-book and electronic versions of this book are fully interactive with each of the Internet sites mentioned (clicking on a hyperlink automatically opens your browser to the site indicated). If you are using the hard copy version of this book, you can access a cited Web site by typing the provided Web address directly into your Internet browser. You may find it useful to refer to synonyms or related terms when accessing these Internet databases. **NOTE:** At the time of publication, the Web addresses were functional. However, some links may fail due to URL address changes, which is a common occurrence on the Internet.

For readers unfamiliar with the Internet, detailed instructions are offered on how to access electronic resources. For readers unfamiliar with medical terminology, a comprehensive glossary is provided. For readers without access to Internet resources, a directory of medical libraries, that have or can locate references cited here, is given. We hope these resources will prove useful to the widest possible audience seeking information on borderline personality disorder.

*The Editors*

---

[1] From the NIH, National Cancer Institute (NCI): **http://www.cancer.gov/cancerinfo/ten-things-to-know.**

# Chapter 1. Studies on Borderline Personality Disorder

## Overview

In this chapter, we will show you how to locate peer-reviewed references and studies on borderline personality disorder.

## Federally Funded Research on Borderline Personality Disorder

The U.S. Government supports a variety of research studies relating to borderline personality disorder. These studies are tracked by the Office of Extramural Research at the National Institutes of Health.[2] CRISP (Computerized Retrieval of Information on Scientific Projects) is a searchable database of federally funded biomedical research projects conducted at universities, hospitals, and other institutions.

Search the CRISP Web site at **http://crisp.cit.nih.gov/crisp/crisp_query.generate_screen**. You will have the option to perform targeted searches by various criteria, including geography, date, and topics related to borderline personality disorder.

For most of the studies, the agencies reporting into CRISP provide summaries or abstracts. As opposed to clinical trial research using patients, many federally funded studies use animals or simulated models to explore borderline personality disorder. The following is typical of the type of information found when searching the CRISP database for borderline personality disorder:

- **Project Title: A COGNITIVE GROUP TREATMENT FOR BORDERLINE OUTPATIENTS**

  Principal Investigator & Institution: Black, Donald W.; Professor; Psychiatry; University of Iowa Iowa City, Ia 52242

---

2 Healthcare projects are funded by the National Institutes of Health (NIH), Substance Abuse and Mental Health Services (SAMHSA), Health Resources and Services Administration (HRSA), Food and Drug Administration (FDA), Centers for Disease Control and Prevention (CDCP), Agency for Healthcare Research and Quality (AHRQ), and Office of Assistant Secretary of Health (OASH).

Timing: Fiscal Year 2002; Project Start 09-JUL-2002; Project End 30-JUN-2006

Summary: The goal of this project is to test the efficacy of a new cognitive-behavioral systems-based group treatment for persons with **borderline personality disorder** (BPD) and to compare it to "treatment as usual" (TAU). We elected to modify a program originally developed by Bartels and Crotty. This led us to develop STEPPS, an acronym that stands for Systems Training for Emotional Predictability and Problem Solving. Briefly, the program involves both cognitive-behavioral techniques and skills training combined with a systems component; the latter involves the patients with BPD and those in their system, including family members, friends, and health care professionals. STEPPS involves twenty 2-hour group meetings with two facilitators; the therapy is manual-based and each week specific goals are set. We propose to recruit approximately 160 adults with DSM-IV BPD during the first 2 1/2 years of the project. Subjects will be recruited through referral from area psychologists, psychiatrists, mental health clinics, and hospitals. Subjects will be screened using the Revised Diagnostic Interview for Borderlines (DIB-R) and relevant sections of the Structured Interview for DSM-IV Personality Disorders (SIDP-IV). Appropriate subjects meeting specified inclusion/exclusion criteria will be randomized to STEPPS or TAU. Subjects in both groups will be allowed to continue to see their psychiatrist, take psychotropic medication, and continue with other therapy. Baseline assessments will include the Structured Clinical Interview for DSM-IV, the SIDP- IV, the Hollingshead Scale, the Social Adjustment Scale, the Beck Depression Inventory, the Positive and Negative Affectivity Scale, the Symptom Checklist-90-R, the Barrett Impulsivity Scale, and the Medical Outcomes Study Short Form Health Survey. A new self-rated scale, the Borderline Evaluation of Severity Over Time (BEST), will also be used to rate BPD symptoms. Subjects will be assessed at baseline, and at weeks 4, 8, 12, 16, and 20. Lay and professional support system members (informants) will be asked to rate the subjects progress at specified intervals. Satisfaction with STEPPS and TAU will be assessed in informants and subjects at the conclusion of the trial. Therapy fidelity will be maintained through regular supervision, and blind ratings of videotaped sessions. Subjects randomized to STEPPS will be followed up at months 1, 3, 6, 9, and 12 post-study completion. We hypothesize that subjects participating in STEPPS will have better symptomatic improvement than subjects receiving TAU; improvement will include greater mood stability, less deliberate self-harm, less anger/impulsivity, and lower rates of health care utilization. We hypothesize that the gains of STEPPS will be maintained over 1 year. These findings should add to our understanding of the appropriate clinical management of BPD. If the efficacy of STEPPS is confirmed, future studies will include larger samples to help test whether specific subgroups will preferentially respond, and comparisons of STEPPS to other programs, including Dialectical Behavior Therapy.

Website: http://crisp.cit.nih.gov/crisp/Crisp_Query.Generate_Screen

- **Project Title: ANATOMICAL BASIS OF DISORDERS OF EXECUTIVE FUNCTION**

  Principal Investigator & Institution: Bechara, Antoine; Assistant Professor; University of Iowa Iowa City, Ia 52242

  Timing: Fiscal Year 2001; Project Start 01-JUL-1983; Project End 30-JUN-2005

  Summary: The overall aim of this project is the investigation of the neurobiological basis of reasoning and decision-making, guided by a specific theoretical framework, the "somatic marker hypothesis". The hypothesis posits that decision-making defects in the personal and social realms are the result of defective engagement of emotion related signals ("somatic markers") that normally operate, covertly or overtly, to facilitate the process of making advantageous choices. In the current funding period, we have investigate anatomical, physiological, and cognitive aspects of a neural network presumed to underlie somatic marker activation and decision making. We confirmed that dysfunction in the ventromedial (VM) prefrontal cortex leads to a failure to enact somatic states and to decision-making defects. However, lesions in other neural regions, including the amygdala and the somatosensory cortices (SII, SI, and insula) also compromise somatic state activation and decision-making, suggesting that these several regions are part of a neural system involved in decision-making. Guided by the results obtained so far, the new studies we propose aim at defining the functional roles played by these components, and by others we propose here. The studies call for the testing of several hypotheses of several hypotheses using the lesion approached in cognitive and psychophysiological experiments. Disorders of decision-making are A prominent feature of the "dysexecutive syndrome" seen in stroke, head injury, and brain tumors. Such disorders are also prevalent in drug addiction, psychopathy, and **borderline personality disorder.** Our results will contribute to the understanding of normal and pathological mechanisms of decision- making and lead to the development of novel behavioral and pharmacological management strategies.

Website: http://crisp.cit.nih.gov/crisp/Crisp_Query.Generate_Screen

- **Project Title: ATTACHMENT AND PSYCHOTHERAPY IN PATIENTS WITH BPD**

  Principal Investigator & Institution: Levy, Kenneth N,.; Assistant Professor; Psychiatry; Weill Medical College of Cornell Univ New York, Ny 10021

  Timing: Fiscal Year 2001; Project Start 24-JUN-2001

  Summary: Borderline personality disorder (BPD) is a highly prevalent and chronic psychiatric problem characterized by a pattern of chaotic, self-defeating interpersonal relationships, emotional instability, poor impulse control, chronic anger, frequent suicidality, self-mutilation and has a high risk of suicide. Not surprisingly, BPD has been associated with higher levels of service use in emergency room, daycare, and inpatient settings. Although, preliminary evidence suggest that psychotherapy treatment is helpful in reducing borderline pathology, controlled studies are rare and the mechanisms that promote change remain unspecified. Clinical investigators have noted that fundamental aspects of **borderline personality disorder** can be understood as stemming from impairments in patients underlying attachment organization. The attachment theory constructs of internal working models, coherence, and reflective function provide an important means for understanding how psychotherapy may directly influence BPD. In a sample of 140 patients with BPD, randomly assigned to either a modified psychodynamic treatment called transference-focused psychotherapy (TFP), a cognitive behavioral therapy called Dialectic Behavioral Therapy (DBT), or a treatment as ususal. Supportive Psychotherapy (SPT), the current study using a multi-method approach to data collection, including self-report, interview, and global and micro- analytic coding of observational data, assesses the efficacy of these treatments and the mediating role of attachment, through examining effect sizes and growth curve analyses and regression analyses. By examining the psychological mechanisms that contribute to and mediate BPD this study hopes to inform psychological interventions and promote adaptation and optimal mental health.

  Website: http://crisp.cit.nih.gov/crisp/Crisp_Query.Generate_Screen

- **Project Title: CLINICAL NEUROSCIENCE RESEARCH TRAINING IN PSYCHIATRY**

  Principal Investigator & Institution: Heninger, George R.; Professor; Psychiatry; Yale University 47 College Street, Suite 203 New Haven, Ct 065208047

Timing: Fiscal Year 2001; Project Start 30-SEP-1996; Project End 30-JUN-2006

Summary: (Provided by applicant): This training program is designed to meet the national goal of increasing the number of fully trained research psychiatrists conducting research in mental health. In order to be effective independent investigators, research psychiatrists must be fully trained in both clinical neuroscience and modern clinical research. The ever increasing complexity of the science and clinical research methods requires that they receive specialized training in order to take full advantage of the rapid advances occurring in the field. This program will utilize a curriculum designed to give the trainee mastery of the fundamentals of basic molecular and cellular neurobiology, neuropharmacology, neuroimaging, psychiatric genetics and the ethics and methods used in clinical research in psychiatry. At the core of the training program is a two-year clinical neuroscience research preceptorship with one or more of the 8 senior training faculty and 19 additional faculty members who have a proven productive research tract record and who are currently involved in intensive clinical neuroscience research in psychiatry. The rich training environment is supported by 9 separate nationally funded research programs within the Department of Psychiatry including: 1) The Clinical Research Center for the Study of Mental Illness, 2) A Program Project on the Neurobiology of Major Psychiatric Disorders, 3) A Schizophrenia Research Center, 4) A Depression Research Center, 5) The National Center for the Neurobiologic Study of Post-traumatic Stress Disorder, 6) An Alcohol Research Center, 7) A Neuroimaging Program that includes SPECT, PET, MRI and Spectroscopy, 8) A Clinical Research Center for the study of Opiate and Cocaine Addiction, and 9) A National Center for the Study of **Borderline Personality Disorder.** Trainees will conduct their research studies in specialized inpatient and outpatient research facilities and clinics and the resources from other basic science programs within the Department and Medical School will also be utilized. For the past twenty-five years the Research Faculty in the Department have had an outstanding record of training nationally prominent researchers in psychiatry. The renewal of this application for stipend support for 4 trainees each year will allow this program to continue to contribute towards the national goal of increasing the number of fully trained research psychiatrists.

Website: http://crisp.cit.nih.gov/crisp/Crisp_Query.Generate_Screen

- **Project Title: CLINICAL TRIALS NETWORK: NEW MEXICO NODE**

  Principal Investigator & Institution: Miller, William R.; Distinguished Professor; Psychology; University of New Mexico Albuquerque Controller's Office Albuquerque, Nm 87131

  Timing: Fiscal Year 2002; Project Start 30-SEP-2002; Project End 31-AUG-2007

  Summary: (provided by applicant): The University of New Mexico Center on Alcoholism, Substance Abuse, and Addictions (CASAA) submits a revised application to join the NIDA Clinical Trials Network as a Regional Research and Training Center and coordinate a New Mexico Node. CASAA and the collaborating Department of Psychiatry of UNM's School of Medicine have well -established infrastructure for behavioral and pharmacotherapy trials, and long experience with collaborative and multisite trials in the addiction field. Particular strengths that the proposed New Mexico Node team can bring to the CTN include: 1) expertise in "Stage III" research on dissemination and training of evidence-based treatments 2) a well -established track record of clinical trials for both behavioral and pharmacotherapies 3) a high concentration (70%) of minority patients in the affiliated CTP's, and substantial experience in research on cultural influences on and adaptations of drug abuse treatment 4) longstanding experience in the development and evaluation of innovative treatment methods for substance use disorders 5) substantial clinical and research experience with challenging populations including dual disorders, the homeless, and runaway adolescents 6) expertise in studying the influence of mutual help (e.g., 12-step) programs on treatment outcomes, and more generally in research on spirituality and addictions 7) geographic representation of the border Southwest To illustrate CTN-wide research that could be initiated from the New Mexico node, protocol concepts for three clinical trials are described, encompassing a behavioral intervention, a pharmacotherapy, and methods for disseminating an evidence-based treatment into clinical practice.

Website: http://crisp.cit.nih.gov/crisp/Crisp_Query.Generate_Screen

- **Project Title: COLLABORATIVE LONGITUDINAL STUDY OF PERSONALITY DISORDER**

  Principal Investigator & Institution: Gunderson, John G.; Professor; Mc Lean Hospital (Belmont, Ma) Belmont, Ma 02478

  Timing: Fiscal Year 2001; Project Start 01-MAR-1996; Project End 31-MAY-2005

  Summary: APPLICANT'S ABSTRACT): This application is a revision of an application for 5 years continuation that was submitted in 1999. At that time a one year extension was awarded; this application is for four years. The overall aim of this study is to provide a comprehensive picture of the course and outcome of four specific personality disorders (PDs): schizotypal (STPD), borderline (BPD), avoidant (AVPD), and obsessive-compulsive (OCPD). The present application continues a multi-site collaborative effort to follow a carefully diagnosed sample of 668 subjects having either these representative PDs or major depressive disorder (MDD) (controls) for the period from 3 to a maximum of 6 years after recruitment. Sixty new minority subjects will be recruited and followed for at least 2 years. Using a prospective, longitudinal, repeated measures design, we will develop the same basic knowledge about course and outcome for the PDs that has previously resulted from similar investigations of affective and anxiety disorders, thus addressing an important gap in our knowledge. The extended period of follow-up is essential to discern clinically meaningful descriptions of course and outcome and their determinants. The sample is large enough and sufficiently diverse demographically to attain a unique array of results generalizable to most clinical settings. To accomplish our overall aim, we propose three approaches: I. descriptive, II. predictive, and III. validating. The descriptive approach will provide data on diagnostic stability of PDs, on presence and course of comorbid Axis I disorders, on persistence of functional impairment, and on utilization of health care resources that allow comparison between the PDs and to similar data on Axis I disorders. The predictive approach will identify clinically meaningful determinants of prognosis within and across PDs. The validating approach will examine the homogeneity of descriptive and longitudinal features for the PDs.

  Website: http://crisp.cit.nih.gov/crisp/Crisp_Query.Generate_Screen

- **Project Title: COLLABORATIVE LONGITUDINAL STUDY OF PERSONALITY DISORDER**

  Principal Investigator & Institution: Morey, Leslie C.; Professor; Psychology; Texas A&M University System College Station, Tx 778433578

  Timing: Fiscal Year 2001; Project Start 01-MAR-1996; Project End 31-MAY-2005

  Summary: (Adapted from Applicant's Abstract) The overall aim of this study is to provide a comprehensive picture of the course and outcome of four specific personality disorders (PDs): schizotypal (STPD), borderline (BPI), avoidant (AVPD), and obsessive-compulsive (OCPD). The present proposal continues a multi-site collaborative effort to follow a carefully diagnosed sample of 668 subjects having either these representative PDs or major depressive disorder (MDD) (controls) for the period from 2 to a minimum of 6 years after recruitment. Using a prospective, longitudinal, repeated measures design, we will develop the same basic knowledge about course and outcome for the PDs that has previously resulted from similar investigations of affective and anxiety disorders, thus addressing an important gap in our knowledge. The extended period of follow-up is essential to discern clinically meaningful descriptions of course and outcome and their determinants. The sample is large enough and sufficiently diverse demographically to attain a unique array of results generalized to most clinical settings. To accomplish our overall aim, we propose three approaches I. Descriptive, II. Predictive, and III. Validating. The descriptive approach will provide data on diagnostic stability of PDs, on presence and course of comorbid Axis I disorders, on persistence of functional impairment, and on utilization of health care resources that allow comparison between the PDs and similar data on Axis I disorders. The predictive approach will identify clinically meaningful determinants of prognosis within and across PDs. The validating approach will examine the homogeneity of descriptive and longitudinal features for the PDs, as defined by the DSM system, and how this compares with alternative schemes.

Website: http://crisp.cit.nih.gov/crisp/Crisp_Query.Generate_Screen

- **Project Title: COLLABORATIVE LONGITUDINAL STUDY OF PERSONALITY DISORDER**

  Principal Investigator & Institution: Shea, M T.; Associate Professor; Psychiatry and Human Behavior; Brown University Providence, Ri 02912

  Timing: Fiscal Year 2001; Project Start 01-MAR-1996; Project End 31-MAY-2005

  Summary: (APPLICANT'S ABSTRACT): The overall aim of this study is to provide a comprehensive picture of the course and outcome of four specific personality disorders (PDs): schizotypal (STPD), borderline (BPD), avoidant (AVPD), and obsessive-compulsive (OCPD). The present application continues a multi-site collaborative effort to follow a carefully diagnosed sample of 668 subjects having either these representative PDs or major depressive disorder (MDD) (controls) for the period from 3 to a maximum of 6 years after recruitment. Sixty new minority subjects will be recruited and followed for at least 2 years. Using a prospective, longitudinal, repeated measures design, we will develop the same basic knowledge about course and outcome for the PDs that has previously resulted from similar investigations of affective and anxiety disorders, thus addressing an important gap in our knowledge. The extended period of follow-up is essential to discern clinically meaningful descriptions of course and outcome and their determinants. The sample is large enough and sufficiently diverse demographically to attain a unique array of results generalizable to most clinical settings. To accomplish our overall aim, we propose three approaches: I. descriptive, II. predictive, and III. validating. The descriptive approach will provide data on diagnostic stability of PDs, on presence and course of comorbid Axis I disorders, on persistence of functional impairment, and on utilization of health care resources that allow comparison between the PDs and to similar data on Axis I disorders. The predictive approach will identify clinically meaningful determinants of prognosis within and across PDs. The validating approach will examine the homogeneity of descriptive and longitudinal features for the PDs.

  Website: http://crisp.cit.nih.gov/crisp/Crisp_Query.Generate_Screen

- **Project Title: CRF AND PERSONALITY DISORDER: BEHAVIORAL CORRELATES**

  Principal Investigator & Institution: Lee, Royce; Psychiatry; University of Chicago 5801 S Ellis Ave Chicago, Il 60637

  Timing: Fiscal Year 2003; Project Start 01-SEP-2003; Project End 31-AUG-2004

  Summary: (provided by applicant): The specifc aim of the proposed project is to test the hypothesis that history of childhood trauma as measured by the Childhood Trauma Questionnaire (CTQ) is associated with elevated CSF corticotropinreleasing factor (CRF) as measured by basal assessment of CSF CRF levels, and associated with elevated ACTH responses to oCRF Challenge in adult personality disorder (i.e. borderline personality disorder) subjects. This study will compare CSF CRF and ACTH response to oCRF in 10 personality disorder subjects with high scores on the Childhood Trauma Questionnaire with 10 personality disorder subjects with low scores on the Childhood Trauma Questionnaire. Personality disorder subjects will be otherwise healthy, without comorbid depression, posttraumatic stress disorder, or substance abuse. The 20 personality disorder subjects will be compared with 10 normal healthy controls with respect to CSF CRF level. A relationship between HPA axis function and childhood maltreatment has been previously described in adults with PTSD or Major depression and in primate and non-primate animal models of emotional/physical neglect. In this study, we seek to: a) replicate the history of childhood trauma/CRF relationship in PD subjects using basal CSF sampling of CRF; b) extend the findings of our previous study by examining both female and male personality disorder subjects; c) extend the findings by examing ACTH response to oCRF Challenge; d) compare CSF CRF and ACTH response to oCRF challenge to healthy normal controls. PD subjects will be prospectively identified as having been exposed to high amounts of childhood maltreatment or low amounts using scores from the Childhood Trauma Questionnaire (CTQ).20 male and female personality disorder subjects stratified into high vs. low CTQ score responders and 10 healthy normal controls will be admitted to our General Clinical Research Center for both lumbar puncture for CSF CRF and oCRF challenge.If this study is able to establish a relationship between history of childhood trauma and altered CSF CRF level and CRF responsivity (elevated ACTH response to oCRF challenge) in personality disordered subjects, this would allow for further work exploring the relationship between childhood trauma, HPA axis function, and stress reactivity in personality disorder.

  Website: http://crisp.cit.nih.gov/crisp/Crisp_Query.Generate_Screen

- **Project Title: DBT EFFECTIVENESS FOR BORDERLINE DEPRESSED PATIENTS**

  Principal Investigator & Institution: Chisholm-Stockard, Sarah M.; Psychiatry; University of Wisconsin Madison 750 University Ave Madison, Wi 53706

  Timing: Fiscal Year 2001; Project Start 01-DEC-2001

  Summary: Although dialectical behavior therapy (DBT) has been efficacious in controlled studies, its effectiveness in community settings, and for patients with **borderline personality disorder** (BPD) and comorbid depression, remain to be determined. My research will address these questions within the framework of effectiveness research, by comparing DBT with treatment as usual. Factors that contribute to patient attrition and outcome from DBT will also be identified, including universal change processes and patient characteristics. Individuals with comorbid BPD and major depressive disorder will be randomly assigned to either DBT or a treatment as usual condition. Assessments will be obtained prior to, during, and at posttreatment (12 months). DBT treatment adherence will be assessed and treatment groups will be compared on a number of outcome variables including severity of depression and number and severity of parasuicidal acts.

Website: http://crisp.cit.nih.gov/crisp/Crisp_Query.Generate_Screen

- **Project Title: DBT SKILLS COMPUTER TRAINING FOR BPD SUBSTANCE ABUSE**

  Principal Investigator & Institution: Dimeff, Linda A.; Behavioral Technology Transfer Group Transfer Group Seattle, Wa 98105

  Timing: Fiscal Year 2002; Project Start 30-SEP-2002; Project End 31-MAR-2003

  Summary: (provided by applicant): Substance use disorders (SUD) co-occurring with **borderline personality disorder** (BPD) pose serious and complex public health problems. Dialectical Behavior Therapy for Substance Abusers (DBT) is an efficacious psychosocial treatment for drug dependent individuals with BPD. Dissemination of evidence-based therapies is remains a high priority at NIDA. We propose to develop and evaluate an innovative computer-based modular training (CBMT) program for use by drug treatment providers to learn DBT. This CBMT will focus exclusively on teaching DBT skills. The Phase I prototype will be limited to teaching a set of "crisis survival" skills from Linehan's (1993) Skills Training for **Borderline Personality Disorder.** The DBT crisis survival CBMT developed in Phase I will include exploration and simulation environments to facilitate knowledge transfer. An iterative process of prototype development will be used where end-user feedback will drive prototype modifications to ensure its usability and acceptability to providers. An advisory board of DBT and behavior therapy experts will also be used to ensure that the prototype is scientifically sound and fidelity to the treatment manual is retained. Feedback will be obtained using focus groups and individual interviews with practitioners, and from the advisory board. Once prototype usability and acceptability is achieved, we will then conduct a randomized controlled trial (N=40) to evaluate gains in DBT skills knowledge, application and recollection of skills, and self-efficacy in applying DBT crisis survival skills.

  Website: http://crisp.cit.nih.gov/crisp/Crisp_Query.Generate_Screen

- **Project Title: DEVELOPMENT OF BORDERLINE PERSONALITY DISORDER FEATURES**

  Principal Investigator & Institution: Trull, Timothy J.; Professor; Psychology; University of Missouri Columbia 310 Jesse Hall Columbia, Mo 65211

  Timing: Fiscal Year 2001; Project Start 30-SEP-1995; Project End 30-APR-2003

  Summary: Borderline personality disorder (BPD) is a sever personality disorder that develops in early adulthood, and is characterized by a lack of control of anger, intense and frequent mood changes, impulsive acts, disturbed interpersonal relationships, and life-threatening behaviors. BPD is relatively prevalent in both clinical and nonclinical populations. Despite the prevalence of this condition, we know very little about how BPD features develop. Although a number of etiological factors have been proposed, studies exploring the etiological relevance of these factors suffer from a number of methodological limitations including: assessing subjects only after they have developed BPD, failing to assess gender effects, and employing cross-sectional designs. This application proposes a two-year prospective multi-cohort study of 500 18 year-old subjects that manifest varying degrees of BPD features; both genders will be equally represented. All subjects will be incoming freshman at the University of Missouri-Columbia, and subjects will complete a number of inventories and interviews at study intake (Time 1) and two-year follow-up (Time 2) that target the following constructs:

BPD and other personality disorder features; parental psychopathology; and abuse experiences in childhood. The proposed study has five major aims: (1) to assess the correspondence between alternative measures of BPD features (self-report and interview); (2) to assess the relationship between personality traits and BPD features and determine whether the relations remain significant after partialling out variance in BPD scores accounted for by gender, parental psychopathology childhood physical and sexual abuse, and Axis I pathology; (3) to assess the two-year stability of scores on BPD measures; (4) To evaluate several models of how BPD features develop over time that include personality trail childhood abuse experiences, and parental psychopathology as moderators or mediators; and (5) to assess the relationship between Time 1 BPD symptom scores and negative outcome across a number of domains functioning, and to evaluate the potential moderating influence of personality traits, childhood abuse, and parental psychopathology on the relationship between Time 1 BPD scores and outcome two years later. By addressing these five aims, factors influencing future BPD pathology will be identified, more comprehensive etiological mode for BPD will be empirically evaluated, the level of dysfunction exhibited by syndromal and subsyndromal subjects will be assessed, and the predictive validity of BPD scores will be determined.

Website: http://crisp.cit.nih.gov/crisp/Crisp_Query.Generate_Screen

- **Project Title: DIVALPROEX SODIUM/PLACEBO IN BORDERLINE PERSONALITY DIS**

  Principal Investigator & Institution: Hollander, Eric; Associate Professor; Mount Sinai School of Medicine of Cuny New York, Ny 10029

  Timing: Fiscal Year 2001

  Summary: There is no text on file for this abstract.

  Website: http://crisp.cit.nih.gov/crisp/Crisp_Query.Generate_Screen

- **Project Title: EATING DISORDERS AND IMPULSIVITY–A LONGITUDINAL STUDY**

  Principal Investigator & Institution: Wonderlich, Stephen A.; Neuropsychiatric Research Institute Fargo, Nd 58103

  Timing: Fiscal Year 2001; Project Start 15-SEP-2000; Project End 31-AUG-2003

  Summary: There is increasing empirical evidence suggesting that a significant subset of eating disordered individuals with high degrees of trait impulsivity display complicated psychopathology, negative course of their eating disorder, and do not respond well to traditional eating disorder treatments. Very little data is available about the day-to-day activities and behavioral patterns of these individuals, frequently referred to as "multi-impulsive" or borderline-type eating disordered patients. Furthermore, there is apparently no effective treatment for these individuals. This grant represents a conceptual model of self-destructive behavior in eating disordered individuals which incorporates both trait-constructs and daily events, moods, and behaviors to account for such self-destructive behavior. This model specifically examines the role of certain personality traits (affective lability, impulsivity), childhood adversity, daily events, daily moods, and daily coping behaviors in the prediction of self-destructive behavior. Furthermore, the present study proposes to test this model utilizing electronic daily diary technology to assess the behaviors of interest. We believe that this methodology will provide reliable data that is less affected by retrospective recall bias which characterizes previous research in this area. One hundred and twenty subjects will complete electronic diaries for thirty consecutive days, which will allow the collection of a sufficient amount of data to adequately test the proposed model. We believe that this methodology will allow us to identify antecedent and consequent conditions surrounding self-destructive behavior in eating disordered individuals. This will provide important information regarding the development of treatments for this group of individuals.

Website: http://crisp.cit.nih.gov/crisp/Crisp_Query.Generate_Screen

- **Project Title: EMOTIONAL AROUSAL AS A PREDICTOR OF SUICIDAL BEHAVIORS**

  Principal Investigator & Institution: Welch, Stacy S.; Psychology; University of Washington Seattle, Wa 98195

  Timing: Fiscal Year 2002; Project Start 16-JUN-2002; Project End 15-JUN-2004

  Summary: (provided by applicant): Patterns of physiological arousal as well as self-reported emotional arousal associated with parasuicidal behavior in **borderline personality disorder** are examined. Women with BPD will participate in personally relevant imagery procedures while both physiological measures of arousal (heart rate, skin conductance, respiration, and blood pressure) as well as self-report measures are conducted. Arousal patterns associated with imagery involving suicide attempts and non-suicidal self-injury will be compared to each other and to arousal patterns elicited during control scenes using a four-stage methodology (cue situation, approach, incident, consequence). The research is based on the theory that parasuicidal behavior is learned via escape conditioning with relief from negative emotional states serving as the negative reinforcer. It is hypothesized that both non-suicidal self-injurious behaviors as well as non-lethal suicide attempts are maintained (i.e., negatively reinforced) by immediate reductions in aversive tension and emotional arousal, which will appear in both physiological and psychological measures. It is further hypothesized that changes in these patterns will predict subsequent changes in the frequency of parasuicide and suicide ideation four months after testing. Analysis of variance techniques and regression analyses are employed. Research of this nature is extremely important to help develop and improve treatments for chronic parasuicide in BPD. It remains a serious public health problem with few efficacious treatments, and is very costly in terms of health services utilization.

  Website: http://crisp.cit.nih.gov/crisp/Crisp_Query.Generate_Screen

- **Project Title: EVALUATION OF DIALECTICAL BEHAVIOR THERAPY (DBT)**

  Principal Investigator & Institution: Lynch, Thomas R.; Assistant Professor; Psychology; Duke University Durham, Nc 27706

  Timing: Fiscal Year 2003; Project Start 30-SEP-2003; Project End 30-JUN-2008

  Summary: (provided by applicant): The primary aim of this research is to determine whether DBT+ suboxone (an opiate drug replacement) is an efficacious treatment for opiate addicts meeting criteria for **Borderline Personality Disorder** (BPD) and to analyze factors that influence efficacy in this population in order to improve the treatment. DBT, originally developed for chronically suicidal women with BPD, is a synthesis of behavior therapy strategies aimed at change and validation strategies aimed at acceptance, both held together by a set of dialectical strategies and underlying assumptions. DBT has been adapted for BPD substance abusers by the addition of 1) specific targets relevant to drug use, 2) a set of attachment strategies, 3) greater reliance on arbitrary reinforcers at treatment start, 4) weekly urinalysis, and, in the case of opiate addicts, 5) an opiate drug replacement program (suboxone, i.e., buprenorphine in combination with naloxone) plus DBT clinical management. The research proposed here is a two arm, multi-site randomized clinical trial comparing a one year treatment program of DBT + suboxone for BPD heroin addicted individuals to a one year program of standard drug counseling + suboxone. Drug counseling will consist of manualized individual sessions + group therapy. Participants in both conditions will be prescribed psychotropic medications following a standardized medication protocol developed specifically for BPD individuals. To minimize the effects of treatment allegiance on outcome, the study will be carried out at Duke University Medical Center and the University of Washington. An expert in DBT at the University of Washington will train, supervise and conduct adherence ratings on DBT therapists at both sites. A Duke expert in drug counseling will do the same for the drug counseling therapists at both sites. One hundred and seventy-two individuals (86 per condition) with opiate dependence and meeting criteria for BPD will be enrolled in a one-year treatment and a one-year follow-up assessment. Assessments measuring drug use, suicidal behaviors, retention and other treatment related behaviors, general psychopathology and functioning, and increases in behavioral skills will be given at four-month intervals for the entire two years. Results will be analyzed using HLM and other regression based procedures.

Website: http://crisp.cit.nih.gov/crisp/Crisp_Query.Generate_Screen

- **Project Title: EXPOSURE TO SHAME IN BORDERLINE PERSONALITY DISORDER**

  Principal Investigator & Institution: Rizvi, Shireen L.; Psychology; University of Washington Seattle, Wa 98195

  Timing: Fiscal Year 2002; Project Start 16-SEP-2002; Project End 31-AUG-2003

  Description (provided by applicant): The study proposed here seeks to develop and test an intervention for the experience of shame in **borderline personality disorder** (BPD). Although the experience of shame is highly prevalent in this population, little is understood about how shame functions to maintain the pathology and even less is known about how to successfully treat it. Past research has indicated that the experience of shame is directly related to suicidal behaviors. These results suggest more attention needs to be paid to developing treatments that attend to the experience of shame. Dialectical Behavior Therapy (DBT), developed by Linehan, has been shown to reduce suicidal behavior in BPD. Although DBT encourages the use of exposure and opposite action techniques applied to negative emotions, such as shame, this component of DBT has not been previously examined. The current study will evaluate this component of DBT by enrolling nine women with **borderline personality disorder** (including three pilot subjects) in an eight-week exposure/opposite action treatment for the experience of shame. The study will utilize a multiple baseline, single-subject design in order to maximize the amount of information obtained about the efficacy of the intervention. Information obtained from this pilot project will be instrumental in further developing short, data-driven treatments for suicidal behavior in BPD.

  Website: http://crisp.cit.nih.gov/crisp/Crisp_Query.Generate_Screen

- **Project Title: FAMILY PERSPECTIVES ON BORDERLINE PERSONALITY DISORDER**

  Principal Investigator & Institution: Hoffman, Perry D.; National Education Alliance Bpd 11 Norman Dr Rye, Ny 10580

  Timing: Fiscal Year 2003; Project Start 10-JUL-2003; Project End 30-JUN-2008

Summary: (provided by applicant): The objectives of the annual Family Perspectives on **Borderline Personality Disorder** Conferences are: 1) the dissemination of scientific information to professionals, consumers, and families for understanding the complex psychiatric condition of **borderline personality disorder** (BPD); 2) the dissemination of family perspectives to researchers and clinicians to understand the challenges, problems and impact of the disorder on relatives; and 3) the promotion of research in the area of family needs with junior and senior researchers. The need for these family/consumer/researcher/clinician forums is based on the fact that BPD is a severe and persistent psychiatric illness and, to date, no conference has addressed consumer and family perspectives. Ten percent of patients suicide which, along with other behaviors, makes BPD a critical public health problem. Estimated prevalence of BPD in the general population is 2-3%, with 11% of outpatients and 20% of psychiatric inpatients meeting DSM-IV criteria. Families and consumers can benefit from the knowledge of professionals and researchers; professionals and researchers can benefit from the perspectives of families and consumers for treatment and research planning. The two-day conferences build on the first conference From Research to Community: Family Perspectives on **Borderline Personality Disorder** 2002, at Columbia University-College of Physicians and Surgeons. Speakers each year are internationally acknowledged researchers, clinicians and family/consumers each speaking to their areas of expertise, and then responding to questions. The format of the conference, which includes break-out sessions at lunchtime, further promotes discussion. The 2003 conference, Family Perspectives on Borderline Personality Disorder: Co-occurring Disorders and BPD, is the second annual conference. The conference for 2004 is entitled Family Perspectives on Borderline Personality Disorder: BPD Across the Life-Span. The 2005 conference Family Perspectives on **Borderline Personality Disorder,** BPD across the Waters, will be at Universite de Geneve. The 2006 conference, back in NYC, will be Family Perspectives on Borderline Personality Disorder: BPD and Treatment Options. The 2007 conference restarts the conference series and focuses again on From Research to Community: Family Perspectives on Borderline Personality.

Website: http://crisp.cit.nih.gov/crisp/Crisp_Query.Generate_Screen

- **Project Title: INTERPERSONAL FUNCTIONING IN BORDERLINE PERSONALITY**

  Principal Investigator & Institution: Pilkonis, Paul A.; Professor of Psychiatry & Psychology; Psychiatry; University of Pittsburgh at Pittsburgh 350 Thackeray Hall Pittsburgh, Pa 15260

  Timing: Fiscal Year 2002; Project Start 10-APR-1998; Project End 30-JUN-2007

  Summary: (provided by applicant): This submission is an amended competing continuation application for MH56888, now titled "Interpersonal Functioning in Borderline Personality." The overall goal is to characterize the interpersonal functioning of patients with **borderline personality disorder** (BPD) in greater detail and with greater clinical relevance than has been done previously. A conceptual hierarchy of interpersonal functioning in BPD will be examined, ranging from long-term patterns of relatedness to moment-to-moment interpersonal appraisals, and the construct and predictive validity of these measures will be tested. The first specific aim is to characterize the adult attachment styles of BPD patients using multiple measures. The second specific aim is to undertake a detailed assessment of the interpersonal functioning of these patients in the areas of romantic relationships, friendships, and work using a state-of-the-art interview, the Revised Adult Personality Functioning Assessment (RAPFA). The third specific aim is to document that both attachment styles and patterns of relatedness identified with the RAPFA are associated with actual day-today interpersonal functioning; for this purpose, a Social Interaction Diary, adapted from the Rochester Interaction Record, will be used. At the most detailed level of analysis, the fourth specific aim is to undertake an assessment of social cognition in BPD patients using a paradigm evaluating biases in the perception of neutral human faces. The research will be conducted with three groups (N = 50 in each group): Patients with BPD and two comparison groups-patients with avoidant personality disorder (AVPD) and patients with no PD, i.e., those with an Axis I mood or anxiety disorder only. All patients will be assessed at intake and followed prospectively for six months. The accomplishment of these aims will be important not only for establishing the construct and predictive validity of these interpersonal variables in BPD but also for promoting the development of improved treatments on behalf of patients who suffer from this disorder. Identification of interpersonal risk factors will help achieve the long-term goal of not only knowing these patients well but also using this knowledge in sc ce-based therapies to improve their lives.

Website: http://crisp.cit.nih.gov/crisp/Crisp_Query.Generate_Screen

- **Project Title: LOW DOSE DEXAMETHASONE CHALLENGE–PERSONALITY DISORDER AND NORMAL CONTROLS**

  Principal Investigator & Institution: Grossman, Robert; Mount Sinai School of Medicine of Cuny New York, Ny 10029

  Timing: Fiscal Year 2001; Project Start 01-DEC-1999; Project End 28-FEB-2001

  Summary: The purpose of this study is to further understand hypothalamic-pituitary-adrenal (HPA) axis functioning in subjects with **borderline personality disorder** (BPD).

  Website: http://crisp.cit.nih.gov/crisp/Crisp_Query.Generate_Screen

- **Project Title: MCLEAN STUDY OF ADULT DEVELOPMENT**

  Principal Investigator & Institution: Zanarini, Mary C.; Associate Professor; Mc Lean Hospital (Belmont, Ma) Belmont, Ma 02478

  Timing: Fiscal Year 2001; Project Start 30-SEP-2000; Project End 31-AUG-2005

  Summary: The overall goal of this study is to continue a prospective study of the long-term course and outcome of **borderline personality disorder** (BPD). BPD is a common, symptomatically severe disorder associated with marked levels of psychosocial impairment and high levels of mental health and other social service utilization. Initial assessment data are available for a sample of 362 inpatients between the ages of 18 and 35; 290 borderline patients and 72 Axis II controls. In addition, the 95 percent of the surviving patients currently eligible for their 2, 4, and 6-year follow-up evaluations have been re-interviewed. The first specific aim is to prospectively assess the six, eight, and ten-year course and outcome of these patients. Four main aspects of the course and outcome will be studied: (1) severity of borderline symptoms, (2) impairment in psychosocial functioning, (3) prevalence of comorbid Axis I and Axis II disorders, and (4) type and amount of psychiatric and medical treatment received. The second specific aim is to determine the best predictive model for each of four outcomes: remission of BPD, recurrence of BPD, the attainment of good psychosocial functioning, and suicide. The third specific aim is to assess the pathways to health reported by those borderline patients who improve substantially. The fourth specific aim is to compare the predictive power of three models of BPD: the categorical model, the severity model of dimensionality, and the 5-Factor Model of dimensionality. Demographic data, social and vocational functioning, psychiatric and medical treatment, borderline symptoms, Axis I and Axis II comorbidity, life stress, basic aspects of temperament, and pathways to health will be assessed at each follow-up period by one of two masters level research assistants blind to all previously collected data. In addition, knowledgeable informants will be interviewed concerning each patient's psychosocial functioning, and medical, work, and school records will be collected and reviewed.

Website: http://crisp.cit.nih.gov/crisp/Crisp_Query.Generate_Screen

- **Project Title: NEGATIVE EMOTION MODERATORS OF TREATMENT FOR PARASUICIDE**

  Principal Investigator & Institution: Brown, Milton Z.; Psychology; University of Washington Seattle, Wa 98195

  Timing: Fiscal Year 2001; Project Start 16-MAR-2001

  Summary: The main aim of this study is to better understand chronic parasuicide in BPD in order to identify specific emotions to target in treatment. Primary emotions will be identified that increase the risk for repeated parasuicide and reduce treatment effectiveness in a chronically and acutely parasuicidal BPD sample. Nonverbal expressions that occur when parasuicide is discussed will be measured. It will be tested which primary emotions are elicited and predict the repetition of parasuicide. The main hypothesis, that in this context patients showing high negative emotions will be more likely to repeat parasuicide, will be tested using a survival analysis model. This study will provide feasible methods for assessing risk for parasuicide and will provide direction for future treatment research. It is essential that basic research such as this be used to develop better treatments for chronic parasuicide in BPD since it is such a serious public health problem, incurring substantial costs both in terms of intense suffering and substantial service utilization. To date, however, there are few treatments with demonstrated efficacy.

  Website: http://crisp.cit.nih.gov/crisp/Crisp_Query.Generate_Screen

- **Project Title: NEURAL CORRELATES OF EMOTION**

  Principal Investigator & Institution: Keele, Norman B.; Psychology and Neuroscience; Baylor University Waco, Tx 76798

  Timing: Fiscal Year 2002; Project Start 10-SEP-2002; Project End 31-AUG-2004

  Summary: (provided by applicant): The long-term goal of this project is to develop and use a clinically relevant animal model of aggressive behavior. We hypothesize that low serotonin-induced aggression is associated with (1) changes in other emotional behavior and (2) increased membrane excitability in amygdala neurons. Impulsive-aggressive humans reportedly have low anxiety and are less sensitive to fear-conditioning. Similar to humans, it is proposed that anxious behaviors and fear-learning are correlated with aggression and low serotonin levels. In addition, aggression has been suggested to result from epilepsy-like processes in limbic areas. One limbic structure, the amygdala, has well-defined roles in both epilepsy and emotion, and seizure activity that involves the amygdala may be associated with aggression in humans. Thus, cellular mechanisms of neuronal excitability in the amygdala may have a functional role in aggressive behavior. Supporting this idea are clinical studies showing anti-aggressive effects of anticonvulsants in prison inmates and psychiatric patients. In this project rats are chronically treated with PCPA, a competitive inhibitor of serotonin synthesis, to significantly inhibit serotonin synthesis. Low serotonin is widely-implicated in aggression in many species. Aggressive behavior is quantified using a simple test of rodent aggression characterized by easily recognized, stereotypical behaviors. Preliminary data have shown that aggressive behavior in this model is inhibited by the anticonvulsant phenytoin, as others have shown with human aggression. The specific aims of this project are to (1) define the salient independent variables required to model impulsive aggression, and to examine the relationship between aggression, low brain serotonin, and changes in amygdala-dependent emotional behaviors such as anxiety and fear-learning; and (2) compare amygdala neuron membrane properties and neurotransmission in control and aggressive animals using whole cell voltage-clamp.An animal model is developed that shares behavioral, neurochemical, and pharmacological similarities with impulsive-aggression in humans. Also, the neural correlates of aggression are investigated using cellular physiological methods never before used to study aggressive behavior. This innovative proposal examines basic biological mechanisms of aberrant emotional behavior that are relevant to human psychopathology. By developing this animal model, future research efforts can yield important insight into the cellular neurobiology of complex emotional behaviors such as aggression, and may have important clinical implications for the treatment of psychiatric disorders involving inappropriate aggression such as bipolar disorder, **borderline personality disorder** or antisocial personality disorder.

Website: http://crisp.cit.nih.gov/crisp/Crisp_Query.Generate_Screen

- **Project Title: PILOT STUDY--SCHEMA FOCUSED COGNITIVE THERAPY FOR BORDERLINE PERSONALITY DISORDER**

  Principal Investigator & Institution: Brown, Gregory; University of Pennsylvania 3451 Walnut Street Philadelphia, Pa 19104

  Timing: Fiscal Year 2001

  Summary: There is no text on file for this abstract.

  Website: http://crisp.cit.nih.gov/crisp/Crisp_Query.Generate_Screen

- **Project Title: PSYCHOBIOLOGY OF SUICIDAL BEHAVIORAL IN BPD**

  Principal Investigator & Institution: Soloff, Paul H.; Psychiatry; University of Pittsburgh at Pittsburgh 350 Thackeray Hall Pittsburgh, Pa 15260

  Timing: Fiscal Year 2001; Project Start 30-SEP-1992; Project End 31-MAY-2006

  Summary: Borderline Personality Disorder is a psychiatric disorder defined, in part, by recurrent impulsive and suicidal behaviors. With a suicide rate of up to 9.5 percent, BPD is among the most lethal of psychiatric disorders, comparable to affective and schizophrenic disorders. This study is the continuation of a first prospective, multidimensional study of the clinical, psychosocial and biological risk factors for suicidal behavior in patients with BPD. Following a stress-diathesis model of suicide, we assess predicted risk factors at baseline and follow patients annually for up to ten years, assessing for suicidal behavior, psychiatric co-morbidities, substance use disorders, episodes of impulsive-aggression, psychosocial stressors, treatment effects, social and clinical outcomes. The role of central serotonergic regulation in impulsive and suicidal behavior is studied using the 5HT2A specific radioligand [F-18] altanserin and PET neuroimaging. The effects of a childhood history of abuse are assessed on suicide risk, impulsive-aggressive behavior and on measures of central serotonergic function. Stressors increasing the risk of suicidal behavior include co-morbidity with Major Depression or Substance Use Disorders, Recent Life Events, and poor social support. Personality characteristics such as impulsivity and aggression represent chronic vulnerabilities to suicidal behavior. Longitudinal follow-up of suicidal patients allows testing of predictor hypotheses concerning risk factors for suicidal behavior in BPD through the application of survival analyses. Risk factors predicting recurrence and medical lethality of attempts will allow early identification of BPD patients at highest risk for suicide and inform treatment efforts.

Website: http://crisp.cit.nih.gov/crisp/Crisp_Query.Generate_Screen

- **Project Title: SKILLS TRAINING VIDEO FOR DIALECTICAL BEHAVIOR THERAPY**

  Principal Investigator & Institution: Waltz, Jennifer A.; Behavioral Technology Transfer Group Transfer Group Seattle, Wa 98105

  Timing: Fiscal Year 2001; Project Start 15-SEP-1999; Project End 31-AUG-2003

  Summary: (provided by applicant): Dialectical Behavior Therapy (DBT) is a multimodal, psychosocial treatment with demonstrated efficacy in treating **borderline personality disorder** (BPD). In Phase I, we developed and evaluated a pilot videotape of Marsha M. Linehan, Ph.D., teaching a DBT emotion regulation skill. Results demonstrated the videotape's efficacy at imparting skill information to BPD subjects. Additionally, three-quarters of the subjects applied the skill in the subsequent week, and reported significant decreases in distress after using the skill. The primary aim of this Phase II proposal is to extend our work by developing a set of four DBT skills training videos taught by Linehan and to evaluate their efficacy. We intend to conduct a randomized controlled trial with 60 BPD subjects, randomly assigned to either the DBT skills video condition or to a psychoeducation video control condition. Outcome measures will again assess knowledge gains and ability to apply the skills. We will also investigate use of these videotapes in naturalistic settings by collecting data on their use within existing DBT programs over a six-month period. As a therapy adjunct, these videos are an innovative approach to increasing the skills capability of BPD clients while facilitating the dissemination of an empirically supported treatment. PROPOSED COMMERCIAL APPLICATION: DBT is a widely used treatment and the skills training manual on which the proposed videotapes will be based is extremely popular. It is currently Guilford Press's best selling book, with 64,000 copies sold since it was first printed in 1993. Since its inception in 1997, the Behavioral Technology Transfer Group has provided over 93 community workshops in the U.S. and many others abroad. In 1999 alone, BTTG provided 40 introductory DBT workshops attended by over 4,566 individuals. Given the demand for DBT training materials, these videos are expected to sell widely to a variety of treatment centers, individual practitioners and to patients.

  Website: http://crisp.cit.nih.gov/crisp/Crisp_Query.Generate_Screen

- **Project Title: TESTING A HYPOTHETICAL DIATHESIS/STRESS MODEL OF SUICIDE**

  Principal Investigator & Institution: Oquendo, Maria A.; Associate Clinical Professor; New York State Psychiatric Institute 1051 Riverside Dr New York, Ny 10032

  Timing: Fiscal Year 2001

  Summary: More than 30,000 Americans die by suicide each year. Over 90% of those who complete suicide have a psychiatric illness; 75% of those with a psychiatric illness who complete suicide have a major depression (MDE), schizophrenia (SC) or **borderline personality disorder** (BPD). We examine the clinical and neurobiological factors related to suicide in high risk samples using a prospective study design. The study is informed by the stress-diathesis model presented in the Overview. No other published study to date has used a multi-variate prospective design focused specifically on suicidal behavior. No other published study to date has used a multi-variate prospective design focused on suicidal behavior. The aims are: 1.) To assess potential clinical predictors of suicide attempts during a two year follow-up in a cohort of 400 patients with major depression (n=200 attempters) and 350 patients with schizophrenia (n=175 attempters). One hundred subjects with MDE will also have BPD; 2.) To study neurobiological and clinical predictors of high versus lower lethality suicide attempts since high lethality attempts can be considered a proxy for complete suicide; 3.) To assess the relationship of serotonergic function (CSF 5-HIAA) to suicide attempt behavior during a two year follow-up of these patients; 4. To assess the relationship of polymorphisms of serotonin-related genes to past and future suicidal behavior and to indices of serotonergic function. Secondary aims are to: 1) examine the role of medication effects on risk for suicidal behavior; 2) examine the interrelationships of SF metabolites, aggression, stress and suicidal behavior. This project relates to Projects #'s 3, 5,6 and 7 of the CCNMD in that it provides neurobiological (CSF metabolite profile and genotyping) assessment, clinical characterization and two year follow up of subjects who participate in other projects (e.g. familial transmission, PET imaging, or statistical methods studies). In addition, this project relies heavily on the cores as follows: 1) The assessment tools of the Clinical Evaluation Core (CEC) are administered; 2) The Clinical Laboratory Core (CLC) analyses neurochemical measures; 3) The Brain Imaging Core (BIC) develops ligands and conducts imaging studies with these well- characterized patients; 4) Finally, all data are entered, managed and analyzed by the Statistics and Computing Core (SCC) of the proposed CCNMD. Using this approach, we can examine risk factors specific to suicide attempters within each of the high-risk groups as well as risk factors consistent across psychiatric diagnostic groups. This will allow testing of the stress-diathesis model for suicidal behavior.

Website: http://crisp.cit.nih.gov/crisp/Crisp_Query.Generate_Screen

- **Project Title: THE NEUROBIOLOGY OF SUICIDAL BEHAVIOR**

  Principal Investigator & Institution: Mann, J John.; Chief; New York State Psychiatric Institute 1051 Riverside Dr New York, Ny 10032

  Timing: Fiscal Year 2001; Project Start 03-JUL-2000; Project End 30-JUN-2005

  Summary: This application requests five years of support for the Conte Center for the Neuroscience of Mental Disorders (CCNMD): The Neurobiology of Suicidal Behavior. The Surgeon General notes that 300,000 suicides per year in the United States and ten times that number of suicide attempts, require a response that involves improving our knowledge regarding the relative importance of multiple predictors of suicide risk. The CCNMD employs a multi-disciplinary approach to develop a predictive and explanatory model for suicidal behavior. Project 1: Involves animal studies of genes regulating serotonin function and related behavioral traits of aggression, impulsivity and anxiety that modulate the risk for suicidal acts. Project 2: In the brainstem of depressed suicides we have found fewer serotonin neurons expressing the serotonin transporter gene. We will determine whether this is related to suicide or major depression and assay gene transcription factors as an explanation. CCNMD investigators have identified altered serotonin function in ventral prefrontal cortex and amygdala of suicide victims that may underlie increased impulsivity and suicide risk. We will now study target neurons in the ventral prefrontal cortex to determine their integrity in suicide Project 3: We will use PET to determine whether the postmortem receptor changes associated with major depression and suicide can be distinguished in vivo. Project 4: CCNMD investigators have found evidence for a stress-diathesis model where lifetime impulsivity is a major correlate of past suicide attempts in a sample of over 340 patients with major depression, schizophrenia or **borderline personality disorder.** Cross-sectional identification of potential risk factors Identifying such predictors will facilitate inception of controlled treatment studies, which are almost non-existent at present. Projects 5 and 6 are studies of familial transmission of suicidality, aggression/impulsivity, serotonin candidate genes, and psychopathology from our adult probands with major depression to their offspring and from parents to our adolescent probands. These studies will evaluate familial influences on the risk for suicide attempts. Project 7 addresses the statistical challenges of large postmortem and in vivo imaging data sets and proposes a set of new and semi -automated strategies.

Website: http://crisp.cit.nih.gov/crisp/Crisp_Query.Generate_Screen

- **Project Title: TREATING SUICIDAL BEHAVIOR AND SELF MUTILATION IN BPD**

  Principal Investigator & Institution: Stanley, Barbara; Professor of Psychology; New York State Psychiatric Institute 1051 Riverside Dr New York, Ny 10032

  Timing: Fiscal Year 2001; Project Start 15-AUG-2000; Project End 30-JUN-2005

  Summary: The purpose of this project is: to conduct a randomized controlled trial for the treatment of suicidal and self-mutilating behaviors with suicidal patients who have **borderline personality disorder** (BPD). Suicidal behavior and self-mutilation are two of the most serious problems confronting contemporary psychiatry, but little is known about the effective prevention and treatment of these behaviors. While clinicians have viewed patients with BPD as manipulative and attention- seeking, suicidal behavior and self-mutilation are especially common in these patients and results in significant mortality and costly morbidity. Unfortunately, systematic investigation of the treatment of suicidal behavior and self-mutilation in BPD is sparse. One psychosocial treatment dialectical behavior therapy (DBT), a cognitive- behavioral treatment-has been shown to significantly decrease self- injurious behaviors in BPD. While DBT has become increasingly popular as the treatment of choice for suicidal patients with BPD, there are no replication studies other than the original study conducted by the developer. Our study will be the first large-scale replication of DBT. With respect to medication, studies of fluoxetine, a selective serotonin reuptake inhibitor (SSRI), and other SSRIs have shown their efficacy in decreasing rates of self-mutilation and suicidal ideation in BPD. Furthermore, biological studies of serotonergic functioning in suicide attempters and BPD suggest the potential benefit of SSRIs in treating self-injurious behavior in BPD. Although the combination of DBT and SSRIs has become one of the most common treatments provided to outpatients with PBD, no systematic investigation of the efficacy of combined psychotherapy and medication in BPD has ever been conducted. In this five-year project, we propose to evaluate the efficacy of DBT, SSRI, and combined DBT and SSRI in the treatment of self-injurious behaviors in BPD and to conduct a replication of DBT. We will use a randomized four cell design comparing DBT+placebo, DBT+fluoxetine, fluoxetine+clinical management, and placebo+clinical management. We will conduct this project at the New York State Psychiatric Institute and will have the support of the MHCRC for Suicidal Behavior under the direction of Dr. J. Mann. Over a 5 year period, 180 subjects with BPD will be randomized to 12 months of treatments and a naturalistic follow- up at 12 months.

  Website: http://crisp.cit.nih.gov/crisp/Crisp_Query.Generate_Screen

## The National Library of Medicine: PubMed

One of the quickest and most comprehensive ways to find academic studies in both English and other languages is to use PubMed, maintained by the National Library of Medicine.[3] The advantage of PubMed over previously mentioned sources is that it covers a greater number of domestic and foreign references. It is also free to use. If the publisher has a Web site that offers full text of its journals, PubMed will provide links to that site, as well as to sites offering other related data. User registration, a subscription fee, or some other type of fee may be required to access the full text of articles in some journals.

To generate your own bibliography of studies dealing with borderline personality disorder, simply go to the PubMed Web site at **http://www.ncbi.nlm.nih.gov/pubmed**. Type "borderline personality disorder" (or synonyms) into the search box, and click "Go." The following is the type of output you can expect from PubMed for borderline personality disorder (hyperlinks lead to article summaries):

- **A 27-year follow-up of patients with borderline personality disorder.**
  Author(s): Paris J, Zweig-Frank H.
  Source: Comprehensive Psychiatry. 2001 November-December; 42(6): 482-7.
  http://www.ncbi.nlm.nih.gov:80/entrez/query.fcgi?cmd=Retrieve&db=PubMed&list_uids=11704940&dopt=Abstract

- **A 44-year-old woman with borderline personality disorder, 1 year later.**
  Author(s): Burns RB, Hartman EE.
  Source: Jama : the Journal of the American Medical Association. 2003 February 26; 289(8): 1026.
  http://www.ncbi.nlm.nih.gov:80/entrez/query.fcgi?cmd=Retrieve&db=PubMed&list_uids=12597756&dopt=Abstract

- **A 44-year-old woman with borderline personality disorder.**
  Author(s): Oldham JM.
  Source: Jama : the Journal of the American Medical Association. 2002 February 27; 287(8): 1029-37.
  http://www.ncbi.nlm.nih.gov:80/entrez/query.fcgi?cmd=Retrieve&db=PubMed&list_uids=11866652&dopt=Abstract

- **A case study of an extremely violent serial rapist with borderline personality disorder in remission.**
  Author(s): Martens WH.
  Source: Acta Psychiatrica Scandinavica. 2003 June; 107(6): 465-6; Discussion 466-7.
  http://www.ncbi.nlm.nih.gov:80/entrez/query.fcgi?cmd=Retrieve&db=PubMed&list_uids=12752024&dopt=Abstract

---

[3] PubMed was developed by the National Center for Biotechnology Information (NCBI) at the National Library of Medicine (NLM) at the National Institutes of Health (NIH). The PubMed database was developed in conjunction with publishers of biomedical literature as a search tool for accessing literature citations and linking to full-text journal articles at Web sites of participating publishers. Publishers that participate in PubMed supply NLM with their citations electronically prior to or at the time of publication.

- **A comparison of posttraumatic stress disorder with and without borderline personality disorder among women with a history of childhood sexual abuse: etiological and clinical characteristics.**
  Author(s): Heffernan K, Cloitre M.
  Source: The Journal of Nervous and Mental Disease. 2000 September; 188(9): 589-95.
  http://www.ncbi.nlm.nih.gov:80/entrez/query.fcgi?cmd=Retrieve&db=PubMed&list_uids=11009332&dopt=Abstract

- **A critique of the American psychiatric practice guideline for the treatment of patients with borderline personality disorder.**
  Author(s): Sanderson C, Swenson C, Bohus M.
  Source: Journal of Personality Disorders. 2002 April; 16(2): 122-9.
  http://www.ncbi.nlm.nih.gov:80/entrez/query.fcgi?cmd=Retrieve&db=PubMed&list_uids=12004488&dopt=Abstract

- **A dialectical behavior therapy program for people with an eating disorder and borderline personality disorder--description and outcome.**
  Author(s): Palmer RL, Birchall H, Damani S, Gatward N, McGrain L, Parker L.
  Source: The International Journal of Eating Disorders. 2003 April; 33(3): 281-6.
  http://www.ncbi.nlm.nih.gov:80/entrez/query.fcgi?cmd=Retrieve&db=PubMed&list_uids=12655624&dopt=Abstract

- **A family study of outpatients with borderline personality disorder and no history of mood disorder.**
  Author(s): Riso LP, Klein DN, Anderson RL, Ouimette PC.
  Source: Journal of Personality Disorders. 2000 Fall; 14(3): 208-17.
  http://www.ncbi.nlm.nih.gov:80/entrez/query.fcgi?cmd=Retrieve&db=PubMed&list_uids=11019745&dopt=Abstract

- **A new beginning for research on borderline personality disorder.**
  Author(s): Hyman SE.
  Source: Biological Psychiatry. 2002 June 15; 51(12): 933-5.
  http://www.ncbi.nlm.nih.gov:80/entrez/query.fcgi?cmd=Retrieve&db=PubMed&list_uids=12062876&dopt=Abstract

- **A preliminary double-blind, placebo-controlled trial of divalproex sodium in borderline personality disorder.**
  Author(s): Hollander E, Allen A, Lopez RP, Bienstock CA, Grossman R, Siever LJ, Merkatz L, Stein DJ.
  Source: The Journal of Clinical Psychiatry. 2001 March; 62(3): 199-203.
  http://www.ncbi.nlm.nih.gov:80/entrez/query.fcgi?cmd=Retrieve&db=PubMed&list_uids=11305707&dopt=Abstract

- **Abusive relationships in families of women with borderline personality disorder, anorexia nervosa and a control group.**
  Author(s): Laporte L, Guttman H.
  Source: The Journal of Nervous and Mental Disease. 2001 August; 189(8): 522-31.
  http://www.ncbi.nlm.nih.gov:80/entrez/query.fcgi?cmd=Retrieve&db=PubMed&list_uids=11531204&dopt=Abstract

- **Affect regulation in women with borderline personality disorder traits.**
  Author(s): Yen S, Zlotnick C, Costello E.
  Source: The Journal of Nervous and Mental Disease. 2002 October; 190(10): 693-6.
  http://www.ncbi.nlm.nih.gov:80/entrez/query.fcgi?cmd=Retrieve&db=PubMed&list_uids=12409863&dopt=Abstract

- **An intensive outpatient program for patients with borderline personality disorder.**
  Author(s): Smith GW, Ruiz-Sancho A, Gunderson JG.
  Source: Psychiatric Services (Washington, D.C.). 2001 April; 52(4): 532-3.
  http://www.ncbi.nlm.nih.gov:80/entrez/query.fcgi?cmd=Retrieve&db=PubMed&list_uids=11274503&dopt=Abstract

- **Another idea for the treatment of patients with borderline personality disorder.**
  Author(s): Marcoux GS, Valnicek SM.
  Source: Canadian Journal of Psychiatry. Revue Canadienne De Psychiatrie. 2000 May; 45(4): 395-6.
  http://www.ncbi.nlm.nih.gov:80/entrez/query.fcgi?cmd=Retrieve&db=PubMed&list_uids=10813079&dopt=Abstract

- **Are the interpersonal and identity disturbances in the borderline personality disorder criteria linked to the traits of affective instability and impulsivity?**
  Author(s): Koenigsberg HW, Harvey PD, Mitropoulou V, New AS, Goodman M, Silverman J, Serby M, Schopick F, Siever LJ.
  Source: Journal of Personality Disorders. 2001 August; 15(4): 358-70.
  http://www.ncbi.nlm.nih.gov:80/entrez/query.fcgi?cmd=Retrieve&db=PubMed&list_uids=11556702&dopt=Abstract

- **Assessment of dysfunctional beliefs in borderline personality disorder.**
  Author(s): Butler AC, Brown GK, Beck AT, Grisham JR.
  Source: Behaviour Research and Therapy. 2002 October; 40(10): 1231-40.
  http://www.ncbi.nlm.nih.gov:80/entrez/query.fcgi?cmd=Retrieve&db=PubMed&list_uids=12375731&dopt=Abstract

- **Attachment and borderline personality disorder.**
  Author(s): Fonagy P.
  Source: J Am Psychoanal Assoc. 2000; 48(4): 1129-46; Discussion 1175-87.
  http://www.ncbi.nlm.nih.gov:80/entrez/query.fcgi?cmd=Retrieve&db=PubMed&list_uids=11212185&dopt=Abstract

- **Attachment, parental bonding and borderline personality disorder features in young adults.**
  Author(s): Nickell AD, Waudby CJ, Trull TJ.
  Source: Journal of Personality Disorders. 2002 April; 16(2): 148-59.
  http://www.ncbi.nlm.nih.gov:80/entrez/query.fcgi?cmd=Retrieve&db=PubMed&list_uids=12004491&dopt=Abstract

- **Attentional mechanisms of borderline personality disorder.**
  Author(s): Posner MI, Rothbart MK, Vizueta N, Levy KN, Evans DE, Thomas KM, Clarkin JF.
  Source: Proceedings of the National Academy of Sciences of the United States of America. 2002 December 10; 99(25): 16366-70. Epub 2002 November 27.
  http://www.ncbi.nlm.nih.gov:80/entrez/query.fcgi?cmd=Retrieve&db=PubMed&list_uids=12456876&dopt=Abstract

- **Autobiographical memory and parasuicide in borderline personality disorder.**
  Author(s): Startup M, Heard H, Swales M, Jones B, Williams JM, Jones RS.
  Source: The British Journal of Clinical Psychology / the British Psychological Society. 2001 June; 40(Pt 2): 113-20.
  http://www.ncbi.nlm.nih.gov:80/entrez/query.fcgi?cmd=Retrieve&db=PubMed&list_uids=11446233&dopt=Abstract

- **Being a case manager for persons with borderline personality disorder: perspectives of community mental health center clinicians.**
  Author(s): Nehls N.
  Source: Archives of Psychiatric Nursing. 2000 February; 14(1): 12-8.
  http://www.ncbi.nlm.nih.gov:80/entrez/query.fcgi?cmd=Retrieve&db=PubMed&list_uids=10692802&dopt=Abstract

- **Biological nature of depressive symptoms in borderline personality disorder: endocrine comparison to recurrent brief and major depression.**
  Author(s): De la Fuente JM, Bobes J, Vizuete C, Mendlewicz J.
  Source: Journal of Psychiatric Research. 2002 May-June; 36(3): 137-45. Erratum In: J Psychiatr Res 2002 July-August; 36(4): 267-8.
  http://www.ncbi.nlm.nih.gov:80/entrez/query.fcgi?cmd=Retrieve&db=PubMed&list_uids=11886691&dopt=Abstract

- **Borderline personality disorder and age of onset in major depression.**
  Author(s): Rothschild L, Zimmerman M.
  Source: Journal of Personality Disorders. 2002 April; 16(2): 189-99.
  http://www.ncbi.nlm.nih.gov:80/entrez/query.fcgi?cmd=Retrieve&db=PubMed&list_uids=12004494&dopt=Abstract

- **Borderline personality disorder and bipolar II disorder in private practice depressed outpatients.**
  Author(s): Benazzi F.
  Source: Comprehensive Psychiatry. 2000 March-April; 41(2): 106-10.
  http://www.ncbi.nlm.nih.gov:80/entrez/query.fcgi?cmd=Retrieve&db=PubMed&list_uids=10741888&dopt=Abstract

- **Borderline Personality Disorder and childhood sexual abuse: a meta-analytic study.**
  Author(s): Fossati A, Madeddu F, Maffei C.
  Source: Journal of Personality Disorders. 1999 Fall; 13(3): 268-80.
  http://www.ncbi.nlm.nih.gov:80/entrez/query.fcgi?cmd=Retrieve&db=PubMed&list_uids=10498039&dopt=Abstract

- **Borderline personality disorder and substance use disorders: a review and integration.**
Author(s): Trull TJ, Sher KJ, Minks-Brown C, Durbin J, Burr R.
Source: Clinical Psychology Review. 2000 March; 20(2): 235-53. Review.
http://www.ncbi.nlm.nih.gov:80/entrez/query.fcgi?cmd=Retrieve&db=PubMed&list_uids=10721499&dopt=Abstract

- **Borderline personality disorder and the chronic headache patient: review and management recommendations.**
Author(s): Saper JR, Lake AE 3rd.
Source: Headache. 2002 July-August; 42(7): 663-74. Review.
http://www.ncbi.nlm.nih.gov:80/entrez/query.fcgi?cmd=Retrieve&db=PubMed&list_uids=12482221&dopt=Abstract

- **Borderline personality disorder comorbidity in early- and late-onset bipolar II disorder.**
Author(s): Benazzi F.
Source: Canadian Journal of Psychiatry. Revue Canadienne De Psychiatrie. 2002 March; 47(2): 195-6.
http://www.ncbi.nlm.nih.gov:80/entrez/query.fcgi?cmd=Retrieve&db=PubMed&list_uids=11926084&dopt=Abstract

- **Borderline personality disorder exists in India.**
Author(s): Pinto C, Dhavale HS, Nair S, Patil B, Dewan M.
Source: The Journal of Nervous and Mental Disease. 2000 June; 188(6): 386-8.
http://www.ncbi.nlm.nih.gov:80/entrez/query.fcgi?cmd=Retrieve&db=PubMed&list_uids=10890350&dopt=Abstract

- **Borderline personality disorder from the perspective of general personality functioning.**
Author(s): Trull TJ, Widiger TA, Lynam DR, Costa PT Jr.
Source: Journal of Abnormal Psychology. 2003 May; 112(2): 193-202.
http://www.ncbi.nlm.nih.gov:80/entrez/query.fcgi?cmd=Retrieve&db=PubMed&list_uids=12784828&dopt=Abstract

- **Borderline personality disorder in major depression: symptomatology, temperament, character, differential drug response, and 6-month outcome.**
Author(s): Joyce PR, Mulder RT, Luty SE, McKenzie JM, Sullivan PF, Cloninger RC.
Source: Comprehensive Psychiatry. 2003 January-February; 44(1): 35-43.
http://www.ncbi.nlm.nih.gov:80/entrez/query.fcgi?cmd=Retrieve&db=PubMed&list_uids=12524634&dopt=Abstract

- **Borderline personality disorder in primary care.**
Author(s): Gross R, Olfson M, Gameroff M, Shea S, Feder A, Fuentes M, Lantigua R, Weissman MM.
Source: Archives of Internal Medicine. 2002 January 14; 162(1): 53-60.
http://www.ncbi.nlm.nih.gov:80/entrez/query.fcgi?cmd=Retrieve&db=PubMed&list_uids=11784220&dopt=Abstract

- **Borderline personality disorder in primary care. Recognizing signs and symptoms.**
  Author(s): Schneidt KS.
  Source: Jaapa. 2000 January; 13(1): 18-22, 28, 31-2 Passim. Review. No Abstract Available.
  http://www.ncbi.nlm.nih.gov:80/entrez/query.fcgi?cmd=Retrieve&db=PubMed&list_uids=11503222&dopt=Abstract

- **Borderline personality disorder symptoms as predictors of 4-year romantic relationship dysfunction in young women: addressing issues of specificity.**
  Author(s): Daley SE, Burge D, Hammen C.
  Source: Journal of Abnormal Psychology. 2000 August; 109(3): 451-60.
  http://www.ncbi.nlm.nih.gov:80/entrez/query.fcgi?cmd=Retrieve&db=PubMed&list_uids=11016115&dopt=Abstract

- **Borderline personality disorder, suicide, and pharmacotherapy.**
  Author(s): Parker GF.
  Source: Psychiatric Services (Washington, D.C.). 2002 October; 53(10): 1330; Author Reply 1330-1.
  http://www.ncbi.nlm.nih.gov:80/entrez/query.fcgi?cmd=Retrieve&db=PubMed&list_uids=12364694&dopt=Abstract

- **Borderline personality disorder.**
  Author(s): Meares R, Stevenson J.
  Source: The Australian and New Zealand Journal of Psychiatry. 2000 October; 34(5): 869-71.
  http://www.ncbi.nlm.nih.gov:80/entrez/query.fcgi?cmd=Retrieve&db=PubMed&list_uids=11037378&dopt=Abstract

- **Borderline personality disorder. Neuropsychological testing results.**
  Author(s): O'Leary KM.
  Source: The Psychiatric Clinics of North America. 2000 March; 23(1): 41-60, Vi. Review.
  http://www.ncbi.nlm.nih.gov:80/entrez/query.fcgi?cmd=Retrieve&db=PubMed&list_uids=10729930&dopt=Abstract

- **Borderline personality disorder. Overview of biologic factors.**
  Author(s): Silk KR.
  Source: The Psychiatric Clinics of North America. 2000 March; 23(1): 61-75. Review.
  http://www.ncbi.nlm.nih.gov:80/entrez/query.fcgi?cmd=Retrieve&db=PubMed&list_uids=10729931&dopt=Abstract

- **Borderline personality disorder. Suicidality and self-mutilation.**
  Author(s): Gunderson JG, Ridolfi ME.
  Source: Annals of the New York Academy of Sciences. 2001 April; 932: 61-73; Discussion 73-7.
  http://www.ncbi.nlm.nih.gov:80/entrez/query.fcgi?cmd=Retrieve&db=PubMed&list_uids=11411191&dopt=Abstract

- **Borderline personality disorder: a motley diagnosis in need of reform.**
  Author(s): Tyrer P.
  Source: Lancet. 1999 December 18-25; 354(9196): 2095-6.
  http://www.ncbi.nlm.nih.gov:80/entrez/query.fcgi?cmd=Retrieve&db=PubMed&list_uids=10609809&dopt=Abstract

- **Characteristics of borderline personality disorder associated with suicidal behavior.**
  Author(s): Brodsky BS, Malone KM, Ellis SP, Dulit RA, Mann JJ.
  Source: The American Journal of Psychiatry. 1997 December; 154(12): 1715-9.
  http://www.ncbi.nlm.nih.gov:80/entrez/query.fcgi?cmd=Retrieve&db=PubMed&list_uids=9396951&dopt=Abstract

- **Characteristics of suicide attempts of patients with major depressive episode and borderline personality disorder: a comparative study.**
  Author(s): Soloff PH, Lynch KG, Kelly TM, Malone KM, Mann JJ.
  Source: The American Journal of Psychiatry. 2000 April; 157(4): 601-8.
  http://www.ncbi.nlm.nih.gov:80/entrez/query.fcgi?cmd=Retrieve&db=PubMed&list_uids=10739420&dopt=Abstract

- **Characterizing affective instability in borderline personality disorder.**
  Author(s): Koenigsberg HW, Harvey PD, Mitropoulou V, Schmeidler J, New AS, Goodman M, Silverman JM, Serby M, Schopick F, Siever LJ.
  Source: The American Journal of Psychiatry. 2002 May; 159(5): 784-8.
  http://www.ncbi.nlm.nih.gov:80/entrez/query.fcgi?cmd=Retrieve&db=PubMed&list_uids=11986132&dopt=Abstract

- **Childhood abuse and platelet tritiated-paroxetine binding in bulimia nervosa: implications of borderline personality disorder.**
  Author(s): Steiger H, Leonard S, Kin NY, Ladouceur C, Ramdoyal D, Young SN.
  Source: The Journal of Clinical Psychiatry. 2000 June; 61(6): 428-35.
  http://www.ncbi.nlm.nih.gov:80/entrez/query.fcgi?cmd=Retrieve&db=PubMed&list_uids=10901341&dopt=Abstract

- **Childhood abuse as a risk factor for suicidal behavior in borderline personality disorder.**
  Author(s): Soloff PH, Lynch KG, Kelly TM.
  Source: Journal of Personality Disorders. 2002 June; 16(3): 201-14.
  http://www.ncbi.nlm.nih.gov:80/entrez/query.fcgi?cmd=Retrieve&db=PubMed&list_uids=12136678&dopt=Abstract

- **Childhood antecedents of self-destructiveness in borderline personality disorder.**
  Author(s): Dubo ED, Zanarini MC, Lewis RE, Williams AA.
  Source: Canadian Journal of Psychiatry. Revue Canadienne De Psychiatrie. 1997 February; 42(1): 63-9.
  http://www.ncbi.nlm.nih.gov:80/entrez/query.fcgi?cmd=Retrieve&db=PubMed&list_uids=9040926&dopt=Abstract

- **Childhood experiences associated with the development of borderline personality disorder.**
  Author(s): Zanarini MC.
  Source: The Psychiatric Clinics of North America. 2000 March; 23(1): 89-101. Review.
  http://www.ncbi.nlm.nih.gov:80/entrez/query.fcgi?cmd=Retrieve&db=PubMed&list_uids=10729933&dopt=Abstract

- **Childhood precursors of borderline personality disorder.**
  Author(s): Paris J.
  Source: The Psychiatric Clinics of North America. 2000 March; 23(1): 77-88, Vii. Review.
  http://www.ncbi.nlm.nih.gov:80/entrez/query.fcgi?cmd=Retrieve&db=PubMed&list_uids=10729932&dopt=Abstract

- **Chronic suicidality among patients with borderline personality disorder.**
  Author(s): Paris J.
  Source: Psychiatric Services (Washington, D.C.). 2002 June; 53(6): 738-42. Review.
  http://www.ncbi.nlm.nih.gov:80/entrez/query.fcgi?cmd=Retrieve&db=PubMed&list_uids=12045312&dopt=Abstract

- **Clinical characteristics of older psychiatric inpatients with borderline personality disorder.**
  Author(s): Trappler B, Backfield J.
  Source: The Psychiatric Quarterly. 2001 Spring; 72(1): 29-40.
  http://www.ncbi.nlm.nih.gov:80/entrez/query.fcgi?cmd=Retrieve&db=PubMed&list_uids=11293200&dopt=Abstract

- **Clinical guidelines for psychotherapy for patients with borderline personality disorder.**
  Author(s): Stone MH.
  Source: The Psychiatric Clinics of North America. 2000 March; 23(1): 193-210, Ix. Review.
  http://www.ncbi.nlm.nih.gov:80/entrez/query.fcgi?cmd=Retrieve&db=PubMed&list_uids=10729939&dopt=Abstract

- **Clinical Practice Guidelines for borderline personality disorder.**
  Author(s): Paris J.
  Source: Journal of Personality Disorders. 2002 April; 16(2): 107-8.
  http://www.ncbi.nlm.nih.gov:80/entrez/query.fcgi?cmd=Retrieve&db=PubMed&list_uids=12004484&dopt=Abstract

- **Clozapine and borderline personality disorder.**
  Author(s): Parker GF.
  Source: Psychiatric Services (Washington, D.C.). 2002 March; 53(3): 348-9.
  http://www.ncbi.nlm.nih.gov:80/entrez/query.fcgi?cmd=Retrieve&db=PubMed&list_uids=11875239&dopt=Abstract

- **Clozapine reduces severe self-mutilation and aggression in psychotic patients with borderline personality disorder.**
  Author(s): Chengappa KN, Ebeling T, Kang JS, Levine J, Parepally H.
  Source: The Journal of Clinical Psychiatry. 1999 July; 60(7): 477-84.
  http://www.ncbi.nlm.nih.gov:80/entrez/query.fcgi?cmd=Retrieve&db=PubMed&list_uids=10453803&dopt=Abstract

- **Commentary on the American Psychiatric Association guidelines for the treatment of borderline personality disorder: evidence-based psychiatry and the quality of evidence.**
  Author(s): Paris J.
  Source: Journal of Personality Disorders. 2002 April; 16(2): 130-4.
  http://www.ncbi.nlm.nih.gov:80/entrez/query.fcgi?cmd=Retrieve&db=PubMed&list_uids=12004489&dopt=Abstract

- **Comorbidity of borderline personality disorder with other personality disorders in hospitalized adolescents and adults.**
  Author(s): Becker DF, Grilo CM, Edell WS, McGlashan TH.
  Source: The American Journal of Psychiatry. 2000 December; 157(12): 2011-6.
  http://www.ncbi.nlm.nih.gov:80/entrez/query.fcgi?cmd=Retrieve&db=PubMed&list_uids=11097968&dopt=Abstract

- **Comorbidity of schizophreniform disorder and borderline personality disorder in an 18-year-old black woman.**
  Author(s): Houry D, Johnson J, Cabrejos C.
  Source: Southern Medical Journal. 1998 March; 91(3): 275-7.
  http://www.ncbi.nlm.nih.gov:80/entrez/query.fcgi?cmd=Retrieve&db=PubMed&list_uids=9521370&dopt=Abstract

- **Confirmatory factor analysis of DSM-IV criteria for borderline personality disorder: findings from the collaborative longitudinal personality disorders study.**
  Author(s): Sanislow CA, Grilo CM, Morey LC, Bender DS, Skodol AE, Gunderson JG, Shea MT, Stout RL, Zanarini MC, McGlashan TH.
  Source: The American Journal of Psychiatry. 2002 February; 159(2): 284-90.
  http://www.ncbi.nlm.nih.gov:80/entrez/query.fcgi?cmd=Retrieve&db=PubMed&list_uids=11823272&dopt=Abstract

- **Co-occurrence of DSM-IV personality disorders with borderline personality disorder.**
  Author(s): Grilo CM, Sanislow CA, McGlashan TH.
  Source: The Journal of Nervous and Mental Disease. 2002 August; 190(8): 552-4.
  http://www.ncbi.nlm.nih.gov:80/entrez/query.fcgi?cmd=Retrieve&db=PubMed&list_uids=12193841&dopt=Abstract

- **Cultural intersections in the psychotherapy of borderline personality disorder.**
  Author(s): Alarcon RD, Leetz KL.
  Source: American Journal of Psychotherapy. 1998 Spring; 52(2): 176-90.
  http://www.ncbi.nlm.nih.gov:80/entrez/query.fcgi?cmd=Retrieve&db=PubMed&list_uids=9656054&dopt=Abstract

- **Depressive response to physostigmine challenge in borderline personality disorder patients.**
  Author(s): Steinberg BJ, Trestman R, Mitropoulou V, Serby M, Silverman J, Coccaro E, Weston S, de Vegvar M, Siever LJ.
  Source: Neuropsychopharmacology : Official Publication of the American College of Neuropsychopharmacology. 1997 October; 17(4): 264-73.
  http://www.ncbi.nlm.nih.gov:80/entrez/query.fcgi?cmd=Retrieve&db=PubMed&list_uids=9326751&dopt=Abstract

- **Development of the American Psychiatric Association Practice Guideline for the Treatment of Borderline Personality Disorder.**
  Author(s): Oldham JM.
  Source: Journal of Personality Disorders. 2002 April; 16(2): 109-12.
  http://www.ncbi.nlm.nih.gov:80/entrez/query.fcgi?cmd=Retrieve&db=PubMed&list_uids=12004485&dopt=Abstract

- **Developmental aspects of borderline personality disorder.**
  Author(s): Reich DB, Zanarini MC.
  Source: Harvard Review of Psychiatry. 2001 November-December; 9(6): 294-301.
  http://www.ncbi.nlm.nih.gov:80/entrez/query.fcgi?cmd=Retrieve&db=PubMed&list_uids=11600488&dopt=Abstract

- **Developmental protective and risk factors in borderline personality disorder: a study using the Adult Attachment Interview.**
  Author(s): Barone L.
  Source: Attachment & Human Development. 2003 March; 5(1): 64-77.
  http://www.ncbi.nlm.nih.gov:80/entrez/query.fcgi?cmd=Retrieve&db=PubMed&list_uids=12745829&dopt=Abstract

- **Diagnostic efficiency of borderline personality disorder criteria in hospitalized adolescents: comparison with hospitalized adults.**
  Author(s): Becker DF, Grilo CM, Edell WS, McGlashan TH.
  Source: The American Journal of Psychiatry. 2002 December; 159(12): 2042-7.
  http://www.ncbi.nlm.nih.gov:80/entrez/query.fcgi?cmd=Retrieve&db=PubMed&list_uids=12450954&dopt=Abstract

- **Dialectical behavior therapy for patients with borderline personality disorder and drug-dependence.**
  Author(s): Linehan MM, Schmidt H 3rd, Dimeff LA, Craft JC, Kanter J, Comtois KA.
  Source: The American Journal on Addictions / American Academy of Psychiatrists in Alcoholism and Addictions. 1999 Fall; 8(4): 279-92.
  http://www.ncbi.nlm.nih.gov:80/entrez/query.fcgi?cmd=Retrieve&db=PubMed&list_uids=10598211&dopt=Abstract

- **Dialectical behavior therapy for patients with borderline personality disorder.**
  Author(s): Alper G, Peterson SJ.
  Source: Journal of Psychosocial Nursing and Mental Health Services. 2001 October; 39(10): 38-45.
  http://www.ncbi.nlm.nih.gov:80/entrez/query.fcgi?cmd=Retrieve&db=PubMed&list_uids=11697073&dopt=Abstract

- **Dialectical behavior therapy in the treatment of persons with borderline personality disorder.**
  Author(s): Hampton MC.
  Source: Archives of Psychiatric Nursing. 1997 April; 11(2): 96-101. Review.
  http://www.ncbi.nlm.nih.gov:80/entrez/query.fcgi?cmd=Retrieve&db=PubMed&list_uids=9105110&dopt=Abstract

- **Dialectical behavior therapy versus comprehensive validation therapy plus 12-step for the treatment of opioid dependent women meeting criteria for borderline personality disorder.**
  Author(s): Linehan MM, Dimeff LA, Reynolds SK, Comtois KA, Welch SS, Heagerty P, Kivlahan DR.
  Source: Drug and Alcohol Dependence. 2002 June 1; 67(1): 13-26.
  http://www.ncbi.nlm.nih.gov:80/entrez/query.fcgi?cmd=Retrieve&db=PubMed&list_uids=12062776&dopt=Abstract

- **Dialectical behaviour therapy for women with borderline personality disorder: 12-month, randomised clinical trialin The Netherlands.**
  Author(s): Verheul R, Van Den Bosch LM, Koeter MW, De Ridder MA, Stijnen T, Van Den Brink W.
  Source: The British Journal of Psychiatry; the Journal of Mental Science. 2003 February; 182: 135-40.
  http://www.ncbi.nlm.nih.gov:80/entrez/query.fcgi?cmd=Retrieve&db=PubMed&list_uids=12562741&dopt=Abstract

- **Differences between clinical and research practices in diagnosing borderline personality disorder.**
  Author(s): Zimmerman M, Mattia JI.
  Source: The American Journal of Psychiatry. 1999 October; 156(10): 1570-4.
  http://www.ncbi.nlm.nih.gov:80/entrez/query.fcgi?cmd=Retrieve&db=PubMed&list_uids=10518168&dopt=Abstract

- **Dimensional personality profiles of borderline personality disorder in comparison with other personality disorders and healthy controls.**
  Author(s): Pukrop R.
  Source: Journal of Personality Disorders. 2002 April; 16(2): 135-47.
  http://www.ncbi.nlm.nih.gov:80/entrez/query.fcgi?cmd=Retrieve&db=PubMed&list_uids=12004490&dopt=Abstract

- **Diminished impulsivity in older patients with borderline personality disorder.**
  Author(s): Stevenson J, Meares R, Comerford A.
  Source: The American Journal of Psychiatry. 2003 January; 160(1): 165-6.
  http://www.ncbi.nlm.nih.gov:80/entrez/query.fcgi?cmd=Retrieve&db=PubMed&list_uids=12505816&dopt=Abstract

- **Directed forgetting of emotional stimuli in borderline personality disorder.**
  Author(s): Korfine L, Hooley JM.
  Source: Journal of Abnormal Psychology. 2000 May; 109(2): 214-21.
  http://www.ncbi.nlm.nih.gov:80/entrez/query.fcgi?cmd=Retrieve&db=PubMed&list_uids=10895559&dopt=Abstract

- **Discriminating among subgroups of borderline personality disorder: an assessment of object representations.**
  Author(s): Tramantano G, Javier RA, Colon M.
  Source: American Journal of Psychoanalysis. 2003 June; 63(2): 149-75.
  http://www.ncbi.nlm.nih.gov:80/entrez/query.fcgi?cmd=Retrieve&db=PubMed&list_uids=12872786&dopt=Abstract

- **Divalproex sodium treatment of women with borderline personality disorder and bipolar II disorder: a double-blind placebo-controlled pilot study.**
  Author(s): Frankenburg FR, Zanarini MC.
  Source: The Journal of Clinical Psychiatry. 2002 May; 63(5): 442-6.
  http://www.ncbi.nlm.nih.gov:80/entrez/query.fcgi?cmd=Retrieve&db=PubMed&list_uids=12019669&dopt=Abstract

- **Do patients with borderline personality disorder belong to the bipolar spectrum?**
  Author(s): Deltito J, Martin L, Riefkohl J, Austria B, Kissilenko A, Corless C Morse P.
  Source: Journal of Affective Disorders. 2001 December; 67(1-3): 221-8.
  http://www.ncbi.nlm.nih.gov:80/entrez/query.fcgi?cmd=Retrieve&db=PubMed&list_uids=11869772&dopt=Abstract

- **Does the ICD 10 classification accurately describe subtypes of borderline personality disorder?**
  Author(s): Whewell P, Ryman A, Bonanno D, Heather N.
  Source: The British Journal of Medical Psychology. 2000 December; 73 Pt 4: 483-94.
  http://www.ncbi.nlm.nih.gov:80/entrez/query.fcgi?cmd=Retrieve&db=PubMed&list_uids=11140789&dopt=Abstract

- **DSM-IV axis II comorbidity with borderline personality disorder in monolingual Hispanic psychiatric outpatients.**
  Author(s): Grilo CM, Miguel Anez L, McGlashan TH.
  Source: The Journal of Nervous and Mental Disease. 2002 May; 190(5): 324-30.
  http://www.ncbi.nlm.nih.gov:80/entrez/query.fcgi?cmd=Retrieve&db=PubMed&list_uids=12011613&dopt=Abstract

- **Dysphoria and aloneness in borderline personality disorder.**
  Author(s): Pazzagli A, Monti MR.
  Source: Psychopathology. 2000 July-August; 33(4): 220-6.
  http://www.ncbi.nlm.nih.gov:80/entrez/query.fcgi?cmd=Retrieve&db=PubMed&list_uids=10867581&dopt=Abstract

- **Early family environments and traumatic experiences associated with borderline personality disorder.**
  Author(s): Weaver TL, Clum GA.
  Source: Journal of Consulting and Clinical Psychology. 1993 December; 61(6): 1068-75.
  http://www.ncbi.nlm.nih.gov:80/entrez/query.fcgi?cmd=Retrieve&db=PubMed&list_uids=8113485&dopt=Abstract

- **EEG in borderline personality disorder.**
  Author(s): Archer RP, Struve FA, Ball JD, Gordon RA.
  Source: Biological Psychiatry. 1988 October; 24(6): 731-2.
  http://www.ncbi.nlm.nih.gov:80/entrez/query.fcgi?cmd=Retrieve&db=PubMed&list_uids=3167160&dopt=Abstract

- **Effect of fluoxetine on anger in symptomatic volunteers with borderline personality disorder.**
  Author(s): Salzman C, Wolfson AN, Schatzberg A, Looper J, Henke R, Albanese M, Schwartz J, Miyawaki E.
  Source: Journal of Clinical Psychopharmacology. 1995 February; 15(1): 23-9.
  http://www.ncbi.nlm.nih.gov:80/entrez/query.fcgi?cmd=Retrieve&db=PubMed&list_uids=7714224&dopt=Abstract

- **Effectiveness of partial hospitalization in the treatment of borderline personality disorder: a randomized controlled trial.**
  Author(s): Bateman A, Fonagy P.
  Source: The American Journal of Psychiatry. 1999 October; 156(10): 1563-9.
  http://www.ncbi.nlm.nih.gov:80/entrez/query.fcgi?cmd=Retrieve&db=PubMed&list_uids=10518167&dopt=Abstract

- **Effectiveness of time-limited cognitive analytic therapy of borderline personality disorder: factors associated with outcome.**
  Author(s): Ryle A, Golynkina K.
  Source: The British Journal of Medical Psychology. 2000 June; 73 ( Pt 2): 197-210.
  http://www.ncbi.nlm.nih.gov:80/entrez/query.fcgi?cmd=Retrieve&db=PubMed&list_uids=10874479&dopt=Abstract

- **Effects of carbamazepine on dexamethasone suppression and sleep electroencephalography in borderline personality disorder.**
  Author(s): De la Fuente JM, Bobes J, Vizuete C, Mendlewicz J.
  Source: Neuropsychobiology. 2002; 45(3): 113-9.
  http://www.ncbi.nlm.nih.gov:80/entrez/query.fcgi?cmd=Retrieve&db=PubMed&list_uids=11979058&dopt=Abstract

- **Electroencephalographic abnormalities in borderline personality disorder.**
  Author(s): De la Fuente JM, Tugendhaft P, Mavroudakis N.
  Source: Psychiatry Research. 1998 February 9; 77(2): 131-8.
  http://www.ncbi.nlm.nih.gov:80/entrez/query.fcgi?cmd=Retrieve&db=PubMed&list_uids=9541149&dopt=Abstract

- **Electrophysiological aberrations in borderline personality disorder: state of the evidence.**
  Author(s): Boutros NN, Torello M, McGlashan TH.
  Source: The Journal of Neuropsychiatry and Clinical Neurosciences. 2003 Spring; 15(2): 145-54. Review.
  http://www.ncbi.nlm.nih.gov:80/entrez/query.fcgi?cmd=Retrieve&db=PubMed&list_uids=12724454&dopt=Abstract

- **Emotion in criminal offenders with psychopathy and borderline personality disorder.**
Author(s): Herpertz SC, Werth U, Lukas G, Qunaibi M, Schuerkens A, Kunert HJ, Freese R, Flesch M, Mueller-Isberner R, Osterheider M, Sass H.
Source: Archives of General Psychiatry. 2001 August; 58(8): 737-45.
http://www.ncbi.nlm.nih.gov:80/entrez/query.fcgi?cmd=Retrieve&db=PubMed&list_uids=11483139&dopt=Abstract

- **Empathy in families of women with borderline personality disorder, anorexia nervosa, and a control group.**
Author(s): Guttman HA, Laporte L.
Source: Family Process. 2000 Fall; 39(3): 345-58.
http://www.ncbi.nlm.nih.gov:80/entrez/query.fcgi?cmd=Retrieve&db=PubMed&list_uids=11008652&dopt=Abstract

- **Enhanced intensity dependence as a marker of low serotonergic neurotransmission in borderline personality disorder.**
Author(s): Norra C, Mrazek M, Tuchtenhagen F, Gobbele R, Buchner H, Sass H, Herpertz SC.
Source: Journal of Psychiatric Research. 2003 January-February; 37(1): 23-33.
http://www.ncbi.nlm.nih.gov:80/entrez/query.fcgi?cmd=Retrieve&db=PubMed&list_uids=12482467&dopt=Abstract

- **Epidemiology of borderline personality disorder.**
Author(s): Widiger TA, Weissman MM.
Source: Hosp Community Psychiatry. 1991 October; 42(10): 1015-21. Review.
http://www.ncbi.nlm.nih.gov:80/entrez/query.fcgi?cmd=Retrieve&db=PubMed&list_uids=1959892&dopt=Abstract

- **Era-related changes in the Japanese cultural and social structure and conformist personality pathology--with a particular emphasis on borderline personality disorder.**
Author(s): Tamai K.
Source: Fukuoka Igaku Zasshi. 1997 April; 88(4): 84-9. Review.
http://www.ncbi.nlm.nih.gov:80/entrez/query.fcgi?cmd=Retrieve&db=PubMed&list_uids=9154712&dopt=Abstract

- **Etiological significance of associations between childhood trauma and borderline personality disorder: conceptual and clinical implications.**
Author(s): Sabo AN.
Source: Journal of Personality Disorders. 1997 Spring; 11(1): 50-70.
http://www.ncbi.nlm.nih.gov:80/entrez/query.fcgi?cmd=Retrieve&db=PubMed&list_uids=9113822&dopt=Abstract

- **Evaluation of diagnostic criteria for borderline personality disorder.**
Author(s): Nurnberg HG, Hurt SW, Feldman A, Suh R.
Source: The American Journal of Psychiatry. 1988 October; 145(10): 1280-4.
http://www.ncbi.nlm.nih.gov:80/entrez/query.fcgi?cmd=Retrieve&db=PubMed&list_uids=3421351&dopt=Abstract

- **Evaluation of inpatient dialectical-behavioral therapy for borderline personality disorder--a prospective study.**
Author(s): Bohus M, Haaf B, Stiglmayr C, Pohl U, Bohme R, Linehan M.
Source: Behaviour Research and Therapy. 2000 September; 38(9): 875-87.
http://www.ncbi.nlm.nih.gov:80/entrez/query.fcgi?cmd=Retrieve&db=PubMed&list_uids=10957822&dopt=Abstract

- **Evidence of abnormal amygdala functioning in borderline personality disorder: a functional MRI study.**
Author(s): Herpertz SC, Dietrich TM, Wenning B, Krings T, Erberich SG, Willmes K, Thron A, Sass H.
Source: Biological Psychiatry. 2001 August 15; 50(4): 292-8.
http://www.ncbi.nlm.nih.gov:80/entrez/query.fcgi?cmd=Retrieve&db=PubMed&list_uids=11522264&dopt=Abstract

- **Experience of aversive tension and dissociation in female patients with borderline personality disorder -- a controlled study.**
Author(s): Stiglmayr CE, Shapiro DA, Stieglitz RD, Limberger MF, Bohus M.
Source: Journal of Psychiatric Research. 2001 March-April; 35(2): 111-8.
http://www.ncbi.nlm.nih.gov:80/entrez/query.fcgi?cmd=Retrieve&db=PubMed&list_uids=11377440&dopt=Abstract

- **Experience, knowledge and attitudes of mental health staff regarding clients with a borderline personality disorder.**
Author(s): Cleary M, Siegfried N, Walter G.
Source: International Journal of Mental Health Nursing. 2002 September; 11(3): 186-91.
http://www.ncbi.nlm.nih.gov:80/entrez/query.fcgi?cmd=Retrieve&db=PubMed&list_uids=12510596&dopt=Abstract

- **Expressed emotion and clinical outcome in borderline personality disorder.**
Author(s): Hooley JM, Hoffman PD.
Source: The American Journal of Psychiatry. 1999 October; 156(10): 1557-62.
http://www.ncbi.nlm.nih.gov:80/entrez/query.fcgi?cmd=Retrieve&db=PubMed&list_uids=10518166&dopt=Abstract

- **Facial expression recognition ability among women with borderline personality disorder: implications for emotion regulation?**
Author(s): Wagner AW, Linehan MM.
Source: Journal of Personality Disorders. 1999 Winter; 13(4): 329-44.
http://www.ncbi.nlm.nih.gov:80/entrez/query.fcgi?cmd=Retrieve&db=PubMed&list_uids=10633314&dopt=Abstract

- **Factor analysis of the DSM-III-R borderline personality disorder criteria in psychiatric inpatients.**
Author(s): Sanislow CA, Grilo CM, McGlashan TH.
Source: The American Journal of Psychiatry. 2000 October; 157(10): 1629-33.
http://www.ncbi.nlm.nih.gov:80/entrez/query.fcgi?cmd=Retrieve&db=PubMed&list_uids=11007717&dopt=Abstract

- **Factors associated with completed suicide in borderline personality disorder.**
  Author(s): Kullgren G.
  Source: The Journal of Nervous and Mental Disease. 1988 January; 176(1): 40-4.
  http://www.ncbi.nlm.nih.gov:80/entrez/query.fcgi?cmd=Retrieve&db=PubMed&list_uids=2826681&dopt=Abstract

- **Factors associated with multiple hospitalizations of patients with borderline personality disorder.**
  Author(s): Hull JW, Yeomans F, Clarkin J, Li C, Goodman G.
  Source: Psychiatric Services (Washington, D.C.). 1996 June; 47(6): 638-41.
  http://www.ncbi.nlm.nih.gov:80/entrez/query.fcgi?cmd=Retrieve&db=PubMed&list_uids=8726493&dopt=Abstract

- **Familial transmission of DSM-III borderline personality disorder.**
  Author(s): Loranger AW, Oldham JM, Tulis EH.
  Source: Archives of General Psychiatry. 1982 July; 39(7): 795-9.
  http://www.ncbi.nlm.nih.gov:80/entrez/query.fcgi?cmd=Retrieve&db=PubMed&list_uids=7165479&dopt=Abstract

- **Familial transmission of schizotypal and borderline personality disorders.**
  Author(s): Baron M, Gruen R, Asnis L, Lord S.
  Source: The American Journal of Psychiatry. 1985 August; 142(8): 927-34.
  http://www.ncbi.nlm.nih.gov:80/entrez/query.fcgi?cmd=Retrieve&db=PubMed&list_uids=4025588&dopt=Abstract

- **Family history of alcoholism in borderline personality disorder.**
  Author(s): Loranger AW, Tulis EH.
  Source: Archives of General Psychiatry. 1985 February; 42(2): 153-7.
  http://www.ncbi.nlm.nih.gov:80/entrez/query.fcgi?cmd=Retrieve&db=PubMed&list_uids=3977541&dopt=Abstract

- **Family problems and relationships for adults with borderline personality disorder.**
  Author(s): Gunderson JG, Lyoo IK.
  Source: Harvard Review of Psychiatry. 1997 January-February; 4(5): 272-8.
  http://www.ncbi.nlm.nih.gov:80/entrez/query.fcgi?cmd=Retrieve&db=PubMed&list_uids=9385003&dopt=Abstract

- **Family relationships of adults with borderline personality disorder.**
  Author(s): Allen DM, Farmer RG.
  Source: Comprehensive Psychiatry. 1996 January-February; 37(1): 43-51. Review.
  http://www.ncbi.nlm.nih.gov:80/entrez/query.fcgi?cmd=Retrieve&db=PubMed&list_uids=8770526&dopt=Abstract

- **Family studies of borderline personality disorder: a review.**
  Author(s): White CN, Gunderson JG, Zanarini MC, Hudson JI.
  Source: Harvard Review of Psychiatry. 2003 January-February; 11(1): 8-19. Review.
  http://www.ncbi.nlm.nih.gov:80/entrez/query.fcgi?cmd=Retrieve&db=PubMed&list_uids=12866737&dopt=Abstract

- **First-cycle REM density in never-depressed subjects with borderline personality disorder.**
  Author(s): Battaglia M, Ferini Strambi L, Bertella S, Bajo S, Bellodi L.
  Source: Biological Psychiatry. 1999 April 15; 45(8): 1056-8.
  http://www.ncbi.nlm.nih.gov:80/entrez/query.fcgi?cmd=Retrieve&db=PubMed&list_uids=10386191&dopt=Abstract

- **Fluoxetine in borderline personality disorder.**
  Author(s): Norden MJ.
  Source: Progress in Neuro-Psychopharmacology & Biological Psychiatry. 1989; 13(6): 885-93.
  http://www.ncbi.nlm.nih.gov:80/entrez/query.fcgi?cmd=Retrieve&db=PubMed&list_uids=2813806&dopt=Abstract

- **Fluoxetine trial in borderline personality disorder.**
  Author(s): Cornelius JR, Soloff PH, Perel JM, Ulrich RF.
  Source: Psychopharmacology Bulletin. 1990; 26(1): 151-4.
  http://www.ncbi.nlm.nih.gov:80/entrez/query.fcgi?cmd=Retrieve&db=PubMed&list_uids=2371370&dopt=Abstract

- **Follow-up study on borderline versus nonborderline personality disorders.**
  Author(s): Modestin J, Villiger C.
  Source: Comprehensive Psychiatry. 1989 May-June; 30(3): 236-44.
  http://www.ncbi.nlm.nih.gov:80/entrez/query.fcgi?cmd=Retrieve&db=PubMed&list_uids=2731422&dopt=Abstract

- **Frequency of borderline personality disorder in a sample of French high school students.**
  Author(s): Chabrol H, Montovany A, Chouicha K, Callahan S, Mullet E.
  Source: Canadian Journal of Psychiatry. Revue Canadienne De Psychiatrie. 2001 November; 46(9): 847-9.
  http://www.ncbi.nlm.nih.gov:80/entrez/query.fcgi?cmd=Retrieve&db=PubMed&list_uids=11761637&dopt=Abstract

- **From Humpty-Dumpty to Rapunzel: theoretical formulations concerning borderline personality disorder.**
  Author(s): Lonie I.
  Source: The Australian and New Zealand Journal of Psychiatry. 1985 December; 19(4): 372-81.
  http://www.ncbi.nlm.nih.gov:80/entrez/query.fcgi?cmd=Retrieve&db=PubMed&list_uids=2421706&dopt=Abstract

- **Frontolimbic brain abnormalities in patients with borderline personality disorder: a volumetric magnetic resonance imaging study.**
  Author(s): Tebartz van Elst L, Hesslinger B, Thiel T, Geiger E, Haegele K, Lemieux L, Lieb K, Bohus M, Hennig J, Ebert D.
  Source: Biological Psychiatry. 2003 July 15; 54(2): 163-71.
  http://www.ncbi.nlm.nih.gov:80/entrez/query.fcgi?cmd=Retrieve&db=PubMed&list_uids=12873806&dopt=Abstract

- **Gender issues and borderline personality disorder: why do females dominate the diagnosis?**
  Author(s): Simmons D.
  Source: Archives of Psychiatric Nursing. 1992 August; 6(4): 219-23.
  http://www.ncbi.nlm.nih.gov:80/entrez/query.fcgi?cmd=Retrieve&db=PubMed&list_uids=1417077&dopt=Abstract

- **Genetic and nosological aspects of schizotypal and borderline personality disorders. A twin study.**
  Author(s): Torgersen S.
  Source: Archives of General Psychiatry. 1984 June; 41(6): 546-54.
  http://www.ncbi.nlm.nih.gov:80/entrez/query.fcgi?cmd=Retrieve&db=PubMed&list_uids=6732416&dopt=Abstract

- **Genetics of patients with borderline personality disorder.**
  Author(s): Torgersen S.
  Source: The Psychiatric Clinics of North America. 2000 March; 23(1): 1-9. Review.
  http://www.ncbi.nlm.nih.gov:80/entrez/query.fcgi?cmd=Retrieve&db=PubMed&list_uids=10729927&dopt=Abstract

- **Group and family treatments for borderline personality disorder.**
  Author(s): Clarkin JF, Marziali E, Munroe-Blum H.
  Source: Hosp Community Psychiatry. 1991 October; 42(10): 1038-43. Review.
  http://www.ncbi.nlm.nih.gov:80/entrez/query.fcgi?cmd=Retrieve&db=PubMed&list_uids=1959895&dopt=Abstract

- **Group therapy for people with borderline personality disorder: interventions associated with positive outcomes.**
  Author(s): Nehls N.
  Source: Issues in Mental Health Nursing. 1992 July-September; 13(3): 255-69.
  http://www.ncbi.nlm.nih.gov:80/entrez/query.fcgi?cmd=Retrieve&db=PubMed&list_uids=1399522&dopt=Abstract

- **Health service utilization costs for borderline personality disorder patients treated with psychoanalytically oriented partial hospitalization versus general psychiatric care.**
  Author(s): Bateman A, Fonagy P.
  Source: The American Journal of Psychiatry. 2003 January; 160(1): 169-71.
  http://www.ncbi.nlm.nih.gov:80/entrez/query.fcgi?cmd=Retrieve&db=PubMed&list_uids=12505818&dopt=Abstract

- **High-risk situations associated with parasuicide and drug use in borderline personality disorder.**
  Author(s): Welch SS, Linehan MM.
  Source: Journal of Personality Disorders. 2002 December; 16(6): 561-9.
  http://www.ncbi.nlm.nih.gov:80/entrez/query.fcgi?cmd=Retrieve&db=PubMed&list_uids=12616831&dopt=Abstract

- **History of childhood attention deficit/hyperactivity disorder symptoms and borderline personality disorder: a controlled study.**
  Author(s): Fossati A, Novella L, Donati D, Donini M, Maffei C.
  Source: Comprehensive Psychiatry. 2002 September-October; 43(5): 369-77.
  http://www.ncbi.nlm.nih.gov:80/entrez/query.fcgi?cmd=Retrieve&db=PubMed&list_uids=12216012&dopt=Abstract

- **Homosexuality in patients with borderline personality disorder.**
  Author(s): Stone MH.
  Source: The American Journal of Psychiatry. 1987 December; 144(12): 1622-3.
  http://www.ncbi.nlm.nih.gov:80/entrez/query.fcgi?cmd=Retrieve&db=PubMed&list_uids=3688295&dopt=Abstract

- **Hospital discharge status and long-term outcome for patients with schizophrenia, schizoaffective disorder, borderline personality disorder, and unipolar affective disorder.**
  Author(s): McGlashan TH, Heinssen RK.
  Source: Archives of General Psychiatry. 1988 April; 45(4): 363-8.
  http://www.ncbi.nlm.nih.gov:80/entrez/query.fcgi?cmd=Retrieve&db=PubMed&list_uids=3355323&dopt=Abstract

- **How nursing staff respond to the label "borderline personality disorder".**
  Author(s): Gallop R, Lancee WJ, Garfinkel P.
  Source: Hosp Community Psychiatry. 1989 August; 40(8): 815-9.
  http://www.ncbi.nlm.nih.gov:80/entrez/query.fcgi?cmd=Retrieve&db=PubMed&list_uids=2759571&dopt=Abstract

- **How useful a diagnosis is borderline personality disorder?**
  Author(s): Davis DR.
  Source: British Medical Journal (Clinical Research Ed.). 1987 January 31; 294(6567): 265-6.
  http://www.ncbi.nlm.nih.gov:80/entrez/query.fcgi?cmd=Retrieve&db=PubMed&list_uids=3101835&dopt=Abstract

- **Hyperresponsiveness of hypothalamic-pituitary-adrenal axis to combined dexamethasone/corticotropin-releasing hormone challenge in female borderline personality disorder subjects with a history of sustained childhood abuse.**
  Author(s): Rinne T, de Kloet ER, Wouters L, Goekoop JG, DeRijk RH, van den Brink W.
  Source: Biological Psychiatry. 2002 December 1; 52(11): 1102-12.
  http://www.ncbi.nlm.nih.gov:80/entrez/query.fcgi?cmd=Retrieve&db=PubMed&list_uids=12460693&dopt=Abstract

- **Hypothesis about borderline personality disorder.**
  Author(s): Knoll JL 3rd.
  Source: The American Journal of Psychiatry. 1991 January; 148(1): 149.
  http://www.ncbi.nlm.nih.gov:80/entrez/query.fcgi?cmd=Retrieve&db=PubMed&list_uids=1984700&dopt=Abstract

- **Identification of borderline personality disorder with the NIMH Diagnostic Interview Schedule.**
  Author(s): Swartz MS, Blazer DG, George LK, Winfield I, Zakris J, Dye E.
  Source: The American Journal of Psychiatry. 1989 February; 146(2): 200-5.
  http://www.ncbi.nlm.nih.gov:80/entrez/query.fcgi?cmd=Retrieve&db=PubMed&list_uids=2643363&dopt=Abstract

- **Identity disturbance in borderline personality disorder: an empirical investigation.**
  Author(s): Wilkinson-Ryan T, Westen D.
  Source: The American Journal of Psychiatry. 2000 April; 157(4): 528-41.
  http://www.ncbi.nlm.nih.gov:80/entrez/query.fcgi?cmd=Retrieve&db=PubMed&list_uids=10739411&dopt=Abstract

- **Impact of borderline personality disorder in late life on systems of care.**
  Author(s): Rosowsky E, Gurian B.
  Source: Hosp Community Psychiatry. 1992 April; 43(4): 386-9. Review.
  http://www.ncbi.nlm.nih.gov:80/entrez/query.fcgi?cmd=Retrieve&db=PubMed&list_uids=1577432&dopt=Abstract

- **Impact of simulating borderline personality disorder on the MMPI-2: a costs-benefits model employing base rates.**
  Author(s): Sivec HJ, Hilsenroth MJ, Lynn SJ.
  Source: Journal of Personality Assessment. 1995 April; 64(2): 295-311.
  http://www.ncbi.nlm.nih.gov:80/entrez/query.fcgi?cmd=Retrieve&db=PubMed&list_uids=7722855&dopt=Abstract

- **Implications of childhood sexual abuse for adult borderline personality disorder and complex posttraumatic stress disorder.**
  Author(s): McLean LM, Gallop R.
  Source: The American Journal of Psychiatry. 2003 February; 160(2): 369-71.
  http://www.ncbi.nlm.nih.gov:80/entrez/query.fcgi?cmd=Retrieve&db=PubMed&list_uids=12562587&dopt=Abstract

- **Implications of long-term outcome research for the management of patients with borderline personality disorder.**
  Author(s): Paris J.
  Source: Harvard Review of Psychiatry. 2002 November-December; 10(6): 315-23. Review.
  http://www.ncbi.nlm.nih.gov:80/entrez/query.fcgi?cmd=Retrieve&db=PubMed&list_uids=12485978&dopt=Abstract

- **Impulsive aggression in borderline personality disorder.**
  Author(s): Goodman M, New A.
  Source: Current Psychiatry Reports. 2000 February; 2(1): 56-61. Review.
  http://www.ncbi.nlm.nih.gov:80/entrez/query.fcgi?cmd=Retrieve&db=PubMed&list_uids=11122933&dopt=Abstract

- **Impulsivity and prefrontal hypometabolism in borderline personality disorder.**
  Author(s): Soloff PH, Meltzer CC, Becker C, Greer PJ, Kelly TM, Constantine D.
  Source: Psychiatry Research. 2003 July 30; 123(3): 153-63.
  http://www.ncbi.nlm.nih.gov:80/entrez/query.fcgi?cmd=Retrieve&db=PubMed&list_uids=12928103&dopt=Abstract

- **Impulsivity, defensive functioning, and borderline personality disorder.**
  Author(s): van Reekum R, Links PS, Mitton MJ, Fedorov C, Patrick J.
  Source: Canadian Journal of Psychiatry. Revue Canadienne De Psychiatrie. 1996 March; 41(2): 81-4.
  http://www.ncbi.nlm.nih.gov:80/entrez/query.fcgi?cmd=Retrieve&db=PubMed&list_uids=8705967&dopt=Abstract

- **Impulsivity: core aspect of borderline personality disorder.**
  Author(s): Links PS, Heslegrave R, van Reekum R.
  Source: Journal of Personality Disorders. 1999 Spring; 13(1): 1-9.
  http://www.ncbi.nlm.nih.gov:80/entrez/query.fcgi?cmd=Retrieve&db=PubMed&list_uids=10228922&dopt=Abstract

- **Increasing staff knowledge of and improving attitudes toward patients with borderline personality disorder.**
  Author(s): Miller SA, Davenport NC.
  Source: Psychiatric Services (Washington, D.C.). 1996 May; 47(5): 533-5.
  http://www.ncbi.nlm.nih.gov:80/entrez/query.fcgi?cmd=Retrieve&db=PubMed&list_uids=8740499&dopt=Abstract

- **Inpatient management of a patient with borderline personality disorder: a case study.**
  Author(s): Freeman SK.
  Source: Archives of Psychiatric Nursing. 1988 December; 2(6): 360-5.
  http://www.ncbi.nlm.nih.gov:80/entrez/query.fcgi?cmd=Retrieve&db=PubMed&list_uids=3233023&dopt=Abstract

- **Inpatient nursing care of patients with borderline personality disorder: a review of the literature.**
  Author(s): O'Brien L.
  Source: The Australian and New Zealand Journal of Mental Health Nursing. 1998 December; 7(4): 172-83. Review.
  http://www.ncbi.nlm.nih.gov:80/entrez/query.fcgi?cmd=Retrieve&db=PubMed&list_uids=10095467&dopt=Abstract

- **Is borderline personality disorder a post-traumatic stress disorder of early childhood?**
  Author(s): Thorpe M.
  Source: Canadian Journal of Psychiatry. Revue Canadienne De Psychiatrie. 1993 June; 38(5): 367-8.
  http://www.ncbi.nlm.nih.gov:80/entrez/query.fcgi?cmd=Retrieve&db=PubMed&list_uids=8348481&dopt=Abstract

- **Is borderline personality disorder an illness?**
  Author(s): Schulz SC, Goldberg SC.
  Source: Psychopharmacology Bulletin. 1984 Summer; 20(3): 554-60.
  http://www.ncbi.nlm.nih.gov:80/entrez/query.fcgi?cmd=Retrieve&db=PubMed&list_uids=6473661&dopt=Abstract

- **Is bulimia associated with borderline personality disorder? A controlled study.**
  Author(s): Pope HG Jr, Frankenburg FR, Hudson JI, Jonas JM, Yurgelun-Todd D.
  Source: The Journal of Clinical Psychiatry. 1987 May; 48(5): 181-4.
  http://www.ncbi.nlm.nih.gov:80/entrez/query.fcgi?cmd=Retrieve&db=PubMed&list_uids=3571171&dopt=Abstract

- **Is comorbidity of posttraumatic stress disorder and borderline personality disorder related to greater pathology and impairment?**
  Author(s): Zlotnick C, Franklin CL, Zimmerman M.
  Source: The American Journal of Psychiatry. 2002 November; 159(11): 1940-3.
  http://www.ncbi.nlm.nih.gov:80/entrez/query.fcgi?cmd=Retrieve&db=PubMed&list_uids=12411235&dopt=Abstract

- **Is couple therapy indicated for borderline personality disorder?**
  Author(s): Links PS, Stockwell M.
  Source: American Journal of Psychotherapy. 2001; 55(4): 491-506.
  http://www.ncbi.nlm.nih.gov:80/entrez/query.fcgi?cmd=Retrieve&db=PubMed&list_uids=11824216&dopt=Abstract

- **Is electroconvulsive therapy effective for the depressed patient with comorbid borderline personality disorder?**
  Author(s): DeBattista C, Mueller K.
  Source: The Journal of Ect. 2001 June; 17(2): 91-8. Review.
  http://www.ncbi.nlm.nih.gov:80/entrez/query.fcgi?cmd=Retrieve&db=PubMed&list_uids=11417933&dopt=Abstract

- **Is psychopharmacological treatment effective for the symptoms of borderline personality disorder (BPD)?**
  Author(s): Paris J.
  Source: Journal of Psychiatry & Neuroscience : Jpn. 1999 May; 24(3): 262.
  http://www.ncbi.nlm.nih.gov:80/entrez/query.fcgi?cmd=Retrieve&db=PubMed&list_uids=10354663&dopt=Abstract

- **Justification for separating schizotypal and borderline personality disorders.**
  Author(s): Spitzer RL, Endicott J.
  Source: Schizophrenia Bulletin. 1979; 5(1): 95-104.
  http://www.ncbi.nlm.nih.gov:80/entrez/query.fcgi?cmd=Retrieve&db=PubMed&list_uids=441693&dopt=Abstract

- **Karen Horney's "resigned person" heralds DSM-III-R's borderline personality disorder.**
  Author(s): Muller RJ.
  Source: Comprehensive Psychiatry. 1993 July-August; 34(4): 264-72.
  http://www.ncbi.nlm.nih.gov:80/entrez/query.fcgi?cmd=Retrieve&db=PubMed&list_uids=8348806&dopt=Abstract

- **Laboratory measures of aggression and impulsivity in women with borderline personality disorder.**
  Author(s): Dougherty DM, Bjork JM, Huckabee HC, Moeller FG, Swann AC.
  Source: Psychiatry Research. 1999 March 22; 85(3): 315-26.
  http://www.ncbi.nlm.nih.gov:80/entrez/query.fcgi?cmd=Retrieve&db=PubMed&list_uids=10333383&dopt=Abstract

- **Lack of effect of dopamine receptor blockade on the TSH response to TRH in borderline personality disorder.**
  Author(s): Garbutt JC, Loosen PT, Glenn M.
  Source: Psychiatry Research. 1987 August; 21(4): 307-11.
  http://www.ncbi.nlm.nih.gov:80/entrez/query.fcgi?cmd=Retrieve&db=PubMed&list_uids=3114780&dopt=Abstract

- **Lamotrigine and borderline personality disorder.**
  Author(s): Rizvi ST.
  Source: Journal of Child and Adolescent Psychopharmacology. 2002 Winter; 12(4): 365-6.
  http://www.ncbi.nlm.nih.gov:80/entrez/query.fcgi?cmd=Retrieve&db=PubMed&list_uids=12625999&dopt=Abstract

- **Latent structure analysis of DSM-IV borderline personality disorder criteria.**
  Author(s): Fossati A, Maffei C, Bagnato M, Donati D, Namia C, Novella L.
  Source: Comprehensive Psychiatry. 1999 January-February; 40(1): 72-9.
  http://www.ncbi.nlm.nih.gov:80/entrez/query.fcgi?cmd=Retrieve&db=PubMed&list_uids=9924881&dopt=Abstract

- **Learning disabilities in children with borderline personality disorder.**
  Author(s): Berg M.
  Source: Bulletin of the Menninger Clinic. 1992 Summer; 56(3): 379-92.
  http://www.ncbi.nlm.nih.gov:80/entrez/query.fcgi?cmd=Retrieve&db=PubMed&list_uids=1504680&dopt=Abstract

- **Life events in borderline personality disorder.**
  Author(s): Labonte E, Paris J.
  Source: Canadian Journal of Psychiatry. Revue Canadienne De Psychiatrie. 1993 December; 38(10): 638-40.
  http://www.ncbi.nlm.nih.gov:80/entrez/query.fcgi?cmd=Retrieve&db=PubMed&list_uids=8313301&dopt=Abstract

- **Low platelet monoamine oxidase activity in borderline personality disorder.**
  Author(s): Yehuda R, Southwick SM, Edell WS, Giller EL Jr.
  Source: Psychiatry Research. 1989 December; 30(3): 265-73.
  http://www.ncbi.nlm.nih.gov:80/entrez/query.fcgi?cmd=Retrieve&db=PubMed&list_uids=2616692&dopt=Abstract

- **Low-dose clozapine in acute and continuation treatment of severe borderline personality disorder.**
  Author(s): Benedetti F, Sforzini L, Colombo C, Maffei C, Smeraldi E.
  Source: The Journal of Clinical Psychiatry. 1998 March; 59(3): 103-7.
  http://www.ncbi.nlm.nih.gov:80/entrez/query.fcgi?cmd=Retrieve&db=PubMed&list_uids=9541151&dopt=Abstract

- **Low-dose olanzapine for self-mutilation behavior in patients with borderline personality disorder.**
  Author(s): Hough DW.
  Source: The Journal of Clinical Psychiatry. 2001 April; 62(4): 296-7.
  http://www.ncbi.nlm.nih.gov:80/entrez/query.fcgi?cmd=Retrieve&db=PubMed&list_uids=11379847&dopt=Abstract

- **Magnetic resonance imaging of hippocampal and amygdala volume in women with childhood abuse and borderline personality disorder.**
  Author(s): Schmahl CG, Vermetten E, Elzinga BM, Douglas Bremner J.
  Source: Psychiatry Research. 2003 April 1; 122(3): 193-8.
  http://www.ncbi.nlm.nih.gov:80/entrez/query.fcgi?cmd=Retrieve&db=PubMed&list_uids=12694893&dopt=Abstract

- **Magnetic resonance imaging volumes of the hippocampus and the amygdala in women with borderline personality disorder and early traumatization.**
  Author(s): Driessen M, Herrmann J, Stahl K, Zwaan M, Meier S, Hill A, Osterheider M, Petersen D.
  Source: Archives of General Psychiatry. 2000 December; 57(12): 1115-22.
  http://www.ncbi.nlm.nih.gov:80/entrez/query.fcgi?cmd=Retrieve&db=PubMed&list_uids=11115325&dopt=Abstract

- **Mahler's developmental theory. Training the nurse to treat older adults with borderline personality disorder.**
  Author(s): Landesman A.
  Source: Journal of Gerontological Nursing. 2003 February; 29(2): 22-8; Quiz 54-5. Review.
  http://www.ncbi.nlm.nih.gov:80/entrez/query.fcgi?cmd=Retrieve&db=PubMed&list_uids=12640861&dopt=Abstract

- **Malevolent object representations in borderline personality disorder and major depression.**
  Author(s): Nigg JT, Lohr NE, Western D, Gold LJ, Silk KR.
  Source: Journal of Abnormal Psychology. 1992 February; 101(1): 61-7.
  http://www.ncbi.nlm.nih.gov:80/entrez/query.fcgi?cmd=Retrieve&db=PubMed&list_uids=1537974&dopt=Abstract

- **Management of borderline personality disorder.**
  Author(s): Flewett T, Bradley P, Redvers A.
  Source: The British Journal of Psychiatry; the Journal of Mental Science. 2003 July; 183: 78-9.
  http://www.ncbi.nlm.nih.gov:80/entrez/query.fcgi?cmd=Retrieve&db=PubMed&list_uids=12835254&dopt=Abstract

- **Managing aggressive behavior in patients with obsessive-compulsive disorder and borderline personality disorder.**
  Author(s): Hollander E.
  Source: The Journal of Clinical Psychiatry. 1999; 60 Suppl 15: 38-44. Review.
  http://www.ncbi.nlm.nih.gov:80/entrez/query.fcgi?cmd=Retrieve&db=PubMed&list_uids=10418814&dopt=Abstract

- **Maternal empathy, family chaos, and the etiology of borderline personality disorder.**
  Author(s): Golomb A, Ludolph P, Westen D, Block MJ, Maurer P, Wiss FC.
  Source: J Am Psychoanal Assoc. 1994; 42(2): 525-48.
  http://www.ncbi.nlm.nih.gov:80/entrez/query.fcgi?cmd=Retrieve&db=PubMed&list_uids=8040554&dopt=Abstract

- **m-Chlorophenylpiperazine challenge in borderline personality disorder: relationship of neuroendocrine response, behavioral response, and clinical measures.**
  Author(s): Stein DJ, Hollander E, DeCaria CM, Simeon D, Cohen L, Aronowitz B.
  Source: Biological Psychiatry. 1996 September 15; 40(6): 508-13.
  http://www.ncbi.nlm.nih.gov:80/entrez/query.fcgi?cmd=Retrieve&db=PubMed&list_uids=8879471&dopt=Abstract

- **MCMI-II diagnosis of borderline personality disorder: base rates versus prototypic items.**
  Author(s): McCann JT, Flynn PM, Gersh DM.
  Source: Journal of Personality Assessment. 1992 February; 58(1): 105-14.
  http://www.ncbi.nlm.nih.gov:80/entrez/query.fcgi?cmd=Retrieve&db=PubMed&list_uids=1545335&dopt=Abstract

- **Methodological variations in the use of the MMPI for diagnosis of borderline personality disorder among alcoholics.**
  Author(s): Horvath P, Jonsdottir-Baldursson T.
  Source: Journal of Clinical Psychology. 1990 March; 46(2): 238-43.
  http://www.ncbi.nlm.nih.gov:80/entrez/query.fcgi?cmd=Retrieve&db=PubMed&list_uids=2324308&dopt=Abstract

- **MMPI critical item characteristics of the DSM-III borderline personality disorder.**
  Author(s): Pitts WM Jr, Gustin QL, Mitchell C, Snyder S.
  Source: The Journal of Nervous and Mental Disease. 1985 October; 173(10): 628-31.
  http://www.ncbi.nlm.nih.gov:80/entrez/query.fcgi?cmd=Retrieve&db=PubMed&list_uids=4031840&dopt=Abstract

- **Mnemonic device for criteria for borderline personality disorder.**
  Author(s): Powers AD, Rustagi PK.
  Source: The American Journal of Psychiatry. 1989 November; 146(11): 1517.
  http://www.ncbi.nlm.nih.gov:80/entrez/query.fcgi?cmd=Retrieve&db=PubMed&list_uids=2817131&dopt=Abstract

- **Mood and global functioning in borderline personality disorder: individual regression models for longitudinal measurements.**
  Author(s): Hoke LA, Lavori PW, Perry JC.
  Source: Journal of Psychiatric Research. 1992 January; 26(1): 1-16.
  http://www.ncbi.nlm.nih.gov:80/entrez/query.fcgi?cmd=Retrieve&db=PubMed&list_uids=1560405&dopt=Abstract

- **Mooney Problem Check List characteristics of DSM-III borderline personality disorder inpatients.**
  Author(s): Pitts WM Jr, Gustin QL, Snyder S, Goodpaster WA.
  Source: Psychological Reports. 1987 June; 60(3 Pt 1): 907-10.
  http://www.ncbi.nlm.nih.gov:80/entrez/query.fcgi?cmd=Retrieve&db=PubMed&list_uids=3615734&dopt=Abstract

- **Mother-child interaction and borderline personality disorder.**
  Author(s): Balon R.
  Source: The American Journal of Psychiatry. 1995 March; 152(3): 477-8.
  http://www.ncbi.nlm.nih.gov:80/entrez/query.fcgi?cmd=Retrieve&db=PubMed&list_uids=7864288&dopt=Abstract

- **Multimodal cognitive-behavior therapy for borderline personality disorder with self-injurious behavior.**
  Author(s): Kern RS, Kuehnel TG, Teuber J, Hayden JL.
  Source: Psychiatric Services (Washington, D.C.). 1997 September; 48(9): 1131-3.
  http://www.ncbi.nlm.nih.gov:80/entrez/query.fcgi?cmd=Retrieve&db=PubMed&list_uids=9285971&dopt=Abstract

- **Multiple determinants of anxiety in a patient with borderline personality disorder.**
  Author(s): Gabbard GO, Nemiah JC.
  Source: Bulletin of the Menninger Clinic. 1985 March; 49(2): 161-72.
  http://www.ncbi.nlm.nih.gov:80/entrez/query.fcgi?cmd=Retrieve&db=PubMed&list_uids=3978305&dopt=Abstract

- **Multiple neuroendocrinological responses in borderline personality disorder patients.**
  Author(s): Kontaxakis V, Markianos M, Vaslamatzis G, Markidis M, Kanellos P, Stefanis C.
  Source: Acta Psychiatrica Scandinavica. 1987 November; 76(5): 593-7.
  http://www.ncbi.nlm.nih.gov:80/entrez/query.fcgi?cmd=Retrieve&db=PubMed&list_uids=3124503&dopt=Abstract

- **Multiple personality and borderline personality disorder.**
  Author(s): Clary WF, Burstin KJ, Carpenter JS.
  Source: The Psychiatric Clinics of North America. 1984 March; 7(1): 89-99.
  http://www.ncbi.nlm.nih.gov:80/entrez/query.fcgi?cmd=Retrieve&db=PubMed&list_uids=6718270&dopt=Abstract

- **Multiple personality disorder and borderline personality disorder.**
  Author(s): Kirsten M.
  Source: The American Journal of Psychiatry. 1990 October; 147(10): 1386-7.
  http://www.ncbi.nlm.nih.gov:80/entrez/query.fcgi?cmd=Retrieve&db=PubMed&list_uids=2400015&dopt=Abstract

- **N of 1 study: methylphenidate in a patient with borderline personality disorder and attention deficit hyperactivity disorder.**
  Author(s): van Reekum R, Links PS.
  Source: Canadian Journal of Psychiatry. Revue Canadienne De Psychiatrie. 1994 April; 39(3): 186-7.
  http://www.ncbi.nlm.nih.gov:80/entrez/query.fcgi?cmd=Retrieve&db=PubMed&list_uids=8033025&dopt=Abstract

- **Naltrexone in the treatment of dissociative symptoms in patients with borderline personality disorder: an open-label trial.**
  Author(s): Bohus MJ, Landwehrmeyer GB, Stiglmayr CE, Limberger MF, Bohme R, Schmahl CG.
  Source: The Journal of Clinical Psychiatry. 1999 September; 60(9): 598-603.
  http://www.ncbi.nlm.nih.gov:80/entrez/query.fcgi?cmd=Retrieve&db=PubMed&list_uids=10520978&dopt=Abstract

- **Narcissistic personality disorder. A validity study and comparison to borderline personality disorder.**
  Author(s): Plakun EM.
  Source: The Psychiatric Clinics of North America. 1989 September; 12(3): 603-20.
  http://www.ncbi.nlm.nih.gov:80/entrez/query.fcgi?cmd=Retrieve&db=PubMed&list_uids=2798199&dopt=Abstract

- **Negativism in evaluative judgments of words among depressed outpatients with borderline personality disorder.**
  Author(s): Kurtz JE, Morey LC.
  Source: Journal of Personality Disorders. 1998 Winter; 12(4): 351-61.
  http://www.ncbi.nlm.nih.gov:80/entrez/query.fcgi?cmd=Retrieve&db=PubMed&list_uids=9891289&dopt=Abstract

- **Neural correlates of memories of abandonment in women with and without borderline personality disorder.**
  Author(s): Schmahl CG, Elzinga BM, Vermetten E, Sanislow C, McGlashan TH, Bremner JD.
  Source: Biological Psychiatry. 2003 July 15; 54(2): 142-51.
  http://www.ncbi.nlm.nih.gov:80/entrez/query.fcgi?cmd=Retrieve&db=PubMed&list_uids=12873804&dopt=Abstract

- **Neurobehavioral study of borderline personality disorder.**
  Author(s): van Reekum R, Conway CA, Gansler D, White R, Bachman DL.
  Source: Journal of Psychiatry & Neuroscience : Jpn. 1993 May; 18(3): 121-9.
  http://www.ncbi.nlm.nih.gov:80/entrez/query.fcgi?cmd=Retrieve&db=PubMed&list_uids=8499428&dopt=Abstract

- **Neurobiological correlates of borderline personality disorder.**
  Author(s): Schmahl CG, McGlashan TH, Bremner JD.
  Source: Psychopharmacology Bulletin. 2002 Spring; 36(2): 69-87. Review.
  http://www.ncbi.nlm.nih.gov:80/entrez/query.fcgi?cmd=Retrieve&db=PubMed&list_uids=12397842&dopt=Abstract

- **Neurocognitive deficits in decision-making and planning of patients with DSM-III-R borderline personality disorder.**
  Author(s): Bazanis E, Rogers RD, Dowson JH, Taylor P, Meux C, Staley C, Nevinson-Andrews D, Taylor C, Robbins TW, Sahakian BJ.
  Source: Psychological Medicine. 2002 November; 32(8): 1395-405.
  http://www.ncbi.nlm.nih.gov:80/entrez/query.fcgi?cmd=Retrieve&db=PubMed&list_uids=12455938&dopt=Abstract

- **Neuroendocrine study of serotonin function in female borderline personality disorder patients: a pilot study.**
  Author(s): Martial J, Paris J, Leyton M, Zweig-Frank H, Schwartz G, Teboul E, Thavundayil J, Larue S, Ng Ying Kin NM, Vasa van Nair NP.
  Source: Biological Psychiatry. 1997 October 15; 42(8): 737-9.
  http://www.ncbi.nlm.nih.gov:80/entrez/query.fcgi?cmd=Retrieve&db=PubMed&list_uids=9325568&dopt=Abstract

- **Neuropsychological function in borderline personality disorder.**
  Author(s): Swirsky-Sacchetti T, Gorton G, Samuel S, Sobel R, Genetta-Wadley A, Burleigh B.
  Source: Journal of Clinical Psychology. 1993 May; 49(3): 385-96.
  http://www.ncbi.nlm.nih.gov:80/entrez/query.fcgi?cmd=Retrieve&db=PubMed&list_uids=8315042&dopt=Abstract

- **Neuropsychological functioning in patients with borderline personality disorder.**
  Author(s): Sprock J, Rader TJ, Kendall JP, Yoder CY.
  Source: Journal of Clinical Psychology. 2000 December; 56(12): 1587-600.
  http://www.ncbi.nlm.nih.gov:80/entrez/query.fcgi?cmd=Retrieve&db=PubMed&list_uids=11132573&dopt=Abstract

- **Neuropsychological testing of patients with borderline personality disorder.**
  Author(s): O'Leary KM, Brouwers P, Gardner DL, Cowdry RW.
  Source: The American Journal of Psychiatry. 1991 January; 148(1): 106-11.
  http://www.ncbi.nlm.nih.gov:80/entrez/query.fcgi?cmd=Retrieve&db=PubMed&list_uids=1984693&dopt=Abstract

- **Neurotransmitter dysfunction in patients with borderline personality disorder.**
Author(s): Gurvits IG, Koenigsberg HW, Siever LJ.
Source: The Psychiatric Clinics of North America. 2000 March; 23(1): 27-40, Vi. Review.
http://www.ncbi.nlm.nih.gov:80/entrez/query.fcgi?cmd=Retrieve&db=PubMed&list_uids=10729929&dopt=Abstract

- **New uses of countertransference for the inpatient treatment of borderline personality disorder.**
Author(s): Rosenbluth M.
Source: Canadian Journal of Psychiatry. Revue Canadienne De Psychiatrie. 1991 May; 36(4): 280-4. Review.
http://www.ncbi.nlm.nih.gov:80/entrez/query.fcgi?cmd=Retrieve&db=PubMed&list_uids=1868421&dopt=Abstract

- **No evidence for overgeneral memories in borderline personality disorder.**
Author(s): Arntz A, Meeren M, Wessel I.
Source: Behaviour Research and Therapy. 2002 September; 40(9): 1063-8.
http://www.ncbi.nlm.nih.gov:80/entrez/query.fcgi?cmd=Retrieve&db=PubMed&list_uids=12296491&dopt=Abstract

- **Nurses' confirming/disconfirming responses to patients diagnosed with borderline personality disorder.**
Author(s): Fraser K, Gallop R.
Source: Archives of Psychiatric Nursing. 1993 December; 7(6): 336-41.
http://www.ncbi.nlm.nih.gov:80/entrez/query.fcgi?cmd=Retrieve&db=PubMed&list_uids=8179357&dopt=Abstract

- **Obsessive-compulsive disorder and borderline personality disorder.**
Author(s): Hermesh H, Shahar A, Munitz H.
Source: The American Journal of Psychiatry. 1987 January; 144(1): 120-2.
http://www.ncbi.nlm.nih.gov:80/entrez/query.fcgi?cmd=Retrieve&db=PubMed&list_uids=3799831&dopt=Abstract

- **Obsessive-compulsive disorder comorbid with borderline personality disorder: a long-term case study.**
Author(s): Hayashi N.
Source: Psychiatry and Clinical Neurosciences. 1996 April; 50(2): 51-4.
http://www.ncbi.nlm.nih.gov:80/entrez/query.fcgi?cmd=Retrieve&db=PubMed&list_uids=8783375&dopt=Abstract

- **Olanzapine safety and efficacy in patients with borderline personality disorder and comorbid dysthymia.**
Author(s): Schulz SC, Camlin KL, Berry SA, Jesberger JA.
Source: Biological Psychiatry. 1999 November 15; 46(10): 1429-35.
http://www.ncbi.nlm.nih.gov:80/entrez/query.fcgi?cmd=Retrieve&db=PubMed&list_uids=10578457&dopt=Abstract

- **Olanzapine treatment of female borderline personality disorder patients: a double-blind, placebo-controlled pilot study.**
  Author(s): Zanarini MC, Frankenburg FR.
  Source: The Journal of Clinical Psychiatry. 2001 November; 62(11): 849-54.
  http://www.ncbi.nlm.nih.gov:80/entrez/query.fcgi?cmd=Retrieve&db=PubMed&list_uids=11775043&dopt=Abstract

- **omega-3 Fatty acid treatment of women with borderline personality disorder: a double-blind, placebo-controlled pilot study.**
  Author(s): Zanarini MC, Frankenburg FR.
  Source: The American Journal of Psychiatry. 2003 January; 160(1): 167-9.
  http://www.ncbi.nlm.nih.gov:80/entrez/query.fcgi?cmd=Retrieve&db=PubMed&list_uids=12505817&dopt=Abstract

- **On the consistency of the MMPI in borderline personality disorder.**
  Author(s): Evans RW, Ruff RM, Braff DL, Cox DR.
  Source: Percept Mot Skills. 1986 April; 62(2): 579-85.
  http://www.ncbi.nlm.nih.gov:80/entrez/query.fcgi?cmd=Retrieve&db=PubMed&list_uids=3503270&dopt=Abstract

- **Open assessment of the safety and efficacy of thioridazine in the treatment of patients with borderline personality disorder.**
  Author(s): Teicher MH, Glod CA, Aaronson ST, Gunter PA, Schatzberg AF, Cole JO.
  Source: Psychopharmacology Bulletin. 1989; 25(4): 535-49.
  http://www.ncbi.nlm.nih.gov:80/entrez/query.fcgi?cmd=Retrieve&db=PubMed&list_uids=2631134&dopt=Abstract

- **Oscillations of attachment in borderline personality disorder.**
  Author(s): Melges FT, Swartz MS.
  Source: The American Journal of Psychiatry. 1989 September; 146(9): 1115-20.
  http://www.ncbi.nlm.nih.gov:80/entrez/query.fcgi?cmd=Retrieve&db=PubMed&list_uids=2764169&dopt=Abstract

- **Otto F. Kernberg, M.D., F.A.P.A., developer of object relations psychoanalytic therapy for borderline personality disorder. Interview by Lata K. McGinn.**
  Author(s): Kernberg OF.
  Source: American Journal of Psychotherapy. 1998 Spring; 52(2): 191-201.
  http://www.ncbi.nlm.nih.gov:80/entrez/query.fcgi?cmd=Retrieve&db=PubMed&list_uids=9656055&dopt=Abstract

- **Pain assessment in self-injurious patients with borderline personality disorder using signal detection theory.**
  Author(s): Kemperman I, Russ MJ, Clark WC, Kakuma T, Zanine E, Harrison K.
  Source: Psychiatry Research. 1997 May 30; 70(3): 175-83.
  http://www.ncbi.nlm.nih.gov:80/entrez/query.fcgi?cmd=Retrieve&db=PubMed&list_uids=9211579&dopt=Abstract

- **Pain perception during self-reported distress and calmness in patients with borderline personality disorder and self-mutilating behavior.**
  Author(s): Bohus M, Limberger M, Ebner U, Glocker FX, Schwarz B, Wernz M, Lieb K.
  Source: Psychiatry Research. 2000 September 11; 95(3): 251-60.
  http://www.ncbi.nlm.nih.gov:80/entrez/query.fcgi?cmd=Retrieve&db=PubMed&list_uids=10974364&dopt=Abstract

- **Partial hospitalization for borderline personality disorder.**
  Author(s): Stern R.
  Source: The American Journal of Psychiatry. 2001 November; 158(11): 1932-3.
  http://www.ncbi.nlm.nih.gov:80/entrez/query.fcgi?cmd=Retrieve&db=PubMed&list_uids=11691712&dopt=Abstract

- **Pathways to the development of borderline personality disorder.**
  Author(s): Zanarini MC, Frankenburg FR.
  Source: Journal of Personality Disorders. 1997 Spring; 11(1): 93-104.
  http://www.ncbi.nlm.nih.gov:80/entrez/query.fcgi?cmd=Retrieve&db=PubMed&list_uids=9113824&dopt=Abstract

- **Pharmacotherapy of borderline personality disorder.**
  Author(s): Hirschfeld RM.
  Source: The Journal of Clinical Psychiatry. 1997; 58 Suppl 14: 48-52; Discussion 53. Review.
  http://www.ncbi.nlm.nih.gov:80/entrez/query.fcgi?cmd=Retrieve&db=PubMed&list_uids=9418746&dopt=Abstract

- **Polythetic diagnostic approach to the borderline personality disorder. the valency of the single criterion in the concept of professional therapists.**
  Author(s): Burgmer M, Jessen F, Freyberger HJ.
  Source: Psychopathology. 2000 May-June; 33(3): 119-24.
  http://www.ncbi.nlm.nih.gov:80/entrez/query.fcgi?cmd=Retrieve&db=PubMed&list_uids=10773769&dopt=Abstract

- **Positron emission tomography in female patients with borderline personality disorder.**
  Author(s): Juengling FD, Schmahl C, Hesslinger B, Ebert D, Bremner JD, Gostomzyk J, Bohus M, Lieb K.
  Source: Journal of Psychiatric Research. 2003 March-April; 37(2): 109-15.
  http://www.ncbi.nlm.nih.gov:80/entrez/query.fcgi?cmd=Retrieve&db=PubMed&list_uids=12842164&dopt=Abstract

- **Practical psychotherapy: borderline personality disorder: the importance of establishing a treatment framework.**
  Author(s): Kraft Goin M.
  Source: Psychiatric Services (Washington, D.C.). 2001 February; 52(2): 167-8.
  http://www.ncbi.nlm.nih.gov:80/entrez/query.fcgi?cmd=Retrieve&db=PubMed&list_uids=11157112&dopt=Abstract

- **Practice guideline for the treatment of borderline personality disorder: a bridge too far.**
  Author(s): Tyrer P.
  Source: Journal of Personality Disorders. 2002 April; 16(2): 113-8. Review.
  http://www.ncbi.nlm.nih.gov:80/entrez/query.fcgi?cmd=Retrieve&db=PubMed&list_uids=12004486&dopt=Abstract

- **Practice guideline for the treatment of patients with borderline personality disorder. American Psychiatric Association.**
  Author(s): American Psychiatric Association Practice Guidelines.
  Source: The American Journal of Psychiatry. 2001 October; 158(10 Suppl): 1-52.
  http://www.ncbi.nlm.nih.gov:80/entrez/query.fcgi?cmd=Retrieve&db=PubMed&list_uids=11665545&dopt=Abstract

- **Predictive factors for borderline personality disorder: patients' early traumatic experiences and losses suffered by the attachment figure. The Italian Group for the Study of Dissociation.**
  Author(s): Liotti G, Pasquini P.
  Source: Acta Psychiatrica Scandinavica. 2000 October; 102(4): 282-9.
  http://www.ncbi.nlm.nih.gov:80/entrez/query.fcgi?cmd=Retrieve&db=PubMed&list_uids=11089728&dopt=Abstract

- **Predictors of outcome in a 27-year follow-up of patients with borderline personality disorder.**
  Author(s): Zweig-Frank H, Paris J.
  Source: Comprehensive Psychiatry. 2002 March-April; 43(2): 103-7.
  http://www.ncbi.nlm.nih.gov:80/entrez/query.fcgi?cmd=Retrieve&db=PubMed&list_uids=11893987&dopt=Abstract

- **Prior head injury in male veterans with borderline personality disorder.**
  Author(s): Streeter CC, Van Reekum R, Shorr RI, Bachman DL.
  Source: The Journal of Nervous and Mental Disease. 1995 September; 183(9): 577-81.
  http://www.ncbi.nlm.nih.gov:80/entrez/query.fcgi?cmd=Retrieve&db=PubMed&list_uids=7561819&dopt=Abstract

- **Professional skills and frame of work organization in managing borderline personality disorder. Shared philosophy or ambivalence--a qualitative study from the view of caregivers.**
  Author(s): Bergman B, Eckerdal A.
  Source: Scandinavian Journal of Caring Sciences. 2000; 14(4): 245-52.
  http://www.ncbi.nlm.nih.gov:80/entrez/query.fcgi?cmd=Retrieve&db=PubMed&list_uids=12035215&dopt=Abstract

- **Prospective follow-up study of borderline personality disorder: prognosis, prediction of outcome, and Axis II comorbidity.**
  Author(s): Links PS, Heslegrave R, van Reekum R.
  Source: Canadian Journal of Psychiatry. Revue Canadienne De Psychiatrie. 1998 April; 43(3): 265-70.
  http://www.ncbi.nlm.nih.gov:80/entrez/query.fcgi?cmd=Retrieve&db=PubMed&list_uids=9561315&dopt=Abstract

- **Prospective studies of outcome. Understanding mechanisms of change in patients with borderline personality disorder.**
  Author(s): Links PS, Heslegrave RJ.
  Source: The Psychiatric Clinics of North America. 2000 March; 23(1): 137-50. Review.
  http://www.ncbi.nlm.nih.gov:80/entrez/query.fcgi?cmd=Retrieve&db=PubMed&list_uids=10729936&dopt=Abstract

- **Providing nursing care for a patient with borderline personality disorder on an acute inpatient unit: a phenomenological study.**
  Author(s): O'Brien L, Flote J.
  Source: The Australian and New Zealand Journal of Mental Health Nursing. 1997 December; 6(4): 137-47.
  http://www.ncbi.nlm.nih.gov:80/entrez/query.fcgi?cmd=Retrieve&db=PubMed&list_uids=9479087&dopt=Abstract

- **Psychodynamic psychotherapy of borderline personality disorder: a contemporary approach.**
  Author(s): Gabbard GO.
  Source: Bulletin of the Menninger Clinic. 2001 Winter; 65(1): 41-57. Review.
  http://www.ncbi.nlm.nih.gov:80/entrez/query.fcgi?cmd=Retrieve&db=PubMed&list_uids=11280958&dopt=Abstract

- **Psychopathology in offspring of mothers with borderline personality disorder: a pilot study.**
  Author(s): Weiss M, Zelkowitz P, Feldman RB, Vogel J, Heyman M, Paris J.
  Source: Canadian Journal of Psychiatry. Revue Canadienne De Psychiatrie. 1996 June; 41(5): 285-90.
  http://www.ncbi.nlm.nih.gov:80/entrez/query.fcgi?cmd=Retrieve&db=PubMed&list_uids=8793148&dopt=Abstract

- **Psychopharmacology of borderline personality disorder.**
  Author(s): Soloff PH.
  Source: The Psychiatric Clinics of North America. 2000 March; 23(1): 169-92, Ix. Review.
  http://www.ncbi.nlm.nih.gov:80/entrez/query.fcgi?cmd=Retrieve&db=PubMed&list_uids=10729938&dopt=Abstract

- **Quetiapine in the treatment of borderline personality disorder.**
  Author(s): Hilger E, Barnas C, Kasper S.
  Source: World J Biol Psychiatry. 2003 January; 4(1): 42-4.
  http://www.ncbi.nlm.nih.gov:80/entrez/query.fcgi?cmd=Retrieve&db=PubMed&list_uids=12582977&dopt=Abstract

- **Re: Impulsivity, defensive functioning, and borderline personality disorder.**
  Author(s): Jerome L.
  Source: Canadian Journal of Psychiatry. Revue Canadienne De Psychiatrie. 1996 September; 41(7): 483.
  http://www.ncbi.nlm.nih.gov:80/entrez/query.fcgi?cmd=Retrieve&db=PubMed&list_uids=8884039&dopt=Abstract

- **Reasons for suicide attempts and nonsuicidal self-injury in women with borderline personality disorder.**
  Author(s): Brown MZ, Comtois KA, Linehan MM.
  Source: Journal of Abnormal Psychology. 2002 February; 111(1): 198-202.
  http://www.ncbi.nlm.nih.gov:80/entrez/query.fcgi?cmd=Retrieve&db=PubMed&list_uids=11866174&dopt=Abstract

- **Recent life events, social adjustment, and suicide attempts in patients with major depression and borderline personality disorder.**
  Author(s): Kelly TM, Soloff PH, Lynch KG, Haas GL, Mann JJ.
  Source: Journal of Personality Disorders. 2000 Winter; 14(4): 316-26.
  http://www.ncbi.nlm.nih.gov:80/entrez/query.fcgi?cmd=Retrieve&db=PubMed&list_uids=11204339&dopt=Abstract

- **Recognizing borderline personality disorder in the family practice setting.**
  Author(s): Hubbard JR, Saathoff GB, Bernardo MJ, Barnett BL Jr.
  Source: American Family Physician. 1995 September 1; 52(3): 908-14. Review.
  http://www.ncbi.nlm.nih.gov:80/entrez/query.fcgi?cmd=Retrieve&db=PubMed&list_uids=7653428&dopt=Abstract

- **Recognizing borderline personality disorder in the primary care client.**
  Author(s): Johnson CE.
  Source: The Nurse Practitioner. 1988 August; 13(8): 11-2, 15-8.
  http://www.ncbi.nlm.nih.gov:80/entrez/query.fcgi?cmd=Retrieve&db=PubMed&list_uids=3173815&dopt=Abstract

- **Relationship between borderline personality disorder and Axis I diagnosis in severity of depression and anxiety.**
  Author(s): Comtois KA, Cowley DS, Dunner DL, Roy-Byrne PP.
  Source: The Journal of Clinical Psychiatry. 1999 November; 60(11): 752-8.
  http://www.ncbi.nlm.nih.gov:80/entrez/query.fcgi?cmd=Retrieve&db=PubMed&list_uids=10584763&dopt=Abstract

- **Relationship between depression and borderline personality disorder.**
  Author(s): Koenigsberg HW, Anwunah I, New AS, Mitropoulou V, Schopick F, Siever LJ.
  Source: Depression and Anxiety. 1999; 10(4): 158-67. Review.
  http://www.ncbi.nlm.nih.gov:80/entrez/query.fcgi?cmd=Retrieve&db=PubMed&list_uids=10690577&dopt=Abstract

- **Relationship between EDNOS and its subtypes and borderline personality disorder.**
  Author(s): Marino MF, Zanarini MC.
  Source: The International Journal of Eating Disorders. 2001 April; 29(3): 349-53.
  http://www.ncbi.nlm.nih.gov:80/entrez/query.fcgi?cmd=Retrieve&db=PubMed&list_uids=11262516&dopt=Abstract

- **Relationship of childhood sexual abuse to borderline personality disorder, posttraumatic stress disorder, and multiple personality disorder.**
  Author(s): Murray JB.
  Source: The Journal of Psychology. 1993 November; 127(6): 657-76. Review.
  http://www.ncbi.nlm.nih.gov:80/entrez/query.fcgi?cmd=Retrieve&db=PubMed&list_uids=8301618&dopt=Abstract

- **Relationship of depression and cognitive impairment to self-injury in borderline personality disorder, major depression, and schizophrenia.**
  Author(s): Burgess JW.
  Source: Psychiatry Research. 1991 July; 38(1): 77-87.
  http://www.ncbi.nlm.nih.gov:80/entrez/query.fcgi?cmd=Retrieve&db=PubMed&list_uids=1946835&dopt=Abstract

- **Relationship of dissociation to self-mutilation and childhood abuse in borderline personality disorder.**
  Author(s): Brodsky BS, Cloitre M, Dulit RA.
  Source: The American Journal of Psychiatry. 1995 December; 152(12): 1788-92.
  http://www.ncbi.nlm.nih.gov:80/entrez/query.fcgi?cmd=Retrieve&db=PubMed&list_uids=8526247&dopt=Abstract

- **Reliability and validity of the borderline personality disorder severity index.**
  Author(s): Arntz A, van den Hoorn M, Cornelis J, Verheul R, van den Bosch WM, de Bie AJ.
  Source: Journal of Personality Disorders. 2003 February; 17(1): 45-59.
  http://www.ncbi.nlm.nih.gov:80/entrez/query.fcgi?cmd=Retrieve&db=PubMed&list_uids=12659546&dopt=Abstract

- **Repeat neurobehavioral study of borderline personality disorder.**
  Author(s): van Reekum R, Links PS, Finlayson MA, Boyle M, Boiago I, Ostrander LA, Moustacalis E.
  Source: Journal of Psychiatry & Neuroscience : Jpn. 1996 January; 21(1): 13-20.
  http://www.ncbi.nlm.nih.gov:80/entrez/query.fcgi?cmd=Retrieve&db=PubMed&list_uids=8580113&dopt=Abstract

- **Reported pathological childhood experiences associated with the development of borderline personality disorder.**
  Author(s): Zanarini MC, Williams AA, Lewis RE, Reich RB, Vera SC, Marino MF, Levin A, Yong L, Frankenburg FR.
  Source: The American Journal of Psychiatry. 1997 August; 154(8): 1101-6.
  http://www.ncbi.nlm.nih.gov:80/entrez/query.fcgi?cmd=Retrieve&db=PubMed&list_uids=9247396&dopt=Abstract

- **Research on dialectical behavior therapy for patients with borderline personality disorder.**
  Author(s): Koerner K, Linehan MM.
  Source: The Psychiatric Clinics of North America. 2000 March; 23(1): 151-67. Review.
  http://www.ncbi.nlm.nih.gov:80/entrez/query.fcgi?cmd=Retrieve&db=PubMed&list_uids=10729937&dopt=Abstract

- **Responses and behaviour of patients with borderline personality disorder during semi-structured interviews.**
Author(s): Mitton J, Huxley G.
Source: Canadian Journal of Psychiatry. Revue Canadienne De Psychiatrie. 1988 June; 33(5): 341-3.
http://www.ncbi.nlm.nih.gov:80/entrez/query.fcgi?cmd=Retrieve&db=PubMed&list_uids=3409152&dopt=Abstract

- **Rethinking the comparison of borderline personality disorder and multiple personality disorder.**
Author(s): Marmer SS, Fink D.
Source: The Psychiatric Clinics of North America. 1994 December; 17(4): 743-71. Review.
http://www.ncbi.nlm.nih.gov:80/entrez/query.fcgi?cmd=Retrieve&db=PubMed&list_uids=7877901&dopt=Abstract

- **Risk factors for suicidal behavior in borderline personality disorder.**
Author(s): Soloff PH, Lis JA, Kelly T, Cornelius J, Ulrich R.
Source: The American Journal of Psychiatry. 1994 September; 151(9): 1316-23.
http://www.ncbi.nlm.nih.gov:80/entrez/query.fcgi?cmd=Retrieve&db=PubMed&list_uids=8067487&dopt=Abstract

- **Risperidone in comorbid borderline personality disorder and dysthymia.**
Author(s): Szigethy EM, Schulz SC.
Source: Journal of Clinical Psychopharmacology. 1997 August; 17(4): 326-7.
http://www.ncbi.nlm.nih.gov:80/entrez/query.fcgi?cmd=Retrieve&db=PubMed&list_uids=9241018&dopt=Abstract

- **Rorschach revised DEPI and CDI with inpatient Major Depressives and Borderline Personality Disorder with major depression: validity issues.**
Author(s): Carlson CF, Kula ML, St Laurent CM.
Source: Journal of Clinical Psychology. 1997 January; 53(1): 51-8.
http://www.ncbi.nlm.nih.gov:80/entrez/query.fcgi?cmd=Retrieve&db=PubMed&list_uids=9120032&dopt=Abstract

- **Self-harm behaviors across the life cycle: a pilot study of inpatients with borderline personality disorder.**
Author(s): Sansone RA, Gaither GA, Songer DA.
Source: Comprehensive Psychiatry. 2002 May-June; 43(3): 215-8.
http://www.ncbi.nlm.nih.gov:80/entrez/query.fcgi?cmd=Retrieve&db=PubMed&list_uids=11994840&dopt=Abstract

- **Self-harming behavior of a parent with borderline personality disorder assessed using revealed preference and attributional approaches: a case study.**
Author(s): Tustin RD.
Source: Journal of Personality Disorders. 2002 August; 16(4): 332-43.
http://www.ncbi.nlm.nih.gov:80/entrez/query.fcgi?cmd=Retrieve&db=PubMed&list_uids=12224126&dopt=Abstract

- **Self-structure in borderline personality disorder.**
  Author(s): Cohen BD, Gara MA.
  Source: The American Journal of Orthopsychiatry. 1992 October; 62(4): 618-25.
  http://www.ncbi.nlm.nih.gov:80/entrez/query.fcgi?cmd=Retrieve&db=PubMed&list_uids=1443071&dopt=Abstract

- **Serotonergic sensitivity in borderline personality disorder: preliminary findings.**
  Author(s): Hollander E, Stein DJ, DeCaria CM, Cohen L, Saoud JB, Skodol AE, Kellman D, Rosnick L, Oldham JM.
  Source: The American Journal of Psychiatry. 1994 February; 151(2): 277-80.
  http://www.ncbi.nlm.nih.gov:80/entrez/query.fcgi?cmd=Retrieve&db=PubMed&list_uids=8296905&dopt=Abstract

- **Serum cholesterol and leptin levels in patients with borderline personality disorder.**
  Author(s): Atmaca M, Kuloglu M, Tezcan E, Gecici O, Ustundag B.
  Source: Neuropsychobiology. 2002; 45(4): 167-71.
  http://www.ncbi.nlm.nih.gov:80/entrez/query.fcgi?cmd=Retrieve&db=PubMed&list_uids=12097803&dopt=Abstract

- **Severity as a diagnostic dimension of borderline personality disorder.**
  Author(s): Marziali E, Munroe-Blum H, Links P.
  Source: Canadian Journal of Psychiatry. Revue Canadienne De Psychiatrie. 1994 November; 39(9): 540-4.
  http://www.ncbi.nlm.nih.gov:80/entrez/query.fcgi?cmd=Retrieve&db=PubMed&list_uids=7874655&dopt=Abstract

- **Sexual abuse and borderline personality disorder.**
  Author(s): Salzman C.
  Source: The American Journal of Psychiatry. 1996 June; 153(6): 848-9.
  http://www.ncbi.nlm.nih.gov:80/entrez/query.fcgi?cmd=Retrieve&db=PubMed&list_uids=8633720&dopt=Abstract

- **Sleep EEG findings in ICD-10 borderline personality disorder in Egypt.**
  Author(s): Asaad T, Okasha T, Okasha A.
  Source: Journal of Affective Disorders. 2002 September; 71(1-3): 11-8.
  http://www.ncbi.nlm.nih.gov:80/entrez/query.fcgi?cmd=Retrieve&db=PubMed&list_uids=12167496&dopt=Abstract

- **Social perceptions and borderline personality disorder: the relation to mood disorders.**
  Author(s): Benjamin LS, Wonderlich SA.
  Source: Journal of Abnormal Psychology. 1994 November; 103(4): 610-24.
  http://www.ncbi.nlm.nih.gov:80/entrez/query.fcgi?cmd=Retrieve&db=PubMed&list_uids=7822562&dopt=Abstract

- **Sociodemography of borderline personality disorder (PD): a comparison with Axis II PDs and psychiatric symptom disorders convergent validation.**
  Author(s): Taub JM.
  Source: The International Journal of Neuroscience. 1996 November; 88(1-2): 27-52.
  http://www.ncbi.nlm.nih.gov:80/entrez/query.fcgi?cmd=Retrieve&db=PubMed&list_uids=9003963&dopt=Abstract

- **Specifying the impulsivity of female inmates with borderline personality disorder.**
  Author(s): Hochhausen NM, Lorenz AR, Newman JP.
  Source: Journal of Abnormal Psychology. 2002 August; 111(3): 495-501.
  http://www.ncbi.nlm.nih.gov:80/entrez/query.fcgi?cmd=Retrieve&db=PubMed&list_uids=12150425&dopt=Abstract

- **Splitting phenomena from a viewpoint of experiencing time: spectrum from multiple personality and hysteria to borderline personality disorder.**
  Author(s): Shoda H.
  Source: Psychopathology. 1993; 26(5-6): 240-54.
  http://www.ncbi.nlm.nih.gov:80/entrez/query.fcgi?cmd=Retrieve&db=PubMed&list_uids=8190843&dopt=Abstract

- **SSRI treatment of borderline personality disorder: a randomized, placebo-controlled clinical trial for female patients with borderline personality disorder.**
  Author(s): Rinne T, van den Brink W, Wouters L, van Dyck R.
  Source: The American Journal of Psychiatry. 2002 December; 159(12): 2048-54.
  http://www.ncbi.nlm.nih.gov:80/entrez/query.fcgi?cmd=Retrieve&db=PubMed&list_uids=12450955&dopt=Abstract

- **STEPPS: a cognitive-behavioral systems-based group treatment for outpatients with borderline personality disorder--a preliminary report.**
  Author(s): Blum N, Pfohl B, John DS, Monahan P, Black DW.
  Source: Comprehensive Psychiatry. 2002 July-August; 43(4): 301-10.
  http://www.ncbi.nlm.nih.gov:80/entrez/query.fcgi?cmd=Retrieve&db=PubMed&list_uids=12107867&dopt=Abstract

- **Structural relations between borderline personality disorder features and putative etiological correlates.**
  Author(s): Trull TJ.
  Source: Journal of Abnormal Psychology. 2001 August; 110(3): 471-81.
  http://www.ncbi.nlm.nih.gov:80/entrez/query.fcgi?cmd=Retrieve&db=PubMed&list_uids=11502090&dopt=Abstract

- **Substance abuse in borderline personality disorder.**
  Author(s): Miller FT, Abrams T, Dulit R, Fyer M.
  Source: The American Journal of Drug and Alcohol Abuse. 1993; 19(4): 491-7.
  http://www.ncbi.nlm.nih.gov:80/entrez/query.fcgi?cmd=Retrieve&db=PubMed&list_uids=8273769&dopt=Abstract

- **Substance abuse in borderline personality disorder: clinical and etiological correlates.**
  Author(s): van den Bosch LM, Verheul R, van den Brink W.
  Source: Journal of Personality Disorders. 2001 October; 15(5): 416-24.
  http://www.ncbi.nlm.nih.gov:80/entrez/query.fcgi?cmd=Retrieve&db=PubMed&list_uids=11723876&dopt=Abstract

- **Subtle prefrontal neuropathology in a pilot magnetic resonance spectroscopy study in patients with borderline personality disorder.**
  Author(s): van Elst LT, Thiel T, Hesslinger B, Lieb K, Bohus M, Hennig J, Ebert D.
  Source: The Journal of Neuropsychiatry and Clinical Neurosciences. 2001 Fall; 13(4): 511-4.
  http://www.ncbi.nlm.nih.gov:80/entrez/query.fcgi?cmd=Retrieve&db=PubMed&list_uids=11748321&dopt=Abstract

- **Subtype differentiation of patients with borderline personality disorder using a circumplex model of interpersonal behavior.**
  Author(s): Leihener F, Wagner A, Haaf B, Schmidt C, Lieb K, Stieglitz R, Bohus M.
  Source: The Journal of Nervous and Mental Disease. 2003 April; 191(4): 248-54.
  http://www.ncbi.nlm.nih.gov:80/entrez/query.fcgi?cmd=Retrieve&db=PubMed&list_uids=12695736&dopt=Abstract

- **Subtypes of self-injurious patients with borderline personality disorder.**
  Author(s): Russ MJ, Shearin EN, Clarkin JF, Harrison K, Hull JW.
  Source: The American Journal of Psychiatry. 1993 December; 150(12): 1869-71.
  http://www.ncbi.nlm.nih.gov:80/entrez/query.fcgi?cmd=Retrieve&db=PubMed&list_uids=8238644&dopt=Abstract

- **Temperament, character, and attachment patterns in borderline personality disorder.**
  Author(s): Fossati A, Donati D, Donini M, Novella L, Bagnato M, Maffei C.
  Source: Journal of Personality Disorders. 2001 October; 15(5): 390-402.
  http://www.ncbi.nlm.nih.gov:80/entrez/query.fcgi?cmd=Retrieve&db=PubMed&list_uids=11723874&dopt=Abstract

- **The application of dialectical behavior therapy for patients with borderline personality disorder on inpatient units.**
  Author(s): Swenson CR, Sanderson C, Dulit RA, Linehan MM.
  Source: The Psychiatric Quarterly. 2001 Winter; 72(4): 307-24. Review.
  http://www.ncbi.nlm.nih.gov:80/entrez/query.fcgi?cmd=Retrieve&db=PubMed&list_uids=11525079&dopt=Abstract

- **The borderline personality disorder practice guidelines: the good, the bad, and the realistic.**
  Author(s): McGlashan TH.
  Source: Journal of Personality Disorders. 2002 April; 16(2): 119-21.
  http://www.ncbi.nlm.nih.gov:80/entrez/query.fcgi?cmd=Retrieve&db=PubMed&list_uids=12004487&dopt=Abstract

- **The development of a psychodynamic treatment for patients with borderline personality disorder: a preliminary study of behavioral change.**
  Author(s): Clarkin JF, Foelsch PA, Levy KN, Hull JW, Delaney JC, Kernberg OF.
  Source: Journal of Personality Disorders. 2001 December; 15(6): 487-95.
  http://www.ncbi.nlm.nih.gov:80/entrez/query.fcgi?cmd=Retrieve&db=PubMed&list_uids=11778390&dopt=Abstract

- **The impact of borderline personality disorder on post-traumatic stress in the community: a study of health status, health utilization, and functioning.**
  Author(s): Connor KM, Davidson JR, Hughes DC, Swartz MS, Blazer DG, George LK.
  Source: Comprehensive Psychiatry. 2002 January-February; 43(1): 41-8.
  http://www.ncbi.nlm.nih.gov:80/entrez/query.fcgi?cmd=Retrieve&db=PubMed&list_uids=11788918&dopt=Abstract

- **The impact of borderline personality disorder on process group outcome among women with posttraumatic stress disorder related to childhood abuse.**
  Author(s): Cloitre M, Koenen KC.
  Source: Int J Group Psychother. 2001 July; 51(3): 379-98.
  http://www.ncbi.nlm.nih.gov:80/entrez/query.fcgi?cmd=Retrieve&db=PubMed&list_uids=11447786&dopt=Abstract

- **The longitudinal course of borderline psychopathology: 6-year prospective follow-up of the phenomenology of borderline personality disorder.**
  Author(s): Zanarini MC, Frankenburg FR, Hennen J, Silk KR.
  Source: The American Journal of Psychiatry. 2003 February; 160(2): 274-83.
  http://www.ncbi.nlm.nih.gov:80/entrez/query.fcgi?cmd=Retrieve&db=PubMed&list_uids=12562573&dopt=Abstract

- **The relation between depressive symptoms and borderline personality disorder features over time in dysthymic disorder.**
  Author(s): Klein DN, Schwartz JE.
  Source: Journal of Personality Disorders. 2002 December; 16(6): 523-35.
  http://www.ncbi.nlm.nih.gov:80/entrez/query.fcgi?cmd=Retrieve&db=PubMed&list_uids=12616828&dopt=Abstract

- **The role of gender in the clinical presentation of patients with borderline personality disorder.**
  Author(s): Zlotnick C, Rothschild L, Zimmerman M.
  Source: Journal of Personality Disorders. 2002 June; 16(3): 277-82.
  http://www.ncbi.nlm.nih.gov:80/entrez/query.fcgi?cmd=Retrieve&db=PubMed&list_uids=12136683&dopt=Abstract

- **The role of the parietal lobe in borderline personality disorder.**
  Author(s): Swinton M.
  Source: Medical Hypotheses. 2003 February; 60(2): 263-7.
  http://www.ncbi.nlm.nih.gov:80/entrez/query.fcgi?cmd=Retrieve&db=PubMed&list_uids=12606245&dopt=Abstract

- **The use of transitional objects in self-directed aggression by patients with borderline personality disorder, anorexia nervosa, or bulimia nervosa.**
  Author(s): Guinjoan SM, Ross DR, Perinot L, Maritato V, Jorda-Fahrer M, Fahrer RD.
  Source: The Journal of the American Academy of Psychoanalysis. 2001 Fall; 29(3): 457-67.
  http://www.ncbi.nlm.nih.gov:80/entrez/query.fcgi?cmd=Retrieve&db=PubMed&list_uids=11816358&dopt=Abstract

- **Topiramate for self-mutilation in a patient with borderline personality disorder.**
  Author(s): Cassano P, Lattanzi L, Pini S, Dell'Osso L, Battistini G, Cassano GB.
  Source: Bipolar Disorders. 2001 June; 3(3): 161.
  http://www.ncbi.nlm.nih.gov:80/entrez/query.fcgi?cmd=Retrieve&db=PubMed&list_uids=11465678&dopt=Abstract

- **Travelling through the system: the lived experience of people with borderline personality disorder in contact with psychiatric services.**
  Author(s): Fallon P.
  Source: Journal of Psychiatric and Mental Health Nursing. 2003 August; 10(4): 393-401.
  http://www.ncbi.nlm.nih.gov:80/entrez/query.fcgi?cmd=Retrieve&db=PubMed&list_uids=12887630&dopt=Abstract

- **Treating personality fragmentation and dissociation in borderline personality disorder: a pilot study of the impact of cognitive analytic therapy.**
  Author(s): Wildgoose A, Clarke S, Waller G.
  Source: The British Journal of Medical Psychology. 2001 March; 74(Pt 1): 47-55.
  http://www.ncbi.nlm.nih.gov:80/entrez/query.fcgi?cmd=Retrieve&db=PubMed&list_uids=11314902&dopt=Abstract

- **Treatment considerations for the patient with borderline personality disorder.**
  Author(s): Antai-Otong D.
  Source: Nurs Clin North Am. 2003 March; 38(1): 101-9. Review.
  http://www.ncbi.nlm.nih.gov:80/entrez/query.fcgi?cmd=Retrieve&db=PubMed&list_uids=12712672&dopt=Abstract

- **Treatment of borderline personality disorder with mood instability with divalproex sodium: series of ten cases.**
  Author(s): Townsend MH, Cambre KM, Barbee JG.
  Source: Journal of Clinical Psychopharmacology. 2001 April; 21(2): 249-51.
  http://www.ncbi.nlm.nih.gov:80/entrez/query.fcgi?cmd=Retrieve&db=PubMed&list_uids=11270932&dopt=Abstract

- **Treatment of borderline personality disorder with psychoanalytically oriented partial hospitalization: an 18-month follow-up.**
  Author(s): Bateman A, Fonagy P.
  Source: The American Journal of Psychiatry. 2001 January; 158(1): 36-42.
  http://www.ncbi.nlm.nih.gov:80/entrez/query.fcgi?cmd=Retrieve&db=PubMed&list_uids=11136631&dopt=Abstract

- **Treatment of borderline personality disorder with risperidone.**
  Author(s): Rocca P, Marchiaro L, Cocuzza E, Bogetto F.
  Source: The Journal of Clinical Psychiatry. 2002 March; 63(3): 241-4.
  http://www.ncbi.nlm.nih.gov:80/entrez/query.fcgi?cmd=Retrieve&db=PubMed&list_uids=11926724&dopt=Abstract

- **Twenty-four-hour urine cortisol in combat veterans with PTSD and comorbid borderline personality disorder.**
  Author(s): Southwick SM, Axelrod SR, Wang S, Yehuda R, Morgan CA 3rd, Charney D, Rosenheck R, Mason JW.
  Source: The Journal of Nervous and Mental Disease. 2003 April; 191(4): 261-2.
  http://www.ncbi.nlm.nih.gov:80/entrez/query.fcgi?cmd=Retrieve&db=PubMed&list_uids=12695738&dopt=Abstract

- **Uncommon self-mutilation in a borderline personality disorder patient.**
  Author(s): Rollnik JD, Schneider U, Wedegaertner F, Huber TJ, Emrich HM.
  Source: The Australian and New Zealand Journal of Psychiatry. 2001 February; 35(1): 133-4.
  http://www.ncbi.nlm.nih.gov:80/entrez/query.fcgi?cmd=Retrieve&db=PubMed&list_uids=11270451&dopt=Abstract

- **Use of dialectical behavior therapy in a partial hospital program for women with borderline personality disorder.**
  Author(s): Simpson EB, Pistorello J, Begin A, Costello E, Levinson J, Mulberry S, Pearlstein T, Rosen K, Stevens M.
  Source: Psychiatric Services (Washington, D.C.). 1998 May; 49(5): 669-73.
  http://www.ncbi.nlm.nih.gov:80/entrez/query.fcgi?cmd=Retrieve&db=PubMed&list_uids=9603574&dopt=Abstract

- **Use of structured self-report assessment to diagnose borderline personality disorder during major depressive episodes.**
  Author(s): Kurtz JE, Morey LC.
  Source: Assessment. 2001 September; 8(3): 291-300.
  http://www.ncbi.nlm.nih.gov:80/entrez/query.fcgi?cmd=Retrieve&db=PubMed&list_uids=11575622&dopt=Abstract

- **Using commercially available films to teach about borderline personality disorder.**
  Author(s): Hyler SE, Schanzer B.
  Source: Bulletin of the Menninger Clinic. 1997 Fall; 61(4): 458-68.
  http://www.ncbi.nlm.nih.gov:80/entrez/query.fcgi?cmd=Retrieve&db=PubMed&list_uids=9401150&dopt=Abstract

- **Using the structural analysis of social behavior (SASB) to differentiate young adults with borderline personality disorder features.**
  Author(s): Ruiz MA, Pincus AL, Bedics JB.
  Source: Journal of Personality Disorders. 1999 Summer; 13(2): 187-98.
  http://www.ncbi.nlm.nih.gov:80/entrez/query.fcgi?cmd=Retrieve&db=PubMed&list_uids=10372351&dopt=Abstract

- **Validation of schizoid personality scales using indices of schizotypal and borderline personality disorder in a criminal population.**
  Author(s): Raine A.
  Source: The British Journal of Clinical Psychology / the British Psychological Society. 1987 November; 26 ( Pt 4): 305-9.
  http://www.ncbi.nlm.nih.gov:80/entrez/query.fcgi?cmd=Retrieve&db=PubMed&list_uids=3427252&dopt=Abstract

- **Validation of the MCMI-I Borderline Personality Disorder Scale with a well-defined criterion sample.**
  Author(s): Patrick J.
  Source: Journal of Clinical Psychology. 1993 January; 49(1): 28-32.
  http://www.ncbi.nlm.nih.gov:80/entrez/query.fcgi?cmd=Retrieve&db=PubMed&list_uids=8425931&dopt=Abstract

- **Venlafaxine in the treatment of borderline personality disorder.**
  Author(s): Markovitz PJ, Wagner SC.
  Source: Psychopharmacology Bulletin. 1995; 31(4): 773-7.
  http://www.ncbi.nlm.nih.gov:80/entrez/query.fcgi?cmd=Retrieve&db=PubMed&list_uids=8851652&dopt=Abstract

- **Voice mail as a transitional object in the treatment of borderline personality disorder.**
  Author(s): Finch SJ.
  Source: Canadian Journal of Psychiatry. Revue Canadienne De Psychiatrie. 2002 December; 47(10): 974-5.
  http://www.ncbi.nlm.nih.gov:80/entrez/query.fcgi?cmd=Retrieve&db=PubMed&list_uids=12553137&dopt=Abstract

- **Vomiting as a manifestation of borderline personality disorder in primary care.**
  Author(s): Johnson TM.
  Source: The Journal of the American Board of Family Practice / American Board of Family Practice. 1993 July-August; 6(4): 385-94.
  http://www.ncbi.nlm.nih.gov:80/entrez/query.fcgi?cmd=Retrieve&db=PubMed&list_uids=8352042&dopt=Abstract

- **What are the borders of borderline personality disorder?**
  Author(s): Tyrer P.
  Source: Acta Psychiatrica Scandinavica. Supplementum. 1994; 379: 38-44. Review.
  http://www.ncbi.nlm.nih.gov:80/entrez/query.fcgi?cmd=Retrieve&db=PubMed&list_uids=8010150&dopt=Abstract

- **When she was bad: borderline personality disorder in a posttraumatic age.**
  Author(s): Becker D.
  Source: The American Journal of Orthopsychiatry. 2000 October; 70(4): 422-32. Review.
  http://www.ncbi.nlm.nih.gov:80/entrez/query.fcgi?cmd=Retrieve&db=PubMed&list_uids=11086521&dopt=Abstract

- **Women in special hospitals: understanding the presenting behaviour of women diagnosed with borderline personality disorder.**
  Author(s): Wilkins TM, Warner S.
  Source: Journal of Psychiatric and Mental Health Nursing. 2001 August; 8(4): 289-97. Review.
  http://www.ncbi.nlm.nih.gov:80/entrez/query.fcgi?cmd=Retrieve&db=PubMed&list_uids=11882141&dopt=Abstract

# CHAPTER 2. NUTRITION AND BORDERLINE PERSONALITY DISORDER

## Overview

In this chapter, we will show you how to find studies dedicated specifically to nutrition and borderline personality disorder.

## Finding Nutrition Studies on Borderline Personality Disorder

The National Institutes of Health's Office of Dietary Supplements (ODS) offers a searchable bibliographic database called the IBIDS (International Bibliographic Information on Dietary Supplements; National Institutes of Health, Building 31, Room 1B29, 31 Center Drive, MSC 2086, Bethesda, Maryland 20892-2086, Tel: 301-435-2920, Fax: 301-480-1845, E-mail: ods@nih.gov). The IBIDS contains over 460,000 scientific citations and summaries about dietary supplements and nutrition as well as references to published international, scientific literature on dietary supplements such as vitamins, minerals, and botanicals.[4] The IBIDS includes references and citations to both human and animal research studies.

As a service of the ODS, access to the IBIDS database is available free of charge at the following Web address: **http://ods.od.nih.gov/databases/ibids.html**. After entering the search area, you have three choices: (1) IBIDS Consumer Database, (2) Full IBIDS Database, or (3) Peer Reviewed Citations Only.

Now that you have selected a database, click on the "Advanced" tab. An advanced search allows you to retrieve up to 100 fully explained references in a comprehensive format. Type "borderline personality disorder" (or synonyms) into the search box, and click "Go." To narrow the search, you can also select the "Title" field.

---

[4] Adapted from **http://ods.od.nih.gov**. IBIDS is produced by the Office of Dietary Supplements (ODS) at the National Institutes of Health to assist the public, healthcare providers, educators, and researchers in locating credible, scientific information on dietary supplements. IBIDS was developed and will be maintained through an interagency partnership with the Food and Nutrition Information Center of the National Agricultural Library, U.S. Department of Agriculture.

The following information is typical of that found when using the "Full IBIDS Database" to search for "borderline personality disorder" (or a synonym):

- **A preliminary double-blind, placebo-controlled trial of divalproex sodium in borderline personality disorder.**
  Author(s): Department of Psychiatry, Mount Sinai School of Medicine, New York, NY 10029-6574, USA. eric.hollander@mssm.edu
  Source: Hollander, E Allen, A Lopez, R P Bienstock, C A Grossman, R Siever, L J Merkatz, L Stein, D J J-Clin-Psychiatry. 2001 March; 62(3): 199-203 0160-6689
- **An open trial of valproate in borderline personality disorder.**
  Author(s): Department of Psychiatry, University of Stellenbosch, Tygerberg, South Africa.
  Source: Stein, D J Simeon, D Frenkel, M Islam, M N Hollander, E J-Clin-Psychiatry. 1995 November; 56(11): 506-10 0160-6689
- **Brain Regional alpha-[11C]methyl-L-tryptophan trapping in impulsive subjects with borderline personality disorder.**
  Author(s): Department of Psychiatry, McGill University, Monteal, Quebec, Canada.
  Source: Leyton, M Okazawa, H Diksic, M Paris, J Rosa, P Mzengeza, S Young, S N Blier, P Benkelfat, C Am-J-Psychiatry. 2001 May; 158(5): 775-82 0002-953X
- **Divalproex sodium as a treatment for borderline personality disorder.**
  Author(s): MECCA, Iowa City, Iowa, USA.
  Source: Wilcox, J A Ann-Clin-Psychiatry. 1995 March; 7(1): 33-7 1040-1237
- **Divalproex sodium treatment of women with borderline personality disorder and bipolar II disorder: a double-blind placebo-controlled pilot study.**
  Author(s): Laboratory for the Study of Adult Development, McLean Hospital, Belmont, MA 02478, USA. ffrankenburg@mclean.harvard.edu
  Source: Frankenburg, Frances R Zanarini, Mary C J-Clin-Psychiatry. 2002 May; 63(5): 442-6 0160-6689
- **Naltrexone in the treatment of dissociative symptoms in patients with borderline personality disorder: an open-label trial.**
  Author(s): Department of Psychiatry, University of Freiburg, Freiburg im Breisgau, Germany. martin_bohus@psyallg.ukl.uni-freiburg.de
  Source: Bohus, M J Landwehrmeyer, G B Stiglmayr, C E Limberger, M F Bohme, R Schmahl, C G J-Clin-Psychiatry. 1999 September; 60(9): 598-603 0160-6689
- **omega-3 Fatty acid treatment of women with borderline personality disorder: a double-blind, placebo-controlled pilot study.**
  Author(s): Laboratory for the Study of Adult Development, McLean Hospital, Belmont, MA 02478, USA. zanarini@mclean.harvard.edu
  Source: Zanarini, M C Frankenburg, F R Am-J-Psychiatry. 2003 January; 160(1): 167-9 0002-953X
- **Pharmacotherapy of borderline personality disorder.**
  Author(s): Department of Psychiatry & Behavioral Sciences, University of Texas Medical Branch, Galveston 77555-0429, USA.
  Source: Hirschfeld, R M J-Clin-Psychiatry. 1997; 58 Suppl 1448-52; discussion 53 0160-6689
- **Platelet alpha 2-adrenergic receptor binding sites in major depressive disorder and borderline personality disorder.**
  Author(s): Posttraumatic Stress Disorder Program, West Haven VA Medical Center, CT.

Source: Southwick, S M Yehuda, R Giller, E L Perry, B D Psychiatry-Res. 1990 November; 34(2): 193-203 0165-1781

- **Practice guideline for the treatment of patients with borderline personality disorder. American Psychiatric Association.**
  Source: Am-J-Psychiatry. 2001 October; 158(10 Suppl): 1-52 0002-953X

## Federal Resources on Nutrition

In addition to the IBIDS, the United States Department of Health and Human Services (HHS) and the United States Department of Agriculture (USDA) provide many sources of information on general nutrition and health. Recommended resources include:

- healthfinder®, HHS's gateway to health information, including diet and nutrition: **http://www.healthfinder.gov/scripts/SearchContext.asp?topic=238&page=0**
- The United States Department of Agriculture's Web site dedicated to nutrition information: **www.nutrition.gov**
- The Food and Drug Administration's Web site for federal food safety information: **www.foodsafety.gov**
- The National Action Plan on Overweight and Obesity sponsored by the United States Surgeon General: **http://www.surgeongeneral.gov/topics/obesity/**
- The Center for Food Safety and Applied Nutrition has an Internet site sponsored by the Food and Drug Administration and the Department of Health and Human Services: **http://vm.cfsan.fda.gov/**
- Center for Nutrition Policy and Promotion sponsored by the United States Department of Agriculture: **http://www.usda.gov/cnpp/**
- Food and Nutrition Information Center, National Agricultural Library sponsored by the United States Department of Agriculture: **http://www.nal.usda.gov/fnic/**
- Food and Nutrition Service sponsored by the United States Department of Agriculture: **http://www.fns.usda.gov/fns/**

## Additional Web Resources

A number of additional Web sites offer encyclopedic information covering food and nutrition. The following is a representative sample:

- AOL: **http://search.aol.com/cat.adp?id=174&layer=&from=subcats**
- Family Village: **http://www.familyvillage.wisc.edu/med_nutrition.html**
- Google: **http://directory.google.com/Top/Health/Nutrition/**
- Healthnotes: **http://www.healthnotes.com/**
- Open Directory Project: **http://dmoz.org/Health/Nutrition/**
- Yahoo.com: **http://dir.yahoo.com/Health/Nutrition/**
- WebMD®Health: **http://my.webmd.com/nutrition**

- WholeHealthMD.com: **http://www.wholehealthmd.com/reflib/0,1529,00.html**

# CHAPTER 3. ALTERNATIVE MEDICINE AND BORDERLINE PERSONALITY DISORDER

## Overview

In this chapter, we will begin by introducing you to official information sources on complementary and alternative medicine (CAM) relating to borderline personality disorder. At the conclusion of this chapter, we will provide additional sources.

## National Center for Complementary and Alternative Medicine

The National Center for Complementary and Alternative Medicine (NCCAM) of the National Institutes of Health (**http://nccam.nih.gov/**) has created a link to the National Library of Medicine's databases to facilitate research for articles that specifically relate to borderline personality disorder and complementary medicine. To search the database, go to the following Web site: **http://www.nlm.nih.gov/nccam/camonpubmed.html**. Select "CAM on PubMed." Enter "borderline personality disorder" (or synonyms) into the search box. Click "Go." The following references provide information on particular aspects of complementary and alternative medicine that are related to borderline personality disorder:

- **A case of probable dissociative disorder.**
  Author(s): Jaschke VA, Spiegel D.
  Source: Bulletin of the Menninger Clinic. 1992 Spring; 56(2): 246-60.
  http://www.ncbi.nlm.nih.gov:80/entrez/query.fcgi?cmd=Retrieve&db=PubMed&list_uids=1352164&dopt=Abstract

- **A developmental model of addictions, and its relationship to the twelve step program of alcoholics anonymous.**
  Author(s): Johnson B.
  Source: Journal of Substance Abuse Treatment. 1993 January-February; 10(1): 23-34.
  http://www.ncbi.nlm.nih.gov:80/entrez/query.fcgi?cmd=Retrieve&db=PubMed&list_uids=8450570&dopt=Abstract

- **A psychoacoustic effect upon mood and its relation to affective instability.**
  Author(s): Gruber LN, Janowsky DS, Mandell AJ, Risch SC, Huey LY.

Source: Comprehensive Psychiatry. 1984 January-February; 25(1): 106-12.
http://www.ncbi.nlm.nih.gov:80/entrez/query.fcgi?cmd=Retrieve&db=PubMed&list_uids=6365431&dopt=Abstract

- **Affect theory and the neurobiology of affective dysregulation.**
  Author(s): Yovell Y.
  Source: The Journal of the American Academy of Psychoanalysis. 2000 Fall; 28(3): 467-81.
  http://www.ncbi.nlm.nih.gov:80/entrez/query.fcgi?cmd=Retrieve&db=PubMed&list_uids=11109226&dopt=Abstract

- **Alchemy, homeopathy and the treatment of borderline cases.**
  Author(s): Whitmont EC.
  Source: The Journal of Analytical Psychology. 1996 July; 41(3): 369-86.
  http://www.ncbi.nlm.nih.gov:80/entrez/query.fcgi?cmd=Retrieve&db=PubMed&list_uids=8760996&dopt=Abstract

- **Alcohol abuse and the borderline patient.**
  Author(s): Hellman JM.
  Source: Psychiatry. 1981 November; 44(4): 307-17.
  http://www.ncbi.nlm.nih.gov:80/entrez/query.fcgi?cmd=Retrieve&db=PubMed&list_uids=7291374&dopt=Abstract

- **An exploratory study of hypnotic capacity of schizophrenic and borderline patients in a clinical setting.**
  Author(s): Murray-Jobsis J.
  Source: Am J Clin Hypn. 1991 January; 33(3): 150-60; Discussion 161-71.
  http://www.ncbi.nlm.nih.gov:80/entrez/query.fcgi?cmd=Retrieve&db=PubMed&list_uids=2012006&dopt=Abstract

- **Bedside stuffed animals and borderline personality.**
  Author(s): Labbate LA, Benedek DM.
  Source: Psychological Reports. 1996 October; 79(2): 624-6.
  http://www.ncbi.nlm.nih.gov:80/entrez/query.fcgi?cmd=Retrieve&db=PubMed&list_uids=8909090&dopt=Abstract

- **Borderline diagnosis and substance abuse in female patients with eating disorders.**
  Author(s): Koepp W, Schildbach S, Schmager C, Rohner R.
  Source: The International Journal of Eating Disorders. 1993 July; 14(1): 107-10.
  http://www.ncbi.nlm.nih.gov:80/entrez/query.fcgi?cmd=Retrieve&db=PubMed&list_uids=8339092&dopt=Abstract

- **Borderline disorder and post-traumatic stress disorder: an equivalence?**
  Author(s): Lonie I.
  Source: The Australian and New Zealand Journal of Psychiatry. 1993 June; 27(2): 233-45. Review.
  http://www.ncbi.nlm.nih.gov:80/entrez/query.fcgi?cmd=Retrieve&db=PubMed&list_uids=8363532&dopt=Abstract

- **Borderline personality and alcohol abuse.**
Author(s): Vaccani JM.
Source: Archives of Psychiatric Nursing. 1989 April; 3(2): 113-9. Review.
http://www.ncbi.nlm.nih.gov:80/entrez/query.fcgi?cmd=Retrieve&db=PubMed&list_uids=2653231&dopt=Abstract

- **Case report of conversion catatonia: indication for hypnosis.**
Author(s): Jensen PS.
Source: American Journal of Psychotherapy. 1984 October; 38(4): 566-70.
http://www.ncbi.nlm.nih.gov:80/entrez/query.fcgi?cmd=Retrieve&db=PubMed&list_uids=6517174&dopt=Abstract

- **Combining individual and homogeneous group psychotherapies for borderline conditions.**
Author(s): Slavinska-Holy N.
Source: Int J Group Psychother. 1983 July; 33(3): 297-312. No Abstract Available.
http://www.ncbi.nlm.nih.gov:80/entrez/query.fcgi?cmd=Retrieve&db=PubMed&list_uids=6885213&dopt=Abstract

- **Diagnosing dissociative disorders.**
Author(s): Allen JG, Smith WH.
Source: Bulletin of the Menninger Clinic. 1993 Summer; 57(3): 328-43. Review.
http://www.ncbi.nlm.nih.gov:80/entrez/query.fcgi?cmd=Retrieve&db=PubMed&list_uids=8401385&dopt=Abstract

- **Dialectical behavior therapy versus comprehensive validation therapy plus 12-step for the treatment of opioid dependent women meeting criteria for borderline personality disorder.**
Author(s): Linehan MM, Dimeff LA, Reynolds SK, Comtois KA, Welch SS, Heagerty P, Kivlahan DR.
Source: Drug and Alcohol Dependence. 2002 June 1; 67(1): 13-26.
http://www.ncbi.nlm.nih.gov:80/entrez/query.fcgi?cmd=Retrieve&db=PubMed&list_uids=12062776&dopt=Abstract

- **Ego-state therapy for self-injurious behavior.**
Author(s): Gainer MJ, Torem MS.
Source: Am J Clin Hypn. 1993 April; 35(4): 257-66.
http://www.ncbi.nlm.nih.gov:80/entrez/query.fcgi?cmd=Retrieve&db=PubMed&list_uids=8480669&dopt=Abstract

- **Electrodermal responses in post-traumatic syndromes. A pilot study of cerebral hemisphere functioning in Vietnam veterans.**
Author(s): Brende JO.
Source: The Journal of Nervous and Mental Disease. 1982 June; 170(6): 352-61.
http://www.ncbi.nlm.nih.gov:80/entrez/query.fcgi?cmd=Retrieve&db=PubMed&list_uids=7077309&dopt=Abstract

- **Enhanced intensity dependence as a marker of low serotonergic neurotransmission in borderline personality disorder.**

Author(s): Norra C, Mrazek M, Tuchtenhagen F, Gobbele R, Buchner H, Sass H, Herpertz SC.
Source: Journal of Psychiatric Research. 2003 January-February; 37(1): 23-33.
http://www.ncbi.nlm.nih.gov:80/entrez/query.fcgi?cmd=Retrieve&db=PubMed&list_uids=12482467&dopt=Abstract

- **From the valley of the shadow of death: a group model for borderline patients.**
  Author(s): Gallagher RE, Manierre A, Castelli C.
  Source: J Pastoral Care. 1994 Spring; 48(1): 45-53.
  http://www.ncbi.nlm.nih.gov:80/entrez/query.fcgi?cmd=Retrieve&db=PubMed&list_uids=10133166&dopt=Abstract

- **Generalized anxiety disorder: new concepts and psychopharmacologic therapies.**
  Author(s): Dubovsky SL.
  Source: The Journal of Clinical Psychiatry. 1990 January; 51 Suppl: 3-10. Review.
  http://www.ncbi.nlm.nih.gov:80/entrez/query.fcgi?cmd=Retrieve&db=PubMed&list_uids=1967248&dopt=Abstract

- **Issues involved in combining drugs with psychotherapy for the borderline inpatient.**
  Author(s): Swenson CR, Wood MJ.
  Source: The Psychiatric Clinics of North America. 1990 June; 13(2): 297-306.
  http://www.ncbi.nlm.nih.gov:80/entrez/query.fcgi?cmd=Retrieve&db=PubMed&list_uids=2352892&dopt=Abstract

- **Multiple personality. 165 years after Mary Reynolds.**
  Author(s): Greaves GB.
  Source: The Journal of Nervous and Mental Disease. 1980 October; 168(10): 577-96.
  http://www.ncbi.nlm.nih.gov:80/entrez/query.fcgi?cmd=Retrieve&db=PubMed&list_uids=7420066&dopt=Abstract

- **Multiple personality: an issue for forensic psychiatry.**
  Author(s): Serban G.
  Source: American Journal of Psychotherapy. 1992 April; 46(2): 269-80.
  http://www.ncbi.nlm.nih.gov:80/entrez/query.fcgi?cmd=Retrieve&db=PubMed&list_uids=1605334&dopt=Abstract

- **omega-3 Fatty acid treatment of women with borderline personality disorder: a double-blind, placebo-controlled pilot study.**
  Author(s): Zanarini MC, Frankenburg FR.
  Source: The American Journal of Psychiatry. 2003 January; 160(1): 167-9.
  http://www.ncbi.nlm.nih.gov:80/entrez/query.fcgi?cmd=Retrieve&db=PubMed&list_uids=12505817&dopt=Abstract

- **Potential contributions of hypnosis to ego-strengthening procedures in EMDR. Eye Movement Desensitization Reprocessing.**
  Author(s): Phillips M.
  Source: Am J Clin Hypn. 2001 January-April; 43(3-4): 247-62. Review.
  http://www.ncbi.nlm.nih.gov:80/entrez/query.fcgi?cmd=Retrieve&db=PubMed&list_uids=11269628&dopt=Abstract

- **Prospective follow-up study of borderline personality disorder: prognosis, prediction of outcome, and Axis II comorbidity.**
Author(s): Links PS, Heslegrave R, van Reekum R.
Source: Canadian Journal of Psychiatry. Revue Canadienne De Psychiatrie. 1998 April; 43(3): 265-70.
http://www.ncbi.nlm.nih.gov:80/entrez/query.fcgi?cmd=Retrieve&db=PubMed&list_uids=9561315&dopt=Abstract

- **Psychoactive substance use disorder in youth suicide.**
Author(s): Runeson B.
Source: Alcohol and Alcoholism (Oxford, Oxfordshire). 1990; 25(5): 561-8.
http://www.ncbi.nlm.nih.gov:80/entrez/query.fcgi?cmd=Retrieve&db=PubMed&list_uids=2088354&dopt=Abstract

- **Relaxation and merging in the treatment of personality disorders.**
Author(s): Glantz K, Goisman RM.
Source: American Journal of Psychotherapy. 1990 July; 44(3): 405-13.
http://www.ncbi.nlm.nih.gov:80/entrez/query.fcgi?cmd=Retrieve&db=PubMed&list_uids=2221212&dopt=Abstract

- **Reliability and validity of a psychotic traits questionnaire (STQ).**
Author(s): Jackson M, Claridge G.
Source: The British Journal of Clinical Psychology / the British Psychological Society. 1991 November; 30 ( Pt 4): 311-23.
http://www.ncbi.nlm.nih.gov:80/entrez/query.fcgi?cmd=Retrieve&db=PubMed&list_uids=1777753&dopt=Abstract

- **Self-injurious behavior: a review of the behavior and biology of self-mutilation.**
Author(s): Winchel RM, Stanley M.
Source: The American Journal of Psychiatry. 1991 March; 148(3): 306-17. Review.
http://www.ncbi.nlm.nih.gov:80/entrez/query.fcgi?cmd=Retrieve&db=PubMed&list_uids=1847025&dopt=Abstract

- **Socio-hygienic and clinico-epidemiological research--the scientific foundation of the prophylaxis of the neuropsychic disorders.**
Author(s): Petrakov BD.
Source: Sante Publique (Bucur). 1985; 28(2): 133-41. No Abstract Available.
http://www.ncbi.nlm.nih.gov:80/entrez/query.fcgi?cmd=Retrieve&db=PubMed&list_uids=4095659&dopt=Abstract

- **Structured interview data on 35 cases of dissociative identity disorder in Turkey.**
Author(s): Sar V, Yargic LI, Tutkun H.
Source: The American Journal of Psychiatry. 1996 October; 153(10): 1329-33.
http://www.ncbi.nlm.nih.gov:80/entrez/query.fcgi?cmd=Retrieve&db=PubMed&list_uids=8831443&dopt=Abstract

- **The application of object relations theory to the hypnotherapy of developmental arrests: the borderline patient.**
Author(s): Copeland DR.

Source: Int J Clin Exp Hypn. 1986 July; 34(3): 157-68. No Abstract Available.
http://www.ncbi.nlm.nih.gov:80/entrez/query.fcgi?cmd=Retrieve&db=PubMed&list_uids=3744609&dopt=Abstract

- **The borderline diagnosis and integration of self.**
  Author(s): Mitchell A.
  Source: American Journal of Psychoanalysis. 1985 Fall; 45(3): 234-50.
  http://www.ncbi.nlm.nih.gov:80/entrez/query.fcgi?cmd=Retrieve&db=PubMed&list_uids=4051045&dopt=Abstract

- **The boy from outer space. An exploration of psychotic catastrophe.**
  Author(s): Macdonald J.
  Source: Psychoanal Study Child. 1992; 47: 299-320.
  http://www.ncbi.nlm.nih.gov:80/entrez/query.fcgi?cmd=Retrieve&db=PubMed&list_uids=1289937&dopt=Abstract

## Additional Web Resources

A number of additional Web sites offer encyclopedic information covering CAM and related topics. The following is a representative sample:

- Alternative Medicine Foundation, Inc.: **http://www.herbmed.org/**
- AOL: **http://search.aol.com/cat.adp?id=169&layer=&from=subcats**
- Chinese Medicine: **http://www.newcenturynutrition.com/**
- drkoop.com®: **http://www.drkoop.com/InteractiveMedicine/IndexC.html**
- Family Village: **http://www.familyvillage.wisc.edu/med_altn.htm**
- Google: **http://directory.google.com/Top/Health/Alternative/**
- Healthnotes: **http://www.healthnotes.com/**
- MedWebPlus: **http://medwebplus.com/subject/Alternative_and_Complementary_Medicine**
- Open Directory Project: **http://dmoz.org/Health/Alternative/**
- HealthGate: **http://www.tnp.com/**
- WebMD®Health: **http://my.webmd.com/drugs_and_herbs**
- WholeHealthMD.com: **http://www.wholehealthmd.com/reflib/0,1529,00.html**
- Yahoo.com: **http://dir.yahoo.com/Health/Alternative_Medicine/**

The following is a specific Web list relating to borderline personality disorder; please note that any particular subject below may indicate either a therapeutic use, or a contraindication (potential danger), and does not reflect an official recommendation:

- **General Overview**

  **Anorexia Nervosa**
  Source: Integrative Medicine Communications; www.drkoop.com

**Depression**
Source: Integrative Medicine Communications; www.drkoop.com

## General References

A good place to find general background information on CAM is the National Library of Medicine. It has prepared within the MEDLINEplus system an information topic page dedicated to complementary and alternative medicine. To access this page, go to the MEDLINEplus site at **http://www.nlm.nih.gov/medlineplus/alternativemedicine.html** This Web site provides a general overview of various topics and can lead to a number of general sources.

# CHAPTER 4. DISSERTATIONS ON BORDERLINE PERSONALITY DISORDER

## Overview

In this chapter, we will give you a bibliography on recent dissertations relating to borderline personality disorder. We will also provide you with information on how to use the Internet to stay current on dissertations. **IMPORTANT NOTE:** When following the search strategy described below, you may discover non-medical dissertations that use the generic term "borderline personality disorder" (or a synonym) in their titles. To accurately reflect the results that you might find while conducting research on borderline personality disorder, we have not necessarily excluded non-medical dissertations in this bibliography.

## Dissertations on Borderline Personality Disorder

*ProQuest Digital Dissertations,* the largest archive of academic dissertations available, is located at the following Web address: **http://wwwlib.umi.com/dissertations**. From this archive, we have compiled the following list covering dissertations devoted to borderline personality disorder. You will see that the information provided includes the dissertation's title, its author, and the institution with which the author is associated. The following covers recent dissertations found when using this search procedure:

- **A Comparison of Neglected Foster Children Who Meet the Criteria for the Diagnosis of Borderline Personality Disorder and Their Undiagnosed Counterparts: a Qualitative Study** by Aquino, Diane, Phd from New York University, 1998, 310 pages
http://wwwlib.umi.com/dissertations/fullcit/9827885
- **A Comparison of Selection of Curative Factors in Group Therapy by Borderline Personality Disorder and Non-borderline Personality Disorder Inpatients** by Jeziorski, Joseph C., Phd from Saint Louis University, 1993, 198 pages
http://wwwlib.umi.com/dissertations/fullcit/9416833
- **A Training Program for Correctional Staff to Treat Incarcerated Individuals with Borderline Personality Disorder** by Ellis Dipadova, Marlo Ann; Psyd from Carlos Albizu University, 2002, 122 pages
http://wwwlib.umi.com/dissertations/fullcit/3082904

- **Action, Somatization, and Language in Borderline Inpatients (borderline Personality Disorder)** by Okie, Jean E., Phd from Adelphi University, the Institute of Advanced Psychological Studies, 1992, 174 pages
http://wwwlib.umi.com/dissertations/fullcit/9211084
- **Adult Emotional Development: a Comparison of Emotion Processing in Borderline Personality Disorders and Non-borderline Subjects** by Levine, Deborah, Phd from University of Toronto (canada), 1992, 181 pages
http://wwwlib.umi.com/dissertations/fullcit/NN73819
- **An Exploration of Ego Development and the Suppression of Anger in Persons with Borderline Personality Disorder As Seen in Art Therapy: a Case Study** by Madden, Alice Judith; Ma from Concordia University (canada), 2002, 85 pages
http://wwwlib.umi.com/dissertations/fullcit/MQ74866
- **Anaclitic and Introjective Dimensions and Depression in Borderline Personality Disorder** by Trifiletti, Robert James; Phd from University of Calgary (canada), 1989
http://wwwlib.umi.com/dissertations/fullcit/NL54340
- **Anorexia Nervosa: a Psychological Birth Anomaly (separation Individuation, Psychoanalytical, Developmental Psychology, Borderline Personality Disorder, Object Relations)** by Brainard, Marythelma Bryant, Phd from The University of New Mexico, 1984, 516 pages
http://wwwlib.umi.com/dissertations/fullcit/8425910
- **Assessing the Perceived Etiological Family System of Outpatient Clients Diagnosed As Having a Borderline Personality Disorder** by Fishel, Lawrence Raymond, Phd from University of Maryland at Baltimore, 1989, 233 pages
http://wwwlib.umi.com/dissertations/fullcit/8917273
- **Borderline and Narcissistic Rage and Emptiness: Their Dramatization and Drama Therapy (borderline Personality Disorder)** by Kaplan, Howard Gary, Phd from Northwestern University, 1990, 410 pages
http://wwwlib.umi.com/dissertations/fullcit/9114570
- **Borderline Personality Disorder and Expressed Emotion** by Hoffman, Perry Ann D., Phd from New York University, 1995, 167 pages
http://wwwlib.umi.com/dissertations/fullcit/9708489
- **Borderline Personality Disorder in Children: Its Possible Relationship to Child Abuse and Neglect** by Seese, Patricia L., Phd from New York University, 1997, 108 pages
http://wwwlib.umi.com/dissertations/fullcit/9710937
- **Borderline Personality Disorder: an Anthropological Perspective** by Miller, Sharon Glick, Phd from University of South Florida, 1993, 287 pages
http://wwwlib.umi.com/dissertations/fullcit/9404909
- **Differences in the Developmental Experiences and Symptomology of High-functioning Women Diagnosed with Borderline Personality Disorder** by Sikora, Elizabeth A.; Phd from Capella University, 2002, 172 pages
http://wwwlib.umi.com/dissertations/fullcit/3061169
- **Evocative Visual and Verbal Memory Functioning of Borderline Personality Disorders** by Curran, Kathleen Ann, Phd from Boston College, 1987, 134 pages
http://wwwlib.umi.com/dissertations/fullcit/8807515

- **Gender and Ethnic Bias in the Diagnosis of Antisocial and Borderline Personality Disorders** by Delphin, Miriam Elizabeth; Phd from Purdue University, 2001, 131 pages
http://wwwlib.umi.com/dissertations/fullcit/3043718
- **Illness-defining As Social Process Borderline Personality Disorder (medical Sociology)** by Elwell, Ronnie Marie, Phd from The American University, 1985, 207 pages
http://wwwlib.umi.com/dissertations/fullcit/8514486
- **Masking Symptoms and Their Relationship to Depression and Borderline Personality Disorder in Adolescent Inpatients** by Diller, Robyne S, Phd from Emory University, 1989, 127 pages
http://wwwlib.umi.com/dissertations/fullcit/8924673
- **Mmpi Characteristics of the Dsm-iii Borderline Personality Disorder in a Forensic Population** by Welch, Larry W., Edd from Tennessee State University, 1987, 137 pages
http://wwwlib.umi.com/dissertations/fullcit/8802639
- **Mothering and the Etiology of Borderline Personality Disorder in Female Adolescents** by Golomb, Anath Chana, Phd from The University of Michigan, 1990, 140 pages
http://wwwlib.umi.com/dissertations/fullcit/9116184
- **Parental Issues of Nurturance and Control with Adolescents with a Borderline Personality Disorder** by Baker, Patricia K. S., Dsw from The Catholic University of America, 1986, 116 pages
http://wwwlib.umi.com/dissertations/fullcit/8611635
- **Rorschach Patterns of Cognitive Processing in Borderline Personality Disorder Adolescents** by Salmeron, Carmen Elizabeth, Phd from Texas A&m University, 1993, 130 pages
http://wwwlib.umi.com/dissertations/fullcit/9403582
- **Self-regulation and Borderline Personality Disorder: Integrating Developmental, Interpersonal, and Cognitive Perspectives** by Davis, Nancy Beth; Phd from The University of Wisconsin - Madison, 2002, 44 pages
http://wwwlib.umi.com/dissertations/fullcit/3072832
- **Separation Anxiety Disorder in Adults with Borderline Personality Disorder** by Aaronson, Cindy J.; Phd from Columbia University, 2001, 114 pages
http://wwwlib.umi.com/dissertations/fullcit/3028492
- **The Conceptualization of Borderline Personality Disorder Within the Framework of Lacanian Thought (otto Kernberg)** by Rusansky Drob, Liliana Monica; Psyd from Pace University, 2002, 271 pages
http://wwwlib.umi.com/dissertations/fullcit/3029610
- **The Effects of a Cognitive-behavioral Treatment on Females with Borderline Personality Disorder** by Manning, Sharon Younis, Phd from University of South Carolina, 1996, 100 pages
http://wwwlib.umi.com/dissertations/fullcit/9637141
- **The Impact of Gestalt Group Therapy on Persons with Borderline Personality Disorder** by Schoenberg, Paul; Phd from Kent State University, 1999, 465 pages
http://wwwlib.umi.com/dissertations/fullcit/9939729

- **The Impact of Negative Emotions on the Efficacy of Treatment for Parasuicide in Borderline Personality Disorder** by Brown, Milton Zebediah; Phd from University of Washington, 2002, 84 pages
  http://wwwlib.umi.com/dissertations/fullcit/3062922
- **The Theory of the Relationship of Child Maltreatment and Dysfunctional Attachment to Borderline Personality Disorder: a Critical Review of the Literature** by Dimascio, Dale; Psyd from Alliant International University, San Diego, 2002, 90 pages
  http://wwwlib.umi.com/dissertations/fullcit/3040664

## Keeping Current

Ask the medical librarian at your library if it has full and unlimited access to the *ProQuest Digital Dissertations* database. From the library, you should be able to do more complete searches via **http://wwwlib.umi.com/dissertations**.

# CHAPTER 5. CLINICAL TRIALS AND BORDERLINE PERSONALITY DISORDER

## Overview

In this chapter, we will show you how to keep informed of the latest clinical trials concerning borderline personality disorder.

## Recent Trials on Borderline Personality Disorder

The following is a list of recent trials dedicated to borderline personality disorder.[5] Further information on a trial is available at the Web site indicated.

- **Treatment for Borderline Personality Disorder**

  Condition(s): Borderline Personality Disorder

  Study Status: This study is currently recruiting patients.

  Sponsor(s): National Institute of Mental Health (NIMH)

  Purpose - Excerpt: The purpose of this study is to determine the most effective therapy for the treatment of borderline personality disorder (BPD).

  Study Type: Interventional

  Contact(s): see Web site below

  Web Site: http://clinicaltrials.gov/ct/show/NCT00055315

## Keeping Current on Clinical Trials

The U.S. National Institutes of Health, through the National Library of Medicine, has developed ClinicalTrials.gov to provide current information about clinical research across the broadest number of diseases and conditions.

[5] These are listed at **www.ClinicalTrials.gov**.

The site was launched in February 2000 and currently contains approximately 5,700 clinical studies in over 59,000 locations worldwide, with most studies being conducted in the United States. ClinicalTrials.gov receives about 2 million hits per month and hosts approximately 5,400 visitors daily. To access this database, simply go to the Web site at **http://www.clinicaltrials.gov/** and search by "borderline personality disorder" (or synonyms).

While ClinicalTrials.gov is the most comprehensive listing of NIH-supported clinical trials available, not all trials are in the database. The database is updated regularly, so clinical trials are continually being added. The following is a list of specialty databases affiliated with the National Institutes of Health that offer additional information on trials:

- For clinical studies at the Warren Grant Magnuson Clinical Center located in Bethesda, Maryland, visit their Web site: **http://clinicalstudies.info.nih.gov/**
- For clinical studies conducted at the Bayview Campus in Baltimore, Maryland, visit their Web site: **http://www.jhbmc.jhu.edu/studies/index.html**
- For cancer trials, visit the National Cancer Institute: **http://cancertrials.nci.nih.gov/**
- For eye-related trials, visit and search the Web page of the National Eye Institute: **http://www.nei.nih.gov/neitrials/index.htm**
- For heart, lung and blood trials, visit the Web page of the National Heart, Lung and Blood Institute: **http://www.nhlbi.nih.gov/studies/index.htm**
- For trials on aging, visit and search the Web site of the National Institute on Aging: **http://www.grc.nia.nih.gov/studies/index.htm**
- For rare diseases, visit and search the Web site sponsored by the Office of Rare Diseases: **http://ord.aspensys.com/asp/resources/rsch_trials.asp**
- For alcoholism, visit the National Institute on Alcohol Abuse and Alcoholism: **http://www.niaaa.nih.gov/intramural/Web_dicbr_hp/particip.htm**
- For trials on infectious, immune, and allergic diseases, visit the site of the National Institute of Allergy and Infectious Diseases: **http://www.niaid.nih.gov/clintrials/**
- For trials on arthritis, musculoskeletal and skin diseases, visit newly revised site of the National Institute of Arthritis and Musculoskeletal and Skin Diseases of the National Institutes of Health: **http://www.niams.nih.gov/hi/studies/index.htm**
- For hearing-related trials, visit the National Institute on Deafness and Other Communication Disorders: **http://www.nidcd.nih.gov/health/clinical/index.htm**
- For trials on diseases of the digestive system and kidneys, and diabetes, visit the National Institute of Diabetes and Digestive and Kidney Diseases: **http://www.niddk.nih.gov/patient/patient.htm**
- For drug abuse trials, visit and search the Web site sponsored by the National Institute on Drug Abuse: **http://www.nida.nih.gov/CTN/Index.htm**
- For trials on mental disorders, visit and search the Web site of the National Institute of Mental Health: **http://www.nimh.nih.gov/studies/index.cfm**
- For trials on neurological disorders and stroke, visit and search the Web site sponsored by the National Institute of Neurological Disorders and Stroke of the NIH: **http://www.ninds.nih.gov/funding/funding_opportunities.htm#Clinical_Trials**

# CHAPTER 6. PATENTS ON BORDERLINE PERSONALITY DISORDER

## Overview

Patents can be physical innovations (e.g. chemicals, pharmaceuticals, medical equipment) or processes (e.g. treatments or diagnostic procedures). The United States Patent and Trademark Office defines a patent as a grant of a property right to the inventor, issued by the Patent and Trademark Office.[6] Patents, therefore, are intellectual property. For the United States, the term of a new patent is 20 years from the date when the patent application was filed. If the inventor wishes to receive economic benefits, it is likely that the invention will become commercially available within 20 years of the initial filing. It is important to understand, therefore, that an inventor's patent does not indicate that a product or service is or will be commercially available. The patent implies only that the inventor has "the right to exclude others from making, using, offering for sale, or selling" the invention in the United States. While this relates to U.S. patents, similar rules govern foreign patents.

In this chapter, we show you how to locate information on patents and their inventors. If you find a patent that is particularly interesting to you, contact the inventor or the assignee for further information. **IMPORTANT NOTE:** When following the search strategy described below, you may discover non-medical patents that use the generic term "borderline personality disorder" (or a synonym) in their titles. To accurately reflect the results that you might find while conducting research on borderline personality disorder, we have not necessarily excluded non-medical patents in this bibliography.

## Patents on Borderline Personality Disorder

By performing a patent search focusing on borderline personality disorder, you can obtain information such as the title of the invention, the names of the inventor(s), the assignee(s) or the company that owns or controls the patent, a short abstract that summarizes the patent, and a few excerpts from the description of the patent. The abstract of a patent tends to be more technical in nature, while the description is often written for the public. Full patent

---

[6] Adapted from the United States Patent and Trademark Office:
**http://www.uspto.gov/web/offices/pac/doc/general/whatis.htm**.

descriptions contain much more information than is presented here (e.g. claims, references, figures, diagrams, etc.). We will tell you how to obtain this information later in the chapter. The following is an example of the type of information that you can expect to obtain from a patent search on borderline personality disorder:

- **Cranial nerve stimulation treatments using neurocybernetic prosthesis**

  Inventor(s): Zabara; Jacob (200 Locust, Apt. 22D, Philadelphia, PA 19106)

  Assignee(s): none reported

  Patent Number: 5,540,734

  Date filed: September 28, 1994

  Abstract: The treatment, control or prevention of medical, psychiatric or neurological disorders may be accomplished by application of modulating electric signals to one or both of a patient's trigeminal and glossopharyngeal nerves. The disorders treatable, controllable or preventable by such nerve stimulation include voluntary and involuntary disorders, migraine, epileptic seizure, motor disorders, Parkinson's disease, cerebral palsy, spasticity, chronic nervous illnesses and involuntary movement; pancreatic endocrine disorders including diabetes and hypoglycemia; dementia including cortical, subcortical, multi-infarct, Alzheimer's disease and Pick's disease; sleep disorders including central sleep apnea, insomnia and hypersomnia; eating disorders including anorexia nervosa, bulimia and compulsive overeating; and neuropsychiatric disorders including schizophrenia, depression and **borderline personality disorder.**

  Excerpt(s): The present invention generally relates to methods for treating, controlling or preventing medical, psychiatric or neurological disorders by application of modulating electrical signals to a selected nerve or nerve bundle of a patient, and more particularly to techniques for treating patients with migraine, epileptic seizures, involuntary motor disorders, chronic nervous illnesses, pancreatic endocrine disorders, dementia, eating disorders and neuropsychiatric disorders. Methods and apparatus for treating or controlling medical, psychiatric or neurological disorders by application of modulating electrical signals to a selected nerve or nerve bundle of the patient, are recognized in the art. The majority of these techniques stimulate one or more nerves which terminate on the target tissue. For example, it is known to stimulate the phrenic nerve, which terminates on the diaphragm, to effect respiration. There are relatively few reports of methods and apparatus which function to stimulate the brain and thereby cause the brain to send signals to the target tissue. The prior art directed to this latter approach to treat or control medical, psychiatric or neurological disorders is directed to the application of electric signals to the vagus and carotid sinus nerves, using an implantable or external neurostimulating device. The use of nerve stimulation to treat endocrine disorders is disclosed in U.S. Pat. No. 5,231,988, which states that electrical stimulation of the vagus nerve can treat the pancreatic disorders of hypoglycemia and diabetes mellitus.

  Web site: http://www.delphion.com/details?pn=US05540734__

- **Method for treating borderline personality disorder with serotonin re-uptake blockers**

  Inventor(s): Norden; Michael J. (348 NW. 113th Pl., Seattle, WA 98177)

  Assignee(s): none reported

  Patent Number: 5,589,512

  Date filed: January 25, 1994

  Abstract: There is disclosed a method for treating **borderline personality disorder** in a patient by administering a nontoxic dose of a serotonin re-uptake blocker. Preferably, the serotonin re-uptake blocker is fluoxetine or norfluoxetine.

  Excerpt(s): The present invention relates to a method of treating various psychiatric disorders and psychiatric symptoms with a class of pharmaceutical compounds called serotonin re-uptake blocking agents. The present invention relates to the treatment of six different types of psychiatric disorders and treatment of several specific symptoms. The disorders and their clinical manifestations are known to practicing psychiatrists, but are briefly described herein from the American Psychiatric Association, The Diagnostic and Statistical Manual of Mental Disorders. The specific symptoms can be recognized by most psychiatrists. Personality traits are enduring patterns of perceiving, relating to, or thinking about the environment and ones self, and are exhibited in wide range of important social and personal contexts. It is only when personality traits are inflexible and maladaptive and cause either significant functional impairment or subject distress that they constitute personality disorders. The manifestations of personality disorders are often recognizable by adolescence or earlier and continue throughout most of adult life. The diagnostic criteria for the personality disorders refer to behaviors or traits that are characteristic of the person's recent and long-term functioning since early adulthood. The constellation of behaviors or traits causes either significant impairment in social or occupational functioning or subjective distress.

  Web site: http://www.delphion.com/details?pn=US05589512__

## Patent Applications on Borderline Personality Disorder

As of December 2000, U.S. patent applications are open to public viewing.[7] Applications are patent requests which have yet to be granted. (The process to achieve a patent can take several years.) The following patent applications have been filed since December 2000 relating to borderline personality disorder:

- **Combinations of SSRI and estrogenic agents**

  Inventor(s): Jenkins, Simon N.; (Audubon, PA)

  Correspondence: Arnold S. Milowsky; American Home Products Corporation; Patent Law Department - 2B; Five Giralda Farms; Madison; NJ; 07940; US

  Patent Application Number: 20020042432

  Date filed: June 29, 2001

  Abstract: This invention comprises methods of depression, anxiety, generalized anxiety disorder (GAD), hot flush, post partum depression, premenstrual syndrome, obesity,

[7] This has been a common practice outside the United States prior to December 2000.

obsessive compulsive disorder, post-traumatic stress disorder, social phobia, disruptive behavior disorders, impulse control disorders, **borderline personality disorder,** chronic fatigue disorder, premature ejaculation, pain, attention deficit disorders, with and without hyperactivity, Gilles de la Tourette syndrome, bulimia nervosa, or Shy Drager Syndrome comprising administration of a selective serotonin reuptake inhibitor and compound of the formulae I or II: 1wherein Z is a moiety selected from the group of: 2wherein: R.sub.1 is selected from H, OH or the C.sub.1-C.sub.12 esters or C.sub.1-C.sub.12 alkyl ethers thereof, benzyloxy, or halogen; or C.sub.1-C.sub.4 halogenated ethers including trifluoromethyl ether and trichloromethyl ether; R.sub.2, R.sub.3, R.sub.4, R.sub.5, and R.sub.6 are H, OH or C.sub.1-C.sub.12 esters or C.sub.1-C.sub.12 alkyl ethers thereof, halogens, or C.sub.1-C.sub.4 halogenated ethers, cyano, C.sub.1-C.sub.6 alkyl, or trifluoromethyl, with the proviso that, when R.sub.1 is H, R.sub.2 is not OH; Y is the moiety: 3R.sub.7 and R.sub.8 are alkyl or concatenated together to form an optionally substituted, nitrogen-containing ring; or a pharmaceutically acceptable salt thereof.

Excerpt(s): This application claims the benefit of U.S. Provisional Application No. 60/216,408, filed Jul. 6, 2000. This invention relates to methods of using substituted indole compounds in the combination with a selective serotonin reuptake inhibitor (SSRI) for the treatment, prevention, inhibition or alleviation of depression, anxiety, generalized anxiety disorder (GAD), hot flush, post partum depression, premenstrual syndrome, obesity, obsessive compulsive disorder, social phobia, disruptive behavior disorders, impulse control disorders, **borderline personality disorder,** chronic fatigue disorder, premature ejaculation, pain, post-traumatic stress disorder, attention deficit disorders, with and without hyperactivity, Gilles de la Tourette syndrome, bulimia nervosa, or Shy Drager Syndrome and related pharmaceutical compositions and kits. as well as their use as estrogenic agents, including the treatment of bone loss, cardiovascular disease, maladies associated with or resulting from the proliferation or abnormal development of endometrial or endometrial-like tissues, and disease states or syndromes associated with estrogen deficiency.

Web site: http://appft1.uspto.gov/netahtml/PTO/search-bool.html

## Keeping Current

In order to stay informed about patents and patent applications dealing with borderline personality disorder, you can access the U.S. Patent Office archive via the Internet at the following Web address: **http://www.uspto.gov/patft/index.html**. You will see two broad options: (1) Issued Patent, and (2) Published Applications. To see a list of issued patents, perform the following steps: Under "Issued Patents," click "Quick Search." Then, type "borderline personality disorder" (or synonyms) into the "Term 1" box. After clicking on the search button, scroll down to see the various patents which have been granted to date on borderline personality disorder.

You can also use this procedure to view pending patent applications concerning borderline personality disorder. Simply go back to **http://www.uspto.gov/patft/index.html**. Select "Quick Search" under "Published Applications." Then proceed with the steps listed above.

# CHAPTER 7. BOOKS ON BORDERLINE PERSONALITY DISORDER

## Overview

This chapter provides bibliographic book references relating to borderline personality disorder. In addition to online booksellers such as **www.amazon.com** and **www.bn.com**, excellent sources for book titles on borderline personality disorder include the Combined Health Information Database and the National Library of Medicine. Your local medical library also may have these titles available for loan.

## Book Summaries: Online Booksellers

Commercial Internet-based booksellers, such as Amazon.com and Barnes&Noble.com, offer summaries which have been supplied by each title's publisher. Some summaries also include customer reviews. Your local bookseller may have access to in-house and commercial databases that index all published books (e.g. Books in Print®). **IMPORTANT NOTE:** Online booksellers typically produce search results for medical and non-medical books. When searching for "borderline personality disorder" at online booksellers' Web sites, you may discover non-medical books that use the generic term "borderline personality disorder" (or a synonym) in their titles. The following is indicative of the results you might find when searching for "borderline personality disorder" (sorted alphabetically by title; follow the hyperlink to view more details at Amazon.com):

- **A Developmental Model of Borderline Personality Disorder: Understanding Variations in Course and Outcome** by Patricia Hoffman Judd, Thomas H. McGlashan; ISBN: 0880485159; http://www.amazon.com/exec/obidos/ASIN/0880485159/icongroupinterna
- **Biological and Neurobehavioral Studies of Borderline Personality Disorder (Progress in Psychiatry, No 45)** by Kenneth R. Silk (Editor) (1994); ISBN: 0880484802; http://www.amazon.com/exec/obidos/ASIN/0880484802/icongroupinterna
- **Borderline Personality Disorder** by John G. Gunderson (1984); ISBN: 0880480203; http://www.amazon.com/exec/obidos/ASIN/0880480203/icongroupinterna

- **Borderline Personality Disorder : The Latest Assessment and Treatment Strategies** by Melanie A. Dean (2001); ISBN: 1887537171; http://www.amazon.com/exec/obidos/ASIN/1887537171/icongroupinterna
- **Borderline Personality Disorder: A Clinical Guide** by John G., Md. Gunderson; ISBN: 1585620165; http://www.amazon.com/exec/obidos/ASIN/1585620165/icongroupinterna
- **Borderline Personality Disorder: A Multidimensional Approach** by Joel, M.D. Paris (1994); ISBN: 0880486554; http://www.amazon.com/exec/obidos/ASIN/0880486554/icongroupinterna
- **Borderline Personality Disorder: A Patient's Guide to Taking Control** by Gina M. Fusco, Arthur Freeman; ISBN: 0393703533; http://www.amazon.com/exec/obidos/ASIN/0393703533/icongroupinterna
- **Borderline Personality Disorder: A Practical Guide to Treatment** by Roy Krawitz, Christine Watson (2003); ISBN: 0198520670; http://www.amazon.com/exec/obidos/ASIN/0198520670/icongroupinterna
- **Borderline Personality Disorder: A Therapist's Guide to Taking Control** by Arthur Freeman, Gina M. Fusco; ISBN: 0393703525; http://www.amazon.com/exec/obidos/ASIN/0393703525/icongroupinterna
- **Borderline Personality Disorder: Clinical and Empirical Perspectives** by John F. Clarkin (Editor), et al; ISBN: 089862262X; http://www.amazon.com/exec/obidos/ASIN/089862262X/icongroupinterna
- **Borderline Personality Disorder: Etiology and Treatment** by Joel Paris (Editor) (1993); ISBN: 088048408X; http://www.amazon.com/exec/obidos/ASIN/088048408X/icongroupinterna
- **Borderline Personality Disorder: Tailoring the Psychotherapy to the Patient** by Leonard Horwitz (Editor), et al; ISBN: 0880486899; http://www.amazon.com/exec/obidos/ASIN/0880486899/icongroupinterna
- **Borderline Personality Disorders: The Concept the Syndrome the Patient** by Peter Hartocollis (1977); ISBN: 0823605752; http://www.amazon.com/exec/obidos/ASIN/0823605752/icongroupinterna
- **Cognitive Analytic Therapy and Borderline Personality Disorder : The Model and the Method** by Anthony Ryle (Author) (1997); ISBN: 0471976172; http://www.amazon.com/exec/obidos/ASIN/0471976172/icongroupinterna
- **Cognitive Therapy of Borderline Personality Disorder** (1993); ISBN: 0205148085; http://www.amazon.com/exec/obidos/ASIN/0205148085/icongroupinterna
- **Cognitive Therapy of Borderline Personality Disorder (Psychology Practitioner Guidebooks)** by Mary Anne Layden, et al; ISBN: 0205148077; http://www.amazon.com/exec/obidos/ASIN/0205148077/icongroupinterna
- **Cognitive-Behavioral Treatment of Borderline Personality Disorder** by Marsha Linehan; ISBN: 0898621836; http://www.amazon.com/exec/obidos/ASIN/0898621836/icongroupinterna
- **Double Bind: A Mystery about Psychiatric Abuse, Trauma, Borderline Personality Disorder and Otto Kernberg, with Research into the Neurophysiology and Consequences of Restraint and Seclusion.** by Linn Cohen-Cole; ISBN: 0970646909; http://www.amazon.com/exec/obidos/ASIN/0970646909/icongroupinterna

- **Eclipses: Behind the Borderline Personality Disorder** by Melissa Ford Thornton, et al; ISBN: 0965939227; http://www.amazon.com/exec/obidos/ASIN/0965939227/icongroupinterna
- **Family Environment and Borderline Personality Disorder** by Paul S. Links (Editor); ISBN: 0880481889; http://www.amazon.com/exec/obidos/ASIN/0880481889/icongroupinterna
- **I'm Not Supposed to Be Here: My Recovery from Borderline Personality Disorder** by Rachel Reiland, Laura Paxton (2002); ISBN: 0971822409; http://www.amazon.com/exec/obidos/ASIN/0971822409/icongroupinterna
- **Imbroglio: Rising to the Challenges of Borderline Personality Disorder** by Janice M. Cauwels (1992); ISBN: 039303349X; http://www.amazon.com/exec/obidos/ASIN/039303349X/icongroupinterna
- **Interpersonal Group Psychotherapy for Borderline Personality Disorder** by Elsa Marziali, et al; ISBN: 0465088937; http://www.amazon.com/exec/obidos/ASIN/0465088937/icongroupinterna
- **Let Me Make It Good: A Chronicle of My Life With Borderline Personality Disorder** by Jane Wanklin (1997); ISBN: 0889626278; http://www.amazon.com/exec/obidos/ASIN/0889626278/icongroupinterna
- **Living in the Dead Zone: Janis Joplin and Jim Morrison: Understanding Borderline Personality Disorders** by Ralph M. Faris, Gerald A. Faris (2001); ISBN: 0971654204; http://www.amazon.com/exec/obidos/ASIN/0971654204/icongroupinterna
- **Lost in the Mirror: An Inside Look at Borderline Personality Disorder** by Richard A. Moskovitz M.D. (2001); ISBN: 0878332669; http://www.amazon.com/exec/obidos/ASIN/0878332669/icongroupinterna
- **New Hope for People with Borderline Personality Disorder: Your Friendly, Authoritative Guide to the Latest in Traditional and Complementary Solutions** by Neil R. Bockian, et al; ISBN: 0761525726; http://www.amazon.com/exec/obidos/ASIN/0761525726/icongroupinterna
- **Personalities: Master Clinicians Confront the Treatment of Borderline Personality Disorder** by Gerben Hellinga (Editor), et al (2001); ISBN: 0765702940; http://www.amazon.com/exec/obidos/ASIN/0765702940/icongroupinterna
- **Practice Guideline for the Treatment of Patients With Borderline Personality Disorder** by American Psychiatric Association; ISBN: 0890423199; http://www.amazon.com/exec/obidos/ASIN/0890423199/icongroupinterna
- **Role of Sexual Abuse in Etiology of Borderline Personality Disorder** by Mary C. Zanarini (Editor); ISBN: 0880484969; http://www.amazon.com/exec/obidos/ASIN/0880484969/icongroupinterna
- **Self-Management Therapy for Borderline Personality Disorder: A Therapist-Guided Approach** by Michael H. Langley; ISBN: 082618300X; http://www.amazon.com/exec/obidos/ASIN/082618300X/icongroupinterna
- **Shorter Term Treatments for Borderline Personality Disorders** by John D. Preston (1997); ISBN: 157224092X; http://www.amazon.com/exec/obidos/ASIN/157224092X/icongroupinterna
- **Skills Training Manual for Treating Borderline Personality Disorder** by Marsha M. Linehan; ISBN: 0898620341; http://www.amazon.com/exec/obidos/ASIN/0898620341/icongroupinterna

- **Sometimes I Act Crazy : Living with Borderline Personality Disorder** by Jerold J. Kreisman (Author), Harold Straus (Author) (2004); ISBN: 0471222860; http://www.amazon.com/exec/obidos/ASIN/0471222860/icongroupinterna
- **Stop Walking on Eggshells; Coping When Someone You Care about Has Borderline Personality Disorder** by Paul T. Mason, et al; ISBN: 157224108X; http://www.amazon.com/exec/obidos/ASIN/157224108X/icongroupinterna
- **The Stop Walking on Eggshells Workbook: Practical Strategies for Living With Someone Who Has Borderline Personality Disorder** by Randi Kreger, James Paul Shirley (2002); ISBN: 1572242760; http://www.amazon.com/exec/obidos/ASIN/1572242760/icongroupinterna
- **Through the Looking Glass: Women and Borderline Personality Disorder (New Directions in Theory and Psychology)** by Dana Becker (1997); ISBN: 0813333105; http://www.amazon.com/exec/obidos/ASIN/0813333105/icongroupinterna
- **Understanding Borderline Personality Disorder: The Dialectical Approach (Book & VHS Tape)** by Marsha M. Linehan (Author); ISBN: 089862567X; http://www.amazon.com/exec/obidos/ASIN/089862567X/icongroupinterna
- **Women and Borderline Personality Disorder: Symptoms and Stories** by Janet Wirth-Cauchon, Janet Wirth Cauchon (2001); ISBN: 0813528917; http://www.amazon.com/exec/obidos/ASIN/0813528917/icongroupinterna

## Chapters on Borderline Personality Disorder

In order to find chapters that specifically relate to borderline personality disorder, an excellent source of abstracts is the Combined Health Information Database. You will need to limit your search to book chapters and borderline personality disorder using the "Detailed Search" option. Go to the following hyperlink: **http://chid.nih.gov/detail/detail.html**. To find book chapters, use the drop boxes at the bottom of the search page where "You may refine your search by." Select the dates and language you prefer, and the format option "Book Chapter." Type "borderline personality disorder" (or synonyms) into the "For these words:" box.

# CHAPTER 8. MULTIMEDIA ON BORDERLINE PERSONALITY DISORDER

## Overview

In this chapter, we show you how to keep current on multimedia sources of information on borderline personality disorder. We start with sources that have been summarized by federal agencies, and then show you how to find bibliographic information catalogued by the National Library of Medicine.

## Bibliography: Multimedia on Borderline Personality Disorder

The National Library of Medicine is a rich source of information on healthcare-related multimedia productions including slides, computer software, and databases. To access the multimedia database, go to the following Web site: **http://locatorplus.gov/**. Select "Search LOCATORplus." Once in the search area, simply type in borderline personality disorder (or synonyms). Then, in the option box provided below the search box, select "Audiovisuals and Computer Files." From there, you can choose to sort results by publication date, author, or relevance. The following multimedia has been indexed on borderline personality disorder:

- **Borderline personality disorders [sound recording]: research issues and new empirical findings (panel)** Source: American Psychoanalytic Association; Year: 1983; Format: Sound recording; [United States: The Association, 1983?]
- **Care of the client with borderline personality disorder [electronic resource]** Source: Computerized Educational Systems; Year: 1992; Format: Electronic resource; Orlando, Fla.: Computerized Educational Systems, c1992
- **Cognitive therapy for borderline personality disorder [videorecording]** Source: American Psychological Association; Year: 1997; Format: Videorecording; Washington, D.C.: The Association, c1997
- **Integrated treatment of borderline personality disorder [videorecording]: pharmacotherapy and psychotherapy** Source: American Psychiatric Video Source; Year: 1995; Format: Videorecording; [Washington, D.C.]: American Psychiatric Press, c1995

- **Psychodynamic concepts and psychotherapy [videorecording]; Borderline personality disorder** Source: Glen O. Gabbard; Year: 1998; Format: Videorecording; [Irvine, Calif.]: CME, c1998
- **Treating borderline personality disorder [videorecording]: the dialectical approach** Source: Kevin Dawkins Productions; Year: 1995; Format: Videorecording; New York, NY: Guilford Publications, c1995
- **Understanding borderline personality disorder [videorecording]: the dialectical approach** Source: Kevin Dawkins Productions; Year: 1995; Format: Videorecording; New York, NY: Guilford Publications, c1995

# Chapter 9. Periodicals and News on Borderline Personality Disorder

## Overview

In this chapter, we suggest a number of news sources and present various periodicals that cover borderline personality disorder.

## News Services and Press Releases

One of the simplest ways of tracking press releases on borderline personality disorder is to search the news wires. In the following sample of sources, we will briefly describe how to access each service. These services only post recent news intended for public viewing.

### PR Newswire

To access the PR Newswire archive, simply go to **http://www.prnewswire.com/**. Select your country. Type "borderline personality disorder" (or synonyms) into the search box. You will automatically receive information on relevant news releases posted within the last 30 days. The search results are shown by order of relevance.

### Reuters Health

The Reuters' Medical News and Health eLine databases can be very useful in exploring news archives relating to borderline personality disorder. While some of the listed articles are free to view, others are available for purchase for a nominal fee. To access this archive, go to **http://www.reutershealth.com/en/index.html** and search by "borderline personality disorder" (or synonyms). The following was recently listed in this archive for borderline personality disorder:

- **Borderline personality disorder associated with deficit in cognitive control**
  Source: Reuters Medical News
  Date: November 27, 2002

- **Guideline issued for treatment of borderline personality disorder**
  Source: Reuters Industry Breifing
  Date: October 15, 2001
- **Drug reduces self-mutilation in borderline personality disorder**
  Source: Reuters Health eLine
  Date: September 01, 1999
- **Borderline personality disorder patients: complex mix of comorbid axis I disorders**
  Source: Reuters Medical News
  Date: January 01, 1999
- **Low-Dose Clozapine Effective For Severe Borderline Personality Disorder**
  Source: Reuters Medical News
  Date: April 06, 1998

### The NIH

Within MEDLINEplus, the NIH has made an agreement with the New York Times Syndicate, the AP News Service, and Reuters to deliver news that can be browsed by the public. Search news releases at **http://www.nlm.nih.gov/medlineplus/alphanews_a.html**. MEDLINEplus allows you to browse across an alphabetical index. Or you can search by date at the following Web page: **http://www.nlm.nih.gov/medlineplus/newsbydate.html**. Often, news items are indexed by MEDLINEplus within its search engine.

### Business Wire

Business Wire is similar to PR Newswire. To access this archive, simply go to **http://www.businesswire.com/**. You can scan the news by industry category or company name.

### Market Wire

Market Wire is more focused on technology than the other wires. To browse the latest press releases by topic, such as alternative medicine, biotechnology, fitness, healthcare, legal, nutrition, and pharmaceuticals, access Market Wire's Medical/Health channel at **http://www.marketwire.com/mw/release_index?channel=MedicalHealth**. Or simply go to Market Wire's home page at **http://www.marketwire.com/mw/home**, type "borderline personality disorder" (or synonyms) into the search box, and click on "Search News." As this service is technology oriented, you may wish to use it when searching for press releases covering diagnostic procedures or tests.

### Search Engines

Medical news is also available in the news sections of commercial Internet search engines. See the health news page at Yahoo (**http://dir.yahoo.com/Health/News_and_Media/**), or you can use this Web site's general news search page at **http://news.yahoo.com/**. Type in "borderline personality disorder" (or synonyms). If you know the name of a company that is relevant to borderline personality disorder, you can go to any stock trading Web site (such as **http://www.etrade.com/**) and search for the company name there. News items across various news sources are reported on indicated hyperlinks. Google offers a similar service at **http://news.google.com/**.

### BBC

Covering news from a more European perspective, the British Broadcasting Corporation (BBC) allows the public free access to their news archive located at **http://www.bbc.co.uk/**. Search by "borderline personality disorder" (or synonyms).

## Newsletter Articles

Use the Combined Health Information Database, and limit your search criteria to "newsletter articles." Again, you will need to use the "Detailed Search" option. Go directly to the following hyperlink: **http://chid.nih.gov/detail/detail.html** Go to the bottom of the search page where "You may refine your search by." Select the dates and language that you prefer. For the format option, select "Newsletter Article." Type "borderline personality disorder" (or synonyms) into the "For these words:" box. You should check back periodically with this database as it is updated every three months. The following is a typical result when searching for newsletter articles on borderline personality disorder:

- **Eating Disorders and Borderline Personality Disorder**

  Source: American Anorexia/Bulimia Association Newsletter. p.1-3. Summer 1998.

  Contact: American Anorexia/Bulimia Association, 165 West 46 Street, Suite 1108, New York, NY 10036. (212) 575- 6200.

  Summary: Dennis suggests that some eating- disordered patients may be suffering from Borderline Personality Disorder (BPD), as recognized in the American Psychiatric Association's `Diagnostic and Statistical Manual 4th ed.' (DSM-IV). According to Dennis, the behaviors associated with eating disorders serve adaptive functions for an individual with BPD. These include: reinforcement of their feelings of low self-esteem, since they can never be thin enough; allowing them to soothe themselves through food, which they find difficult otherwise; and purging to allow them to feel a sense of self-control. Finally, the behaviors associated with eating disorders are self- destructive and may be used as self-punishment by the BPD patient, and these behaviors may also serve as a numbing agent against the emotional pain they feel. As a result, says Dennis, treatment should be different, more intensive and lengthy.

## Academic Periodicals covering Borderline Personality Disorder

Numerous periodicals are currently indexed within the National Library of Medicine's PubMed database that are known to publish articles relating to borderline personality disorder. In addition to these sources, you can search for articles covering borderline personality disorder that have been published by any of the periodicals listed in previous chapters. To find the latest studies published, go to **http://www.ncbi.nlm.nih.gov/pubmed**, type the name of the periodical into the search box, and click "Go."

If you want complete details about the historical contents of a journal, you can also visit the following Web site: **http://www.ncbi.nlm.nih.gov/entrez/jrbrowser.cgi**. Here, type in the name of the journal or its abbreviation, and you will receive an index of published articles. At **http://locatorplus.gov/**, you can retrieve more indexing information on medical periodicals (e.g. the name of the publisher). Select the button "Search LOCATORplus." Then type in the name of the journal and select the advanced search option "Journal Title Search."

# CHAPTER 10. RESEARCHING MEDICATIONS

## Overview

While a number of hard copy or CD-ROM resources are available for researching medications, a more flexible method is to use Internet-based databases. Broadly speaking, there are two sources of information on approved medications: public sources and private sources. We will emphasize free-to-use public sources.

## U.S. Pharmacopeia

Because of historical investments by various organizations and the emergence of the Internet, it has become rather simple to learn about the medications recommended for borderline personality disorder. One such source is the United States Pharmacopeia. In 1820, eleven physicians met in Washington, D.C. to establish the first compendium of standard drugs for the United States. They called this compendium the U.S. Pharmacopeia (USP). Today, the USP is a non-profit organization consisting of 800 volunteer scientists, eleven elected officials, and 400 representatives of state associations and colleges of medicine and pharmacy. The USP is located in Rockville, Maryland, and its home page is located at **http://www.usp.org/**. The USP currently provides standards for over 3,700 medications. The resulting USP DI® Advice for the Patient® can be accessed through the National Library of Medicine of the National Institutes of Health. The database is partially derived from lists of federally approved medications in the Food and Drug Administration's (FDA) Drug Approvals database, located at **http://www.fda.gov/cder/da/da.htm**.

While the FDA database is rather large and difficult to navigate, the Phamacopeia is both user-friendly and free to use. It covers more than 9,000 prescription and over-the-counter medications. To access this database, simply type the following hyperlink into your Web browser: **http://www.nlm.nih.gov/medlineplus/druginformation.html**. To view examples of a given medication (brand names, category, description, preparation, proper use, precautions, side effects, etc.), simply follow the hyperlinks indicated within the United States Pharmacopeia (USP).

Below, we have compiled a list of medications associated with borderline personality disorder. If you would like more information on a particular medication, the provided hyperlinks will direct you to ample documentation (e.g. typical dosage, side effects, drug-interaction risks, etc.). The following drugs have been mentioned in the Pharmacopeia and other sources as being potentially applicable to borderline personality disorder:

**Carbamazepine**

- **Systemic - U.S. Brands:** Atretol; Carbatrol; Epitol; Tegretol; Tegretol-XR
  http://www.nlm.nih.gov/medlineplus/druginfo/uspdi/202111.html

**Lithium**

- **Systemic - U.S. Brands:** Cibalith-S; Eskalith; Lithane; Lithobid; Lithonate; Lithotabs
  http://www.nlm.nih.gov/medlineplus/druginfo/uspdi/202330.html

## Commercial Databases

In addition to the medications listed in the USP above, a number of commercial sites are available by subscription to physicians and their institutions. Or, you may be able to access these sources from your local medical library.

### Mosby's Drug Consult™

Mosby's Drug Consult™ database (also available on CD-ROM and book format) covers 45,000 drug products including generics and international brands. It provides prescribing information, drug interactions, and patient information. Subscription information is available at the following hyperlink: **http://www.mosbysdrugconsult.com/**.

### PDR*health*

The PDR*health* database is a free-to-use, drug information search engine that has been written for the public in layman's terms. It contains FDA-approved drug information adapted from the Physicians' Desk Reference (PDR) database. PDR*health* can be searched by brand name, generic name, or indication. It features multiple drug interactions reports. Search PDR*health* at **http://www.pdrhealth.com/drug_info/index.html**.

### Other Web Sites

Drugs.com (**www.drugs.com**) reproduces the information in the Pharmacopeia as well as commercial information. You may also want to consider the Web site of the Medical Letter, Inc. (**http://www.medletter.com/**) which allows users to download articles on various drugs and therapeutics for a nominal fee.

If you have any questions about a medical treatment, the FDA may have an office near you. Look for their number in the blue pages of the phone book. You can also contact the FDA through its toll-free number, 1-888-INFO-FDA (1-888-463-6332), or on the World Wide Web at **www.fda.gov**.

# APPENDICES

# Appendix A. Physician Resources

## Overview

In this chapter, we focus on databases and Internet-based guidelines and information resources created or written for a professional audience.

## NIH Guidelines

Commonly referred to as "clinical" or "professional" guidelines, the National Institutes of Health publish physician guidelines for the most common diseases. Publications are available at the following by relevant Institute[8]:

- Office of the Director (OD); guidelines consolidated across agencies available at **http://www.nih.gov/health/consumer/conkey.htm**
- National Institute of General Medical Sciences (NIGMS); fact sheets available at **http://www.nigms.nih.gov/news/facts/**
- National Library of Medicine (NLM); extensive encyclopedia (A.D.A.M., Inc.) with guidelines: **http://www.nlm.nih.gov/medlineplus/healthtopics.html**
- National Cancer Institute (NCI); guidelines available at **http://www.cancer.gov/cancerinfo/list.aspx?viewid=5f35036e-5497-4d86-8c2c-714a9f7c8d25**
- National Eye Institute (NEI); guidelines available at **http://www.nei.nih.gov/order/index.htm**
- National Heart, Lung, and Blood Institute (NHLBI); guidelines available at **http://www.nhlbi.nih.gov/guidelines/index.htm**
- National Human Genome Research Institute (NHGRI); research available at **http://www.genome.gov/page.cfm?pageID=10000375**
- National Institute on Aging (NIA); guidelines available at **http://www.nia.nih.gov/health/**

[8] These publications are typically written by one or more of the various NIH Institutes.

- National Institute on Alcohol Abuse and Alcoholism (NIAAA); guidelines available at **http://www.niaaa.nih.gov/publications/publications.htm**
- National Institute of Allergy and Infectious Diseases (NIAID); guidelines available at **http://www.niaid.nih.gov/publications/**
- National Institute of Arthritis and Musculoskeletal and Skin Diseases (NIAMS); fact sheets and guidelines available at **http://www.niams.nih.gov/hi/index.htm**
- National Institute of Child Health and Human Development (NICHD); guidelines available at **http://www.nichd.nih.gov/publications/pubskey.cfm**
- National Institute on Deafness and Other Communication Disorders (NIDCD); fact sheets and guidelines at **http://www.nidcd.nih.gov/health/**
- National Institute of Dental and Craniofacial Research (NIDCR); guidelines available at **http://www.nidr.nih.gov/health/**
- National Institute of Diabetes and Digestive and Kidney Diseases (NIDDK); guidelines available at **http://www.niddk.nih.gov/health/health.htm**
- National Institute on Drug Abuse (NIDA); guidelines available at **http://www.nida.nih.gov/DrugAbuse.html**
- National Institute of Environmental Health Sciences (NIEHS); environmental health information available at **http://www.niehs.nih.gov/external/facts.htm**
- National Institute of Mental Health (NIMH); guidelines available at **http://www.nimh.nih.gov/practitioners/index.cfm**
- National Institute of Neurological Disorders and Stroke (NINDS); neurological disorder information pages available at **http://www.ninds.nih.gov/health_and_medical/disorder_index.htm**
- National Institute of Nursing Research (NINR); publications on selected illnesses at **http://www.nih.gov/ninr/news-info/publications.html**
- National Institute of Biomedical Imaging and Bioengineering; general information at **http://grants.nih.gov/grants/becon/becon_info.htm**
- Center for Information Technology (CIT); referrals to other agencies based on keyword searches available at **http://kb.nih.gov/www_query_main.asp**
- National Center for Complementary and Alternative Medicine (NCCAM); health information available at **http://nccam.nih.gov/health/**
- National Center for Research Resources (NCRR); various information directories available at **http://www.ncrr.nih.gov/publications.asp**
- Office of Rare Diseases; various fact sheets available at **http://rarediseases.info.nih.gov/html/resources/rep_pubs.html**
- Centers for Disease Control and Prevention; various fact sheets on infectious diseases available at **http://www.cdc.gov/publications.htm**

## NIH Databases

In addition to the various Institutes of Health that publish professional guidelines, the NIH has designed a number of databases for professionals.[9] Physician-oriented resources provide a wide variety of information related to the biomedical and health sciences, both past and present. The format of these resources varies. Searchable databases, bibliographic citations, full-text articles (when available), archival collections, and images are all available. The following are referenced by the National Library of Medicine:[10]

- **Bioethics:** Access to published literature on the ethical, legal, and public policy issues surrounding healthcare and biomedical research. This information is provided in conjunction with the Kennedy Institute of Ethics located at Georgetown University, Washington, D.C.: **http://www.nlm.nih.gov/databases/databases_bioethics.html**

- **HIV/AIDS Resources:** Describes various links and databases dedicated to HIV/AIDS research: **http://www.nlm.nih.gov/pubs/factsheets/aidsinfs.html**

- **NLM Online Exhibitions:** Describes "Exhibitions in the History of Medicine": **http://www.nlm.nih.gov/exhibition/exhibition.html**. Additional resources for historical scholarship in medicine: **http://www.nlm.nih.gov/hmd/hmd.html**

- **Biotechnology Information:** Access to public databases. The National Center for Biotechnology Information conducts research in computational biology, develops software tools for analyzing genome data, and disseminates biomedical information for the better understanding of molecular processes affecting human health and disease: **http://www.ncbi.nlm.nih.gov/**

- **Population Information:** The National Library of Medicine provides access to worldwide coverage of population, family planning, and related health issues, including family planning technology and programs, fertility, and population law and policy: **http://www.nlm.nih.gov/databases/databases_population.html**

- **Cancer Information:** Access to cancer-oriented databases: **http://www.nlm.nih.gov/databases/databases_cancer.html**

- **Profiles in Science:** Offering the archival collections of prominent twentieth-century biomedical scientists to the public through modern digital technology: **http://www.profiles.nlm.nih.gov/**

- **Chemical Information:** Provides links to various chemical databases and references: **http://sis.nlm.nih.gov/Chem/ChemMain.html**

- **Clinical Alerts:** Reports the release of findings from the NIH-funded clinical trials where such release could significantly affect morbidity and mortality: **http://www.nlm.nih.gov/databases/alerts/clinical_alerts.html**

- **Space Life Sciences:** Provides links and information to space-based research (including NASA): **http://www.nlm.nih.gov/databases/databases_space.html**

- **MEDLINE:** Bibliographic database covering the fields of medicine, nursing, dentistry, veterinary medicine, the healthcare system, and the pre-clinical sciences: **http://www.nlm.nih.gov/databases/databases_medline.html**

---

[9] Remember, for the general public, the National Library of Medicine recommends the databases referenced in MEDLINE*plus* (**http://medlineplus.gov/** or **http://www.nlm.nih.gov/medlineplus/databases.html**).

[10] See **http://www.nlm.nih.gov/databases/databases.html**.

- **Toxicology and Environmental Health Information (TOXNET):** Databases covering toxicology and environ mental health: **http://sis.nlm.nih.gov/Tox/ToxMain.html**
- **Visible Human Interface:** Anatomically detailed, three-dimensional representations of normal male and female human bodies: **http://www.nlm.nih.gov/research/visible/visible_human.html**

### The NLM Gateway[11]

The NLM (National Library of Medicine) Gateway is a Web-based system that lets users search simultaneously in multiple retrieval systems at the U.S. National Library of Medicine (NLM). It allows users of NLM services to initiate searches from one Web interface, providing one-stop searching for many of NLM's information resources or databases.[12] To use the NLM Gateway, simply go to the search site at **http://gateway.nlm.nih.gov/gw/Cmd**. Type "borderline personality disorder" (or synonyms) into the search box and click "Search." The results will be presented in a tabular form, indicating the number of references in each database category.

**Results Summary**

| Category | Items Found |
|---|---|
| Journal Articles | 2801 |
| Books / Periodicals / Audio Visual | 191 |
| Consumer Health | 751 |
| Meeting Abstracts | 5 |
| Other Collections | 1 |
| Total | 3749 |

### HSTAT[13]

HSTAT is a free, Web-based resource that provides access to full-text documents used in healthcare decision-making.[14] These documents include clinical practice guidelines, quick-reference guides for clinicians, consumer health brochures, evidence reports and technology assessments from the Agency for Healthcare Research and Quality (AHRQ), as well as AHRQ's Put Prevention Into Practice.[15] Simply search by "borderline personality disorder" (or synonyms) at the following Web site: **http://text.nlm.nih.gov**.

---

11 Adapted from NLM: **http://gateway.nlm.nih.gov/gw/Cmd?Overview.x**.

12 The NLM Gateway is currently being developed by the Lister Hill National Center for Biomedical Communications (LHNCBC) at the National Library of Medicine (NLM) of the National Institutes of Health (NIH).

13 Adapted from HSTAT: **http://www.nlm.nih.gov/pubs/factsheets/hstat.html**.

14 The HSTAT URL is **http://hstat.nlm.nih.gov/**.

15 Other important documents in HSTAT include: the National Institutes of Health (NIH) Consensus Conference Reports and Technology Assessment Reports; the HIV/AIDS Treatment Information Service (ATIS) resource documents; the Substance Abuse and Mental Health Services Administration's Center for Substance Abuse Treatment (SAMHSA/CSAT) Treatment Improvement Protocols (TIP) and Center for Substance Abuse Prevention (SAMHSA/CSAP) Prevention Enhancement Protocols System (PEPS); the Public Health Service (PHS) Preventive Services Task Force's *Guide to Clinical Preventive Services;* the independent, nonfederal Task Force on Community Services' *Guide to Community Preventive Services;* and the Health Technology Advisory Committee (HTAC) of the Minnesota Health Care Commission (MHCC) health technology evaluations.

### Coffee Break: Tutorials for Biologists[16]

Coffee Break is a general healthcare site that takes a scientific view of the news and covers recent breakthroughs in biology that may one day assist physicians in developing treatments. Here you will find a collection of short reports on recent biological discoveries. Each report incorporates interactive tutorials that demonstrate how bioinformatics tools are used as a part of the research process. Currently, all Coffee Breaks are written by NCBI staff.[17] Each report is about 400 words and is usually based on a discovery reported in one or more articles from recently published, peer-reviewed literature.[18] This site has new articles every few weeks, so it can be considered an online magazine of sorts. It is intended for general background information. You can access the Coffee Break Web site at the following hyperlink: **http://www.ncbi.nlm.nih.gov/Coffeebreak/**.

## Other Commercial Databases

In addition to resources maintained by official agencies, other databases exist that are commercial ventures addressing medical professionals. Here are some examples that may interest you:

- **CliniWeb International:** Index and table of contents to selected clinical information on the Internet; see **http://www.ohsu.edu/cliniweb/**.
- **Medical World Search:** Searches full text from thousands of selected medical sites on the Internet; see **http://www.mwsearch.com/**.

---

16 Adapted from **http://www.ncbi.nlm.nih.gov/Coffeebreak/Archive/FAQ.html**.

17 The figure that accompanies each article is frequently supplied by an expert external to NCBI, in which case the source of the figure is cited. The result is an interactive tutorial that tells a biological story.

18 After a brief introduction that sets the work described into a broader context, the report focuses on how a molecular understanding can provide explanations of observed biology and lead to therapies for diseases. Each vignette is accompanied by a figure and hypertext links that lead to a series of pages that interactively show how NCBI tools and resources are used in the research process.

# APPENDIX B. PATIENT RESOURCES

## Overview

Official agencies, as well as federally funded institutions supported by national grants, frequently publish a variety of guidelines written with the patient in mind. These are typically called "Fact Sheets" or "Guidelines." They can take the form of a brochure, information kit, pamphlet, or flyer. Often they are only a few pages in length. Since new guidelines on borderline personality disorder can appear at any moment and be published by a number of sources, the best approach to finding guidelines is to systematically scan the Internet-based services that post them.

## Patient Guideline Sources

The remainder of this chapter directs you to sources which either publish or can help you find additional guidelines on topics related to borderline personality disorder. Due to space limitations, these sources are listed in a concise manner. Do not hesitate to consult the following sources by either using the Internet hyperlink provided, or, in cases where the contact information is provided, contacting the publisher or author directly.

### The National Institutes of Health

The NIH gateway to patients is located at **http://health.nih.gov/**. From this site, you can search across various sources and institutes, a number of which are summarized below.

### Topic Pages: MEDLINEplus

The National Library of Medicine has created a vast and patient-oriented healthcare information portal called MEDLINEplus. Within this Internet-based system are "health topic pages" which list links to available materials relevant to borderline personality disorder. To access this system, log on to **http://www.nlm.nih.gov/medlineplus/healthtopics.html**. From there you can either search using the alphabetical index or browse by broad topic areas. Recently, MEDLINEplus listed the following when searched for "borderline personality disorder":

- Other guides

  **Bipolar Disorder**
  http://www.nlm.nih.gov/medlineplus/bipolardisorder.html

  **Mental Health**
  http://www.nlm.nih.gov/medlineplus/mentalhealth.html

  **Panic Disorder**
  http://www.nlm.nih.gov/medlineplus/panicdisorder.html

  **Post-Traumatic Stress Disorder**
  http://www.nlm.nih.gov/medlineplus/posttraumaticstressdisorder.html

You may also choose to use the search utility provided by MEDLINEplus at the following Web address: **http://www.nlm.nih.gov/medlineplus/**. Simply type a keyword into the search box and click "Search." This utility is similar to the NIH search utility, with the exception that it only includes materials that are linked within the MEDLINEplus system (mostly patient-oriented information). It also has the disadvantage of generating unstructured results. We recommend, therefore, that you use this method only if you have a very targeted search.

### The National Guideline Clearinghouse™

The National Guideline Clearinghouse™ offers hundreds of evidence-based clinical practice guidelines published in the United States and other countries. You can search this site located at **http://www.guideline.gov/** by using the keyword "borderline personality disorder" (or synonyms). The following was recently posted:

- **Practice guideline for the treatment of patients with borderline personality disorder**

  Source: American Psychiatric Association - Medical Specialty Society; 2001 October; 52 pages

  http://www.guideline.gov/summary/summary.aspx?doc_id=2972&nbr=2198&string=borderline+AND+personality+AND+disorder

### Healthfinder™

Healthfinder™ is sponsored by the U.S. Department of Health and Human Services and offers links to hundreds of other sites that contain healthcare information. This Web site is located at **http://www.healthfinder.gov**. Again, keyword searches can be used to find guidelines. The following was recently found in this database:

- **Borderline Personality Disorder**

  Summary: Borderline personality disorder (BPD) is a serious mental illness characterized by pervasive instability in moods, interpersonal relationships, self-image, and behavior.

  Source: National Institute of Mental Health, National Institutes of Health

  http://www.healthfinder.gov/scripts/recordpass.asp?RecordType=0&RecordID=6610

### The NIH Search Utility

The NIH search utility allows you to search for documents on over 100 selected Web sites that comprise the NIH-WEB-SPACE. Each of these servers is "crawled" and indexed on an ongoing basis. Your search will produce a list of various documents, all of which will relate in some way to borderline personality disorder. The drawbacks of this approach are that the information is not organized by theme and that the references are often a mix of information for professionals and patients. Nevertheless, a large number of the listed Web sites provide useful background information. We can only recommend this route, therefore, for relatively rare or specific disorders, or when using highly targeted searches. To use the NIH search utility, visit the following Web page: **http://search.nih.gov/index.html**.

### Additional Web Sources

A number of Web sites are available to the public that often link to government sites. These can also point you in the direction of essential information. The following is a representative sample:

- AOL: **http://search.aol.com/cat.adp?id=168&layer=&from=subcats**
- Family Village: **http://www.familyvillage.wisc.edu/specific.htm**
- Google: **http://directory.google.com/Top/Health/Conditions_and_Diseases/**
- Med Help International: **http://www.medhelp.org/HealthTopics/A.html**
- Open Directory Project: **http://dmoz.org/Health/Conditions_and_Diseases/**
- Yahoo.com: **http://dir.yahoo.com/Health/Diseases_and_Conditions/**
- WebMD®Health: **http://my.webmd.com/health_topics**

## Finding Associations

There are several Internet directories that provide lists of medical associations with information on or resources relating to borderline personality disorder. By consulting all of associations listed in this chapter, you will have nearly exhausted all sources for patient associations concerned with borderline personality disorder.

### The National Health Information Center (NHIC)

The National Health Information Center (NHIC) offers a free referral service to help people find organizations that provide information about borderline personality disorder. For more information, see the NHIC's Web site at **http://www.health.gov/NHIC/** or contact an information specialist by calling 1-800-336-4797.

### Directory of Health Organizations

The Directory of Health Organizations, provided by the National Library of Medicine Specialized Information Services, is a comprehensive source of information on associations. The Directory of Health Organizations database can be accessed via the Internet at

**http://www.sis.nlm.nih.gov/Dir/DirMain.html**. It is composed of two parts: DIRLINE and Health Hotlines.

The DIRLINE database comprises some 10,000 records of organizations, research centers, and government institutes and associations that primarily focus on health and biomedicine. To access DIRLINE directly, go to the following Web site: **http://dirline.nlm.nih.gov/**. Simply type in "borderline personality disorder" (or a synonym), and you will receive information on all relevant organizations listed in the database.

Health Hotlines directs you to toll-free numbers to over 300 organizations. You can access this database directly at **http://www.sis.nlm.nih.gov/hotlines/**. On this page, you are given the option to search by keyword or by browsing the subject list. When you have received your search results, click on the name of the organization for its description and contact information.

### The Combined Health Information Database

Another comprehensive source of information on healthcare associations is the Combined Health Information Database. Using the "Detailed Search" option, you will need to limit your search to "Organizations" and "borderline personality disorder". Type the following hyperlink into your Web browser: **http://chid.nih.gov/detail/detail.html**. To find associations, use the drop boxes at the bottom of the search page where "You may refine your search by." For publication date, select "All Years." Then, select your preferred language and the format option "Organization Resource Sheet." Type "borderline personality disorder" (or synonyms) into the "For these words:" box. You should check back periodically with this database since it is updated every three months.

### The National Organization for Rare Disorders, Inc.

The National Organization for Rare Disorders, Inc. has prepared a Web site that provides, at no charge, lists of associations organized by health topic. You can access this database at the following Web site: **http://www.rarediseases.org/search/orgsearch.html**. Type "borderline personality disorder" (or a synonym) into the search box, and click "Submit Query."

# APPENDIX C. FINDING MEDICAL LIBRARIES

## Overview

In this Appendix, we show you how to quickly find a medical library in your area.

## Preparation

Your local public library and medical libraries have interlibrary loan programs with the National Library of Medicine (NLM), one of the largest medical collections in the world. According to the NLM, most of the literature in the general and historical collections of the National Library of Medicine is available on interlibrary loan to any library. If you would like to access NLM medical literature, then visit a library in your area that can request the publications for you.[19]

## Finding a Local Medical Library

The quickest method to locate medical libraries is to use the Internet-based directory published by the National Network of Libraries of Medicine (NN/LM). This network includes 4626 members and affiliates that provide many services to librarians, health professionals, and the public. To find a library in your area, simply visit **http://nnlm.gov/members/adv.html** or call 1-800-338-7657.

## Medical Libraries in the U.S. and Canada

In addition to the NN/LM, the National Library of Medicine (NLM) lists a number of libraries with reference facilities that are open to the public. The following is the NLM's list and includes hyperlinks to each library's Web site. These Web pages can provide information on hours of operation and other restrictions. The list below is a small sample of

[19] Adapted from the NLM: **http://www.nlm.nih.gov/psd/cas/interlibrary.html**.

libraries recommended by the National Library of Medicine (sorted alphabetically by name of the U.S. state or Canadian province where the library is located)[20]:

- **Alabama:** Health InfoNet of Jefferson County (Jefferson County Library Cooperative, Lister Hill Library of the Health Sciences), **http://www.uab.edu/infonet/**
- **Alabama:** Richard M. Scrushy Library (American Sports Medicine Institute)
- **Arizona:** Samaritan Regional Medical Center: The Learning Center (Samaritan Health System, Phoenix, Arizona), **http://www.samaritan.edu/library/bannerlibs.htm**
- **California:** Kris Kelly Health Information Center (St. Joseph Health System, Humboldt), **http://www.humboldt1.com/~kkhic/index.html**
- **California:** Community Health Library of Los Gatos, **http://www.healthlib.org/orgresources.html**
- **California:** Consumer Health Program and Services (CHIPS) (County of Los Angeles Public Library, Los Angeles County Harbor-UCLA Medical Center Library) - Carson, CA, **http://www.colapublib.org/services/chips.html**
- **California:** Gateway Health Library (Sutter Gould Medical Foundation)
- **California:** Health Library (Stanford University Medical Center), **http://www-med.stanford.edu/healthlibrary/**
- **California:** Patient Education Resource Center - Health Information and Resources (University of California, San Francisco), **http://sfghdean.ucsf.edu/barnett/PERC/default.asp**
- **California:** Redwood Health Library (Petaluma Health Care District), **http://www.phcd.org/rdwdlib.html**
- **California:** Los Gatos PlaneTree Health Library, **http://planetreesanjose.org/**
- **California:** Sutter Resource Library (Sutter Hospitals Foundation, Sacramento), **http://suttermedicalcenter.org/library/**
- **California:** Health Sciences Libraries (University of California, Davis), **http://www.lib.ucdavis.edu/healthsci/**
- **California:** ValleyCare Health Library & Ryan Comer Cancer Resource Center (ValleyCare Health System, Pleasanton), **http://gaelnet.stmarys-ca.edu/other.libs/gbal/east/vchl.html**
- **California:** Washington Community Health Resource Library (Fremont), **http://www.healthlibrary.org/**
- **Colorado:** William V. Gervasini Memorial Library (Exempla Healthcare), **http://www.saintjosephdenver.org/yourhealth/libraries/**
- **Connecticut:** Hartford Hospital Health Science Libraries (Hartford Hospital), **http://www.harthosp.org/library/**
- **Connecticut:** Healthnet: Connecticut Consumer Health Information Center (University of Connecticut Health Center, Lyman Maynard Stowe Library), **http://library.uchc.edu/departm/hnet/**

---

[20] Abstracted from **http://www.nlm.nih.gov/medlineplus/libraries.html**.

- **Connecticut:** Waterbury Hospital Health Center Library (Waterbury Hospital, Waterbury), **http://www.waterburyhospital.com/library/consumer.shtml**
- **Delaware:** Consumer Health Library (Christiana Care Health System, Eugene du Pont Preventive Medicine & Rehabilitation Institute, Wilmington), **http://www.christianacare.org/health_guide/health_guide_pmri_health_info.cfm**
- **Delaware:** Lewis B. Flinn Library (Delaware Academy of Medicine, Wilmington), **http://www.delamed.org/chls.html**
- **Georgia:** Family Resource Library (Medical College of Georgia, Augusta), **http://cmc.mcg.edu/kids_families/fam_resources/fam_res_lib/frl.htm**
- **Georgia:** Health Resource Center (Medical Center of Central Georgia, Macon), **http://www.mccg.org/hrc/hrchome.asp**
- **Hawaii:** Hawaii Medical Library: Consumer Health Information Service (Hawaii Medical Library, Honolulu), **http://hml.org/CHIS/**
- **Idaho:** DeArmond Consumer Health Library (Kootenai Medical Center, Coeur d'Alene), **http://www.nicon.org/DeArmond/index.htm**
- **Illinois:** Health Learning Center of Northwestern Memorial Hospital (Chicago), **http://www.nmh.org/health_info/hlc.html**
- **Illinois:** Medical Library (OSF Saint Francis Medical Center, Peoria), **http://www.osfsaintfrancis.org/general/library/**
- **Kentucky:** Medical Library - Services for Patients, Families, Students & the Public (Central Baptist Hospital, Lexington), **http://www.centralbap.com/education/community/library.cfm**
- **Kentucky:** University of Kentucky - Health Information Library (Chandler Medical Center, Lexington), **http://www.mc.uky.edu/PatientEd/**
- **Louisiana:** Alton Ochsner Medical Foundation Library (Alton Ochsner Medical Foundation, New Orleans), **http://www.ochsner.org/library/**
- **Louisiana:** Louisiana State University Health Sciences Center Medical Library-Shreveport, **http://lib-sh.lsuhsc.edu/**
- **Maine:** Franklin Memorial Hospital Medical Library (Franklin Memorial Hospital, Farmington), **http://www.fchn.org/fmh/lib.htm**
- **Maine:** Gerrish-True Health Sciences Library (Central Maine Medical Center, Lewiston), **http://www.cmmc.org/library/library.html**
- **Maine:** Hadley Parrot Health Science Library (Eastern Maine Healthcare, Bangor), **http://www.emh.org/hll/hpl/guide.htm**
- **Maine:** Maine Medical Center Library (Maine Medical Center, Portland), **http://www.mmc.org/library/**
- **Maine:** Parkview Hospital (Brunswick), **http://www.parkviewhospital.org/**
- **Maine:** Southern Maine Medical Center Health Sciences Library (Southern Maine Medical Center, Biddeford), **http://www.smmc.org/services/service.php3?choice=10**
- **Maine:** Stephens Memorial Hospital's Health Information Library (Western Maine Health, Norway), **http://www.wmhcc.org/Library/**

- **Manitoba, Canada:** Consumer & Patient Health Information Service (University of Manitoba Libraries), **http://www.umanitoba.ca/libraries/units/health/reference/chis.html**
- **Manitoba, Canada:** J.W. Crane Memorial Library (Deer Lodge Centre, Winnipeg), **http://www.deerlodge.mb.ca/crane_library/about.asp**
- **Maryland:** Health Information Center at the Wheaton Regional Library (Montgomery County, Dept. of Public Libraries, Wheaton Regional Library), **http://www.mont.lib.md.us/healthinfo/hic.asp**
- **Massachusetts:** Baystate Medical Center Library (Baystate Health System), **http://www.baystatehealth.com/1024/**
- **Massachusetts:** Boston University Medical Center Alumni Medical Library (Boston University Medical Center), **http://med-libwww.bu.edu/library/lib.html**
- **Massachusetts:** Lowell General Hospital Health Sciences Library (Lowell General Hospital, Lowell), **http://www.lowellgeneral.org/library/HomePageLinks/WWW.htm**
- **Massachusetts:** Paul E. Woodard Health Sciences Library (New England Baptist Hospital, Boston), **http://www.nebh.org/health_lib.asp**
- **Massachusetts:** St. Luke's Hospital Health Sciences Library (St. Luke's Hospital, Southcoast Health System, New Bedford), **http://www.southcoast.org/library/**
- **Massachusetts:** Treadwell Library Consumer Health Reference Center (Massachusetts General Hospital), **http://www.mgh.harvard.edu/library/chrcindex.html**
- **Massachusetts:** UMass HealthNet (University of Massachusetts Medical School, Worchester), **http://healthnet.umassmed.edu/**
- **Michigan:** Botsford General Hospital Library - Consumer Health (Botsford General Hospital, Library & Internet Services), **http://www.botsfordlibrary.org/consumer.htm**
- **Michigan:** Helen DeRoy Medical Library (Providence Hospital and Medical Centers), **http://www.providence-hospital.org/library/**
- **Michigan:** Marquette General Hospital - Consumer Health Library (Marquette General Hospital, Health Information Center), **http://www.mgh.org/center.html**
- **Michigan:** Patient Education Resouce Center - University of Michigan Cancer Center (University of Michigan Comprehensive Cancer Center, Ann Arbor), **http://www.cancer.med.umich.edu/learn/leares.htm**
- **Michigan:** Sladen Library & Center for Health Information Resources - Consumer Health Information (Detroit), **http://www.henryford.com/body.cfm?id=39330**
- **Montana:** Center for Health Information (St. Patrick Hospital and Health Sciences Center, Missoula)
- **National:** Consumer Health Library Directory (Medical Library Association, Consumer and Patient Health Information Section), **http://caphis.mlanet.org/directory/index.html**
- **National:** National Network of Libraries of Medicine (National Library of Medicine) - provides library services for health professionals in the United States who do not have access to a medical library, **http://nnlm.gov/**
- **National:** NN/LM List of Libraries Serving the Public (National Network of Libraries of Medicine), **http://nnlm.gov/members/**

- **Nevada:** Health Science Library, West Charleston Library (Las Vegas-Clark County Library District, Las Vegas), **http://www.lvccld.org/special_collections/medical/index.htm**
- **New Hampshire:** Dartmouth Biomedical Libraries (Dartmouth College Library, Hanover), **http://www.dartmouth.edu/~biomed/resources.htmld/conshealth.htmld/**
- **New Jersey:** Consumer Health Library (Rahway Hospital, Rahway), **http://www.rahwayhospital.com/library.htm**
- **New Jersey:** Dr. Walter Phillips Health Sciences Library (Englewood Hospital and Medical Center, Englewood), **http://www.englewoodhospital.com/links/index.htm**
- **New Jersey:** Meland Foundation (Englewood Hospital and Medical Center, Englewood), **http://www.geocities.com/ResearchTriangle/9360/**
- **New York:** Choices in Health Information (New York Public Library) - NLM Consumer Pilot Project participant, **http://www.nypl.org/branch/health/links.html**
- **New York:** Health Information Center (Upstate Medical University, State University of New York, Syracuse), **http://www.upstate.edu/library/hic/**
- **New York:** Health Sciences Library (Long Island Jewish Medical Center, New Hyde Park), **http://www.lij.edu/library/library.html**
- **New York:** ViaHealth Medical Library (Rochester General Hospital), **http://www.nyam.org/library/**
- **Ohio:** Consumer Health Library (Akron General Medical Center, Medical & Consumer Health Library), **http://www.akrongeneral.org/hwlibrary.htm**
- **Oklahoma:** The Health Information Center at Saint Francis Hospital (Saint Francis Health System, Tulsa), **http://www.sfh-tulsa.com/services/healthinfo.asp**
- **Oregon:** Planetree Health Resource Center (Mid-Columbia Medical Center, The Dalles), **http://www.mcmc.net/phrc/**
- **Pennsylvania:** Community Health Information Library (Milton S. Hershey Medical Center, Hershey), **http://www.hmc.psu.edu/commhealth/**
- **Pennsylvania:** Community Health Resource Library (Geisinger Medical Center, Danville), **http://www.geisinger.edu/education/commlib.shtml**
- **Pennsylvania:** HealthInfo Library (Moses Taylor Hospital, Scranton), **http://www.mth.org/healthwellness.html**
- **Pennsylvania:** Hopwood Library (University of Pittsburgh, Health Sciences Library System, Pittsburgh), **http://www.hsls.pitt.edu/guides/chi/hopwood/index_html**
- **Pennsylvania:** Koop Community Health Information Center (College of Physicians of Philadelphia), **http://www.collphyphil.org/kooppg1.shtml**
- **Pennsylvania:** Learning Resources Center - Medical Library (Susquehanna Health System, Williamsport), **http://www.shscares.org/services/lrc/index.asp**
- **Pennsylvania:** Medical Library (UPMC Health System, Pittsburgh), **http://www.upmc.edu/passavant/library.htm**
- **Quebec, Canada:** Medical Library (Montreal General Hospital), **http://www.mghlib.mcgill.ca/**

- **South Dakota:** Rapid City Regional Hospital Medical Library (Rapid City Regional Hospital), **http://www.rcrh.org/Services/Library/Default.asp**
- **Texas:** Houston HealthWays (Houston Academy of Medicine-Texas Medical Center Library), **http://hhw.library.tmc.edu/**
- **Washington:** Community Health Library (Kittitas Valley Community Hospital), **http://www.kvch.com/**
- **Washington:** Southwest Washington Medical Center Library (Southwest Washington Medical Center, Vancouver), **http://www.swmedicalcenter.com/body.cfm?id=72**

# ONLINE GLOSSARIES

The Internet provides access to a number of free-to-use medical dictionaries. The National Library of Medicine has compiled the following list of online dictionaries:

- ADAM Medical Encyclopedia (A.D.A.M., Inc.), comprehensive medical reference: **http://www.nlm.nih.gov/medlineplus/encyclopedia.html**
- MedicineNet.com Medical Dictionary (MedicineNet, Inc.): **http://www.medterms.com/Script/Main/hp.asp**
- Merriam-Webster Medical Dictionary (Inteli-Health, Inc.): **http://www.intelihealth.com/IH/**
- Multilingual Glossary of Technical and Popular Medical Terms in Eight European Languages (European Commission) - Danish, Dutch, English, French, German, Italian, Portuguese, and Spanish: **http://allserv.rug.ac.be/~rvdstich/eugloss/welcome.html**
- On-line Medical Dictionary (CancerWEB): **http://cancerweb.ncl.ac.uk/omd/**
- Rare Diseases Terms (Office of Rare Diseases): **http://ord.aspensys.com/asp/diseases/diseases.asp**
- Technology Glossary (National Library of Medicine) - Health Care Technology: **http://www.nlm.nih.gov/nichsr/ta101/ta10108.htm**

Beyond these, MEDLINEplus contains a very patient-friendly encyclopedia covering every aspect of medicine (licensed from A.D.A.M., Inc.). The ADAM Medical Encyclopedia can be accessed at **http://www.nlm.nih.gov/medlineplus/encyclopedia.html**. ADAM is also available on commercial Web sites such as drkoop.com (**http://www.drkoop.com/**) and Web MD (**http://my.webmd.com/adam/asset/adam_disease_articles/a_to_z/a**). The NIH suggests the following Web sites in the ADAM Medical Encyclopedia when searching for information on borderline personality disorder:

- **Basic Guidelines for Borderline Personality Disorder**

  **Borderline personality disorder**
  Web site: http://www.nlm.nih.gov/medlineplus/ency/article/000935.htm

- **Signs & Symptoms for Borderline Personality Disorder**

  **Binge eating**
  Web site: http://www.nlm.nih.gov/medlineplus/ency/article/003265.htm

  **Depression**
  Web site: http://www.nlm.nih.gov/medlineplus/ency/article/003213.htm

- **Diagnostics and Tests for Borderline Personality Disorder**

  **Orientation**
  Web site: http://www.nlm.nih.gov/medlineplus/ency/article/003326.htm

- **Background Topics for Borderline Personality Disorder**

  **Drug abuse**
  Web site: http://www.nlm.nih.gov/medlineplus/ency/article/001945.htm

  **Substance abuse**
  Web site: http://www.nlm.nih.gov/medlineplus/ency/article/001945.htm

## Online Dictionary Directories

The following are additional online directories compiled by the National Library of Medicine, including a number of specialized medical dictionaries:

- Medical Dictionaries: Medical & Biological (World Health Organization): **http://www.who.int/hlt/virtuallibrary/English/diction.htm#Medical**
- MEL-Michigan Electronic Library List of Online Health and Medical Dictionaries (Michigan Electronic Library): **http://mel.lib.mi.us/health/health-dictionaries.html**
- Patient Education: Glossaries (DMOZ Open Directory Project): **http://dmoz.org/Health/Education/Patient_Education/Glossaries/**
- Web of Online Dictionaries (Bucknell University): **http://www.yourdictionary.com/diction5.html#medicine**

# BORDERLINE PERSONALITY DISORDER DICTIONARY

The definitions below are derived from official public sources, including the National Institutes of Health [NIH] and the European Union [EU].

**Abdominal:** Having to do with the abdomen, which is the part of the body between the chest and the hips that contains the pancreas, stomach, intestines, liver, gallbladder, and other organs. [NIH]

**Aberrant:** Wandering or deviating from the usual or normal course. [EU]

**Acoustic:** Having to do with sound or hearing. [NIH]

**Adaptation:** 1. The adjustment of an organism to its environment, or the process by which it enhances such fitness. 2. The normal ability of the eye to adjust itself to variations in the intensity of light; the adjustment to such variations. 3. The decline in the frequency of firing of a neuron, particularly of a receptor, under conditions of constant stimulation. 4. In dentistry, (a) the proper fitting of a denture, (b) the degree of proximity and interlocking of restorative material to a tooth preparation, (c) the exact adjustment of bands to teeth. 5. In microbiology, the adjustment of bacterial physiology to a new environment. [EU]

**Adipocytes:** Fat-storing cells found mostly in the abdominal cavity and subcutaneous tissue. Fat is usually stored in the form of tryglycerides. [NIH]

**Adjustment:** The dynamic process wherein the thoughts, feelings, behavior, and biophysiological mechanisms of the individual continually change to adjust to the environment. [NIH]

**Adolescence:** The period of life beginning with the appearance of secondary sex characteristics and terminating with the cessation of somatic growth. The years usually referred to as adolescence lie between 13 and 18 years of age. [NIH]

**Adrenal Cortex:** The outer layer of the adrenal gland. It secretes mineralocorticoids, androgens, and glucocorticoids. [NIH]

**Adrenergic:** Activated by, characteristic of, or secreting epinephrine or substances with similar activity; the term is applied to those nerve fibres that liberate norepinephrine at a synapse when a nerve impulse passes, i.e., the sympathetic fibres. [EU]

**Adverse Effect:** An unwanted side effect of treatment. [NIH]

**Afferent:** Concerned with the transmission of neural impulse toward the central part of the nervous system. [NIH]

**Affinity:** 1. Inherent likeness or relationship. 2. A special attraction for a specific element, organ, or structure. 3. Chemical affinity; the force that binds atoms in molecules; the tendency of substances to combine by chemical reaction. 4. The strength of noncovalent chemical binding between two substances as measured by the dissociation constant of the complex. 5. In immunology, a thermodynamic expression of the strength of interaction between a single antigen-binding site and a single antigenic determinant (and thus of the stereochemical compatibility between them), most accurately applied to interactions among simple, uniform antigenic determinants such as haptens. Expressed as the association constant (K litres mole -1), which, owing to the heterogeneity of affinities in a population of antibody molecules of a given specificity, actually represents an average value (mean intrinsic association constant). 6. The reciprocal of the dissociation constant. [EU]

**Age of Onset:** The age or period of life at which a disease or the initial symptoms or manifestations of a disease appear in an individual. [NIH]

**Agonist:** In anatomy, a prime mover. In pharmacology, a drug that has affinity for and stimulates physiologic activity at cell receptors normally stimulated by naturally occurring substances. [EU]

**Agoraphobia:** Obsessive, persistent, intense fear of open places. [NIH]

**Airway:** A device for securing unobstructed passage of air into and out of the lungs during general anesthesia. [NIH]

**Algorithms:** A procedure consisting of a sequence of algebraic formulas and/or logical steps to calculate or determine a given task. [NIH]

**Alkaloid:** A member of a large group of chemicals that are made by plants and have nitrogen in them. Some alkaloids have been shown to work against cancer. [NIH]

**Alternative medicine:** Practices not generally recognized by the medical community as standard or conventional medical approaches and used instead of standard treatments. Alternative medicine includes the taking of dietary supplements, megadose vitamins, and herbal preparations; the drinking of special teas; and practices such as massage therapy, magnet therapy, spiritual healing, and meditation. [NIH]

**Amenorrhea:** Absence of menstruation. [NIH]

**Amygdala:** Almond-shaped group of basal nuclei anterior to the inferior horn of the lateral ventricle of the brain, within the temporal lobe. The amygdala is part of the limbic system. [NIH]

**Anal:** Having to do with the anus, which is the posterior opening of the large bowel. [NIH]

**Analgesic:** An agent that alleviates pain without causing loss of consciousness. [EU]

**Anatomical:** Pertaining to anatomy, or to the structure of the organism. [EU]

**Animal model:** An animal with a disease either the same as or like a disease in humans. Animal models are used to study the development and progression of diseases and to test new treatments before they are given to humans. Animals with transplanted human cancers or other tissues are called xenograft models. [NIH]

**Anorexia:** Lack or loss of appetite for food. Appetite is psychologic, dependent on memory and associations. Anorexia can be brought about by unattractive food, surroundings, or company. [NIH]

**Anorexia Nervosa:** The chief symptoms are inability to eat, weight loss, and amenorrhea. [NIH]

**Antagonism:** Interference with, or inhibition of, the growth of a living organism by another living organism, due either to creation of unfavorable conditions (e. g. exhaustion of food supplies) or to production of a specific antibiotic substance (e. g. penicillin). [NIH]

**Antecedent:** Existing or occurring before in time or order often with consequential effects. [EU]

**Antibacterial:** A substance that destroys bacteria or suppresses their growth or reproduction. [EU]

**Antibiotic:** A drug used to treat infections caused by bacteria and other microorganisms. [NIH]

**Antibody:** A type of protein made by certain white blood cells in response to a foreign substance (antigen). Each antibody can bind to only a specific antigen. The purpose of this binding is to help destroy the antigen. Antibodies can work in several ways, depending on the nature of the antigen. Some antibodies destroy antigens directly. Others make it easier for white blood cells to destroy the antigen. [NIH]

**Anticholinergic:** An agent that blocks the parasympathetic nerves. Called also parasympatholytic. [EU]

**Anticonvulsant:** An agent that prevents or relieves convulsions. [EU]

**Antidepressant:** A drug used to treat depression. [NIH]

**Anti-inflammatory:** Having to do with reducing inflammation. [NIH]

**Antipsychotic:** Effective in the treatment of psychosis. Antipsychotic drugs (called also neuroleptic drugs and major tranquilizers) are a chemically diverse (including phenothiazines, thioxanthenes, butyrophenones, dibenzoxazepines, dibenzodiazepines, and diphenylbutylpiperidines) but pharmacologically similar class of drugs used to treat schizophrenic, paranoid, schizoaffective, and other psychotic disorders; acute delirium and dementia, and manic episodes (during induction of lithium therapy); to control the movement disorders associated with Huntington's chorea, Gilles de la Tourette's syndrome, and ballismus; and to treat intractable hiccups and severe nausea and vomiting. Antipsychotic agents bind to dopamine, histamine, muscarinic cholinergic, a-adrenergic, and serotonin receptors. Blockade of dopaminergic transmission in various areas is thought to be responsible for their major effects : antipsychotic action by blockade in the mesolimbic and mesocortical areas; extrapyramidal side effects (dystonia, akathisia, parkinsonism, and tardive dyskinesia) by blockade in the basal ganglia; and antiemetic effects by blockade in the chemoreceptor trigger zone of the medulla. Sedation and autonomic side effects (orthostatic hypotension, blurred vision, dry mouth, nasal congestion and constipation) are caused by blockade of histamine, cholinergic, and adrenergic receptors. [EU]

**Anus:** The opening of the rectum to the outside of the body. [NIH]

**Anxiety:** Persistent feeling of dread, apprehension, and impending disaster. [NIH]

**Anxiety Disorders:** Disorders in which anxiety (persistent feelings of apprehension, tension, or uneasiness) is the predominant disturbance. [NIH]

**Apnea:** A transient absence of spontaneous respiration. [NIH]

**Aqueous:** Having to do with water. [NIH]

**Arterial:** Pertaining to an artery or to the arteries. [EU]

**Arteries:** The vessels carrying blood away from the heart. [NIH]

**Assay:** Determination of the amount of a particular constituent of a mixture, or of he biological or pharmacological potency of a drug. [EU]

**Astrocytes:** The largest and most numerous neuroglial cells in the brain and spinal cord. Astrocytes (from "star" cells) are irregularly shaped with many long processes, including those with "end feet" which form the glial (limiting) membrane and directly and indirectly contribute to the blood brain barrier. They regulate the extracellular ionic and chemical environment, and "reactive astrocytes" (along with microglia) respond to injury. Astrocytes have high- affinity transmitter uptake systems, voltage-dependent and transmitter-gated ion channels, and can release transmitter, but their role in signaling (as in many other functions) is not well understood. [NIH]

**Atrial:** Pertaining to an atrium. [EU]

**Atrioventricular:** Pertaining to an atrium of the heart and to a ventricle. [EU]

**Atrium:** A chamber; used in anatomical nomenclature to designate a chamber affording entrance to another structure or organ. Usually used alone to designate an atrium of the heart. [EU]

**Atypical:** Irregular; not conformable to the type; in microbiology, applied specifically to strains of unusual type. [EU]

**Auditory:** Pertaining to the sense of hearing. [EU]

**Autonomic:** Self-controlling; functionally independent. [EU]

**Bacteria:** Unicellular prokaryotic microorganisms which generally possess rigid cell walls, multiply by cell division, and exhibit three principal forms: round or coccal, rodlike or bacillary, and spiral or spirochetal. [NIH]

**Bacterial Physiology:** Physiological processes and activities of bacteria. [NIH]

**Bacteriuria:** The presence of bacteria in the urine with or without consequent urinary tract infection. Since bacteriuria is a clinical entity, the term does not preclude the use of urine/microbiology for technical discussions on the isolation and segregation of bacteria in the urine. [NIH]

**Base:** In chemistry, the nonacid part of a salt; a substance that combines with acids to form salts; a substance that dissociates to give hydroxide ions in aqueous solutions; a substance whose molecule or ion can combine with a proton (hydrogen ion); a substance capable of donating a pair of electrons (to an acid) for the formation of a coordinate covalent bond. [EU]

**Behavior Therapy:** The application of modern theories of learning and conditioning in the treatment of behavior disorders. [NIH]

**Benign:** Not cancerous; does not invade nearby tissue or spread to other parts of the body. [NIH]

**Binding Sites:** The reactive parts of a macromolecule that directly participate in its specific combination with another molecule. [NIH]

**Biochemical:** Relating to biochemistry; characterized by, produced by, or involving chemical reactions in living organisms. [EU]

**Biotechnology:** Body of knowledge related to the use of organisms, cells or cell-derived constituents for the purpose of developing products which are technically, scientifically and clinically useful. Alteration of biologic function at the molecular level (i.e., genetic engineering) is a central focus; laboratory methods used include transfection and cloning technologies, sequence and structure analysis algorithms, computer databases, and gene and protein structure function analysis and prediction. [NIH]

**Bipolar Disorder:** A major affective disorder marked by severe mood swings (manic or major depressive episodes) and a tendency to remission and recurrence. [NIH]

**Bladder:** The organ that stores urine. [NIH]

**Blood Platelets:** Non-nucleated disk-shaped cells formed in the megakaryocyte and found in the blood of all mammals. They are mainly involved in blood coagulation. [NIH]

**Blood pressure:** The pressure of blood against the walls of a blood vessel or heart chamber. Unless there is reference to another location, such as the pulmonary artery or one of the heart chambers, it refers to the pressure in the systemic arteries, as measured, for example, in the forearm. [NIH]

**Blood vessel:** A tube in the body through which blood circulates. Blood vessels include a network of arteries, arterioles, capillaries, venules, and veins. [NIH]

**Blood-Brain Barrier:** Specialized non-fenestrated tightly-joined endothelial cells (tight junctions) that form a transport barrier for certain substances between the cerebral capillaries and the brain tissue. [NIH]

**Body Fluids:** Liquid components of living organisms. [NIH]

**Bowel:** The long tube-shaped organ in the abdomen that completes the process of digestion. There is both a small and a large bowel. Also called the intestine. [NIH]

**Bowel Movement:** Body wastes passed through the rectumand anus. [NIH]

**Branch:** Most commonly used for branches of nerves, but applied also to other structures. [NIH]

**Bulimia:** Episodic binge eating. The episodes may be associated with the fear of not being able to stop eating, depressed mood, or self-deprecating thoughts (binge-eating disorder) and may frequently be terminated by self-induced vomiting (bulimia nervosa). [NIH]

**Buprenorphine:** A derivative of the opioid alkaloid thebaine that is a more potent and longer lasting analgesic than morphine. It appears to act as a partial agonist at mu and kappa opioid receptors and as an antagonist at delta receptors. The lack of delta-agonist activity has been suggested to account for the observation that buprenorphine tolerance may not develop with chronic use. [NIH]

**Carbamazepine:** An anticonvulsant used to control grand mal and psychomotor or focal seizures. Its mode of action is not fully understood, but some of its actions resemble those of phenytoin; although there is little chemical resemblance between the two compounds, their three-dimensional structure is similar. [NIH]

**Carbon Dioxide:** A colorless, odorless gas that can be formed by the body and is necessary for the respiration cycle of plants and animals. [NIH]

**Cardiac:** Having to do with the heart. [NIH]

**Cardiovascular:** Having to do with the heart and blood vessels. [NIH]

**Cardiovascular disease:** Any abnormal condition characterized by dysfunction of the heart and blood vessels. CVD includes atherosclerosis (especially coronary heart disease, which can lead to heart attacks), cerebrovascular disease (e.g., stroke), and hypertension (high blood pressure). [NIH]

**Carotid Sinus:** The dilated portion of the common carotid artery at its bifurcation into external and internal carotids. It contains baroreceptors which, when stimulated, cause slowing of the heart, vasodilatation, and a fall in blood pressure. [NIH]

**Catecholamine:** A group of chemical substances manufactured by the adrenal medulla and secreted during physiological stress. [NIH]

**Cell:** The individual unit that makes up all of the tissues of the body. All living things are made up of one or more cells. [NIH]

**Cell Respiration:** The metabolic process of all living cells (animal and plant) in which oxygen is used to provide a source of energy for the cell. [NIH]

**Central Nervous System:** The main information-processing organs of the nervous system, consisting of the brain, spinal cord, and meninges. [NIH]

**Central Nervous System Infections:** Pathogenic infections of the brain, spinal cord, and meninges. DNA virus infections; RNA virus infections; bacterial infections; mycoplasma infections; Spirochaetales infections; fungal infections; protozoan infections; helminthiasis; and prion diseases may involve the central nervous system as a primary or secondary process. [NIH]

**Cerebellum:** Part of the metencephalon that lies in the posterior cranial fossa behind the brain stem. It is concerned with the coordination of movement. [NIH]

**Cerebral:** Of or pertaining of the cerebrumor the brain. [EU]

**Cerebral Palsy:** Refers to a motor disability caused by a brain dysfunction. [NIH]

**Cerebrospinal:** Pertaining to the brain and spinal cord. [EU]

**Cerebrospinal fluid:** CSF. The fluid flowing around the brain and spinal cord. Cerebrospinal fluid is produced in the ventricles in the brain. [NIH]

**Cerebrovascular:** Pertaining to the blood vessels of the cerebrum, or brain. [EU]

**Cerebrum:** The largest part of the brain. It is divided into two hemispheres, or halves, called the cerebral hemispheres. The cerebrum controls muscle functions of the body and also controls speech, emotions, reading, writing, and learning. [NIH]

**Cervical:** Relating to the neck, or to the neck of any organ or structure. Cervical lymph nodes are located in the neck; cervical cancer refers to cancer of the uterine cervix, which is the lower, narrow end (the "neck") of the uterus. [NIH]

**Cervical Plexus:** A network of nerve fibers originating in the upper four cervical spinal cord segments. The cervical plexus distributes cutaneous nerves to parts of the neck, shoulders, and back of the head, and motor fibers to muscles of the cervical spinal column, infrahyoid muscles, and the diaphragm. [NIH]

**Chaos:** Complex behavior that seems random but actually has some hidden order. [NIH]

**Character:** In current usage, approximately equivalent to personality. The sum of the relatively fixed personality traits and habitual modes of response of an individual. [NIH]

**Chemoreceptors:** Cells specialized to detect chemical substances and relay that information centrally in the nervous system. Chemoreceptors may monitor external stimuli, as in taste and olfaction, or internal stimuli, such as the concentrations of oxygen and carbon dioxide in the blood. [NIH]

**Cholesterol:** The principal sterol of all higher animals, distributed in body tissues, especially the brain and spinal cord, and in animal fats and oils. [NIH]

**Chronic:** A disease or condition that persists or progresses over a long period of time. [NIH]

**Clamp:** A u-shaped steel rod used with a pin or wire for skeletal traction in the treatment of certain fractures. [NIH]

**Clinical study:** A research study in which patients receive treatment in a clinic or other medical facility. Reports of clinical studies can contain results for single patients (case reports) or many patients (case series or clinical trials). [NIH]

**Clinical trial:** A research study that tests how well new medical treatments or other interventions work in people. Each study is designed to test new methods of screening, prevention, diagnosis, or treatment of a disease. [NIH]

**Cloning:** The production of a number of genetically identical individuals; in genetic engineering, a process for the efficient replication of a great number of identical DNA molecules. [NIH]

**Clozapine:** A tricylic dibenzodiazepine, classified as an atypical antipsychotic agent. It binds several types of central nervous system receptors, and displays a unique pharmacological profile. Clozapine is a serotonin antagonist, with strong binding to 5-HT 2A/2C receptor subtype. It also displays strong affinity to several dopaminergic receptors, but shows only weak antagonism at the dopamine D2 receptor, a receptor commonly thought to modulate neuroleptic activity. Agranulocytosis is a major adverse effect associated with administration of this agent. [NIH]

**Cofactor:** A substance, microorganism or environmental factor that activates or enhances the action of another entity such as a disease-causing agent. [NIH]

**Cognition:** Intellectual or mental process whereby an organism becomes aware of or obtains knowledge. [NIH]

**Collapse:** 1. A state of extreme prostration and depression, with failure of circulation. 2. Abnormal falling in of the walls of any part of organ. [EU]

**Commitment of Mentally Ill:** Legal process required for the institutionalization of a patient with severe mental problems. [NIH]

**Comorbidity:** The presence of co-existing or additional diseases with reference to an initial diagnosis or with reference to the index condition that is the subject of study. Comorbidity may affect the ability of affected individuals to function and also their survival; it may be used as a prognostic indicator for length of hospital stay, cost factors, and outcome or survival. [NIH]

**Complement:** A term originally used to refer to the heat-labile factor in serum that causes immune cytolysis, the lysis of antibody-coated cells, and now referring to the entire functionally related system comprising at least 20 distinct serum proteins that is the effector not only of immune cytolysis but also of other biologic functions. Complement activation occurs by two different sequences, the classic and alternative pathways. The proteins of the classic pathway are termed 'components of complement' and are designated by the symbols C1 through C9. C1 is a calcium-dependent complex of three distinct proteins C1q, C1r and C1s. The proteins of the alternative pathway (collectively referred to as the properdin system) and complement regulatory proteins are known by semisystematic or trivial names. Fragments resulting from proteolytic cleavage of complement proteins are designated with lower-case letter suffixes, e.g., C3a. Inactivated fragments may be designated with the suffix 'i', e.g. C3bi. Activated components or complexes with biological activity are designated by a bar over the symbol e.g. C1 or C4b,2a. The classic pathway is activated by the binding of C1 to classic pathway activators, primarily antigen-antibody complexes containing IgM, IgG1, IgG3; C1q binds to a single IgM molecule or two adjacent IgG molecules. The alternative pathway can be activated by IgA immune complexes and also by nonimmunologic materials including bacterial endotoxins, microbial polysaccharides, and cell walls. Activation of the classic pathway triggers an enzymatic cascade involving C1, C4, C2 and C3; activation of the alternative pathway triggers a cascade involving C3 and factors B, D and P. Both result in the cleavage of C5 and the formation of the membrane attack complex. Complement activation also results in the formation of many biologically active complement fragments that act as anaphylatoxins, opsonins, or chemotactic factors. [EU]

**Complementary and alternative medicine:** CAM. Forms of treatment that are used in addition to (complementary) or instead of (alternative) standard treatments. These practices are not considered standard medical approaches. CAM includes dietary supplements, megadose vitamins, herbal preparations, special teas, massage therapy, magnet therapy, spiritual healing, and meditation. [NIH]

**Complementary medicine:** Practices not generally recognized by the medical community as standard or conventional medical approaches and used to enhance or complement the standard treatments. Complementary medicine includes the taking of dietary supplements, megadose vitamins, and herbal preparations; the drinking of special teas; and practices such as massage therapy, magnet therapy, spiritual healing, and meditation. [NIH]

**Complete remission:** The disappearance of all signs of cancer. Also called a complete response. [NIH]

**Computational Biology:** A field of biology concerned with the development of techniques for the collection and manipulation of biological data, and the use of such data to make biological discoveries or predictions. This field encompasses all computational methods and theories applicable to molecular biology and areas of computer-based techniques for solving biological problems including manipulation of models and datasets. [NIH]

**Conjunctiva:** The mucous membrane that lines the inner surface of the eyelids and the anterior part of the sclera. [NIH]

**Consciousness:** Sense of awareness of self and of the environment. [NIH]

**Contraindications:** Any factor or sign that it is unwise to pursue a certain kind of action or treatment, e. g. giving a general anesthetic to a person with pneumonia. [NIH]

**Control group:** In a clinical trial, the group that does not receive the new treatment being studied. This group is compared to the group that receives the new treatment, to see if the new treatment works. [NIH]

**Controlled clinical trial:** A clinical study that includes a comparison (control) group. The comparison group receives a placebo, another treatment, or no treatment at all. [NIH]

**Controlled study:** An experiment or clinical trial that includes a comparison (control) group. [NIH]

**Convulsions:** A general term referring to sudden and often violent motor activity of cerebral or brainstem origin. Convulsions may also occur in the absence of an electrical cerebral discharge (e.g., in response to hypotension). [NIH]

**Cor:** The muscular organ that maintains the circulation of the blood. c. adiposum a heart that has undergone fatty degeneration or that has an accumulation of fat around it; called also fat or fatty, heart. c. arteriosum the left side of the heart, so called because it contains oxygenated (arterial) blood. c. biloculare a congenital anomaly characterized by failure of formation of the atrial and ventricular septums, the heart having only two chambers, a single atrium and a single ventricle, and a common atrioventricular valve. c. bovinum (L. 'ox heart') a greatly enlarged heart due to a hypertrophied left ventricle; called also c. taurinum and bucardia. c. dextrum (L. 'right heart') the right atrium and ventricle. c. hirsutum, c. villosum. c. mobile (obs.) an abnormally movable heart. c. pendulum a heart so movable that it seems to be hanging by the great blood vessels. c. pseudotriloculare biatriatum a congenital cardiac anomaly in which the heart functions as a three-chambered heart because of tricuspid atresia, the right ventricle being extremely small or rudimentary and the right atrium greatly dilated. Blood passes from the right to the left atrium and thence disease due to pulmonary hypertension secondary to disease of the lung, or its blood vessels, with hypertrophy of the right ventricle. [EU]

**Coronary:** Encircling in the manner of a crown; a term applied to vessels; nerves, ligaments, etc. The term usually denotes the arteries that supply the heart muscle and, by extension, a pathologic involvement of them. [EU]

**Coronary heart disease:** A type of heart disease caused by narrowing of the coronary arteries that feed the heart, which needs a constant supply of oxygen and nutrients carried by the blood in the coronary arteries. When the coronary arteries become narrowed or clogged by fat and cholesterol deposits and cannot supply enough blood to the heart, CHD results. [NIH]

**Coronary Thrombosis:** Presence of a thrombus in a coronary artery, often causing a myocardial infarction. [NIH]

**Cortex:** The outer layer of an organ or other body structure, as distinguished from the internal substance. [EU]

**Cortical:** Pertaining to or of the nature of a cortex or bark. [EU]

**Cortices:** The outer layer of an organ; used especially of the cerebrum and cerebellum. [NIH]

**Corticotropin-Releasing Hormone:** A neuropeptide released by the hypothalamus that stimulates the release of corticotropin by the anterior pituitary gland. [NIH]

**Cortisol:** A steroid hormone secreted by the adrenal cortex as part of the body's response to stress. [NIH]

**Cortisone:** A natural steroid hormone produced in the adrenal gland. It can also be made in the laboratory. Cortisone reduces swelling and can suppress immune responses. [NIH]

**Cranial:** Pertaining to the cranium, or to the anterior (in animals) or superior (in humans) end of the body. [EU]

**Craniocerebral Trauma:** Traumatic injuries involving the cranium and intracranial structures (i.e., brain; cranial nerves; meninges; and other structures). Injuries may be classified by whether or not the skull is penetrated (i.e., penetrating vs. nonpenetrating) or whether there is an associated hemorrhage. [NIH]

**Criminology:** The study of crime and criminals with special reference to the personality factors and social conditions leading toward, or away from crime. [NIH]

**Criterion:** A standard by which something may be judged. [EU]

**Curative:** Tending to overcome disease and promote recovery. [EU]

**Data Collection:** Systematic gathering of data for a particular purpose from various sources, including questionnaires, interviews, observation, existing records, and electronic devices. The process is usually preliminary to statistical analysis of the data. [NIH]

**Databases, Bibliographic:** Extensive collections, reputedly complete, of references and citations to books, articles, publications, etc., generally on a single subject or specialized subject area. Databases can operate through automated files, libraries, or computer disks. The concept should be differentiated from factual databases which is used for collections of data and facts apart from bibliographic references to them. [NIH]

**Deamination:** The removal of an amino group (NH2) from a chemical compound. [NIH]

**Decision Making:** The process of making a selective intellectual judgment when presented with several complex alternatives consisting of several variables, and usually defining a course of action or an idea. [NIH]

**Dementia:** An acquired organic mental disorder with loss of intellectual abilities of sufficient severity to interfere with social or occupational functioning. The dysfunction is multifaceted and involves memory, behavior, personality, judgment, attention, spatial relations, language, abstract thought, and other executive functions. The intellectual decline is usually progressive, and initially spares the level of consciousness. [NIH]

**Dendrites:** Extensions of the nerve cell body. They are short and branched and receive stimuli from other neurons. [NIH]

**Density:** The logarithm to the base 10 of the opacity of an exposed and processed film. [NIH]

**Dentate Gyrus:** Gray matter situated above the gyrus hippocampi. It is composed of three layers. The molecular layer is continuous with the hippocampus in the hippocampal fissure. The granular layer consists of closely arranged spherical or oval neurons, called granule cells, whose axons pass through the polymorphic layer ending on the dendrites of pyramidal cells in the hippocampus. [NIH]

**Depressive Disorder:** An affective disorder manifested by either a dysphoric mood or loss of interest or pleasure in usual activities. The mood disturbance is prominent and relatively persistent. [NIH]

**Dexamethasone:** (11 beta,16 alpha)-9-Fluoro-11,17,21-trihydroxy-16-methylpregna-1,4-diene-3,20-dione. An anti-inflammatory glucocorticoid used either in the free alcohol or esterified form in treatment of conditions that respond generally to cortisone. [NIH]

**Dextroamphetamine:** The d-form of amphetamine. It is a central nervous system stimulant and a sympathomimetic. It has also been used in the treatment of narcolepsy and of attention deficit disorders and hyperactivity in children. Dextroamphetamine has multiple mechanisms of action including blocking uptake of adrenergics and dopamine, stimulating release of monamines, and inhibiting monoamine oxidase. It is also a drug of abuse and a psychotomimetic. [NIH]

**Diabetes Mellitus:** A heterogeneous group of disorders that share glucose intolerance in common. [NIH]

**Diagnostic procedure:** A method used to identify a disease. [NIH]

**Diaphragm:** The musculofibrous partition that separates the thoracic cavity from the abdominal cavity. Contraction of the diaphragm increases the volume of the thoracic cavity aiding inspiration. [NIH]

**Diathesis:** A constitution or condition of the body which makes the tissues react in special ways to certain extrinsic stimuli and thus tends to make the person more than usually susceptible to certain diseases. [EU]

**Diencephalon:** The paired caudal parts of the prosencephalon from which the thalamus, hypothalamus, epithalamus, and subthalamus are derived. [NIH]

**Digestive system:** The organs that take in food and turn it into products that the body can use to stay healthy. Waste products the body cannot use leave the body through bowel movements. The digestive system includes the salivary glands, mouth, esophagus, stomach, liver, pancreas, gallbladder, small and large intestines, and rectum. [NIH]

**Direct:** 1. Straight; in a straight line. 2. Performed immediately and without the intervention of subsidiary means. [EU]

**Dissociation:** 1. The act of separating or state of being separated. 2. The separation of a molecule into two or more fragments (atoms, molecules, ions, or free radicals) produced by the absorption of light or thermal energy or by solvation. 3. In psychology, a defense mechanism in which a group of mental processes are segregated from the rest of a person's mental activity in order to avoid emotional distress, as in the dissociative disorders (q.v.), or in which an idea or object is segregated from its emotional significance; in the first sense it is roughly equivalent to splitting, in the second, to isolation. 4. A defect of mental integration in which one or more groups of mental processes become separated off from normal consciousness and, thus separated, function as a unitary whole. [EU]

**Dissociative Disorders:** Sudden temporary alterations in the normally integrative functions of consciousness. [NIH]

**Dopamine:** An endogenous catecholamine and prominent neurotransmitter in several systems of the brain. In the synthesis of catecholamines from tyrosine, it is the immediate precursor to norepinephrine and epinephrine. Dopamine is a major transmitter in the extrapyramidal system of the brain, and important in regulating movement. A family of dopaminergic receptor subtypes mediate its action. Dopamine is used pharmacologically for its direct (beta adrenergic agonist) and indirect (adrenergic releasing) sympathomimetic effects including its actions as an inotropic agent and as a renal vasodilator. [NIH]

**Drive:** A state of internal activity of an organism that is a necessary condition before a given stimulus will elicit a class of responses; e.g., a certain level of hunger (drive) must be present before food will elicit an eating response. [NIH]

**Drug Interactions:** The action of a drug that may affect the activity, metabolism, or toxicity of another drug. [NIH]

**Dysphoric:** A feeling of unpleasantness and discomfort. [NIH]

**Eating Disorders:** A group of disorders characterized by physiological and psychological disturbances in appetite or food intake. [NIH]

**Efficacy:** The extent to which a specific intervention, procedure, regimen, or service produces a beneficial result under ideal conditions. Ideally, the determination of efficacy is based on the results of a randomized control trial. [NIH]

**Ego:** The conscious portion of the personality structure which serves to mediate between the demands of the primitive instinctual drives, (the id), of internalized parental and social prohibitions or the conscience, (the superego), and of reality. [NIH]

**Ejaculation:** The release of semen through the penis during orgasm. [NIH]

**Electroconvulsive Therapy:** Electrically induced convulsions primarily used in the treatment of severe affective disorders and schizophrenia. [NIH]

**Electroencephalography:** Recording of electric currents developed in the brain by means of electrodes applied to the scalp, to the surface of the brain, or placed within the substance of the brain. [NIH]

**Electrolyte:** A substance that dissociates into ions when fused or in solution, and thus becomes capable of conducting electricity; an ionic solute. [EU]

**Electrons:** Stable elementary particles having the smallest known negative charge, present in all elements; also called negatrons. Positively charged electrons are called positrons. The numbers, energies and arrangement of electrons around atomic nuclei determine the chemical identities of elements. Beams of electrons are called cathode rays or beta rays, the latter being a high-energy biproduct of nuclear decay. [NIH]

**Elementary Particles:** Individual components of atoms, usually subatomic; subnuclear particles are usually detected only when the atomic nucleus decays and then only transiently, as most of them are unstable, often yielding pure energy without substance, i.e., radiation. [NIH]

**Empirical:** A treatment based on an assumed diagnosis, prior to receiving confirmatory laboratory test results. [NIH]

**Endocrine System:** The system of glands that release their secretions (hormones) directly into the circulatory system. In addition to the endocrine glands, included are the chromaffin system and the neurosecretory systems. [NIH]

**Endometrial:** Having to do with the endometrium (the layer of tissue that lines the uterus). [NIH]

**Endometrium:** The layer of tissue that lines the uterus. [NIH]

**Energy balance:** Energy is the capacity of a body or a physical system for doing work. Energy balance is the state in which the total energy intake equals total energy needs. [NIH]

**Entorhinal Cortex:** Cortex where the signals are combined with those from other sensory systems. [NIH]

**Environmental Health:** The science of controlling or modifying those conditions, influences, or forces surrounding man which relate to promoting, establishing, and maintaining health. [NIH]

**Enzyme:** A protein that speeds up chemical reactions in the body. [NIH]

**Epidemiological:** Relating to, or involving epidemiology. [EU]

**Epinephrine:** The active sympathomimetic hormone from the adrenal medulla in most species. It stimulates both the alpha- and beta- adrenergic systems, causes systemic vasoconstriction and gastrointestinal relaxation, stimulates the heart, and dilates bronchi and cerebral vessels. It is used in asthma and cardiac failure and to delay absorption of local anesthetics. [NIH]

**Esophagus:** The muscular tube through which food passes from the throat to the stomach. [NIH]

**Estrogen:** One of the two female sex hormones. [NIH]

**Ether:** One of a class of organic compounds in which any two organic radicals are attached directly to a single oxygen atom. [NIH]

**Excitability:** Property of a cardiac cell whereby, when the cell is depolarized to a critical level (called threshold), the membrane becomes permeable and a regenerative inward current causes an action potential. [NIH]

**Expert Testimony:** Presentation of pertinent data by one with special skill or knowledge representing mastery of a particular subject. [NIH]

**Expiration:** The act of breathing out, or expelling air from the lungs. [EU]

**Extracellular:** Outside a cell or cells. [EU]

**Extrapyramidal:** Outside of the pyramidal tracts. [EU]

**Family Planning:** Programs or services designed to assist the family in controlling reproduction by either improving or diminishing fertility. [NIH]

**Family Practice:** A medical specialty concerned with the provision of continuing, comprehensive primary health care for the entire family. [NIH]

**Fat:** Total lipids including phospholipids. [NIH]

**Fatigue:** The state of weariness following a period of exertion, mental or physical, characterized by a decreased capacity for work and reduced efficiency to respond to stimuli. [NIH]

**Fissure:** Any cleft or groove, normal or otherwise; especially a deep fold in the cerebral cortex which involves the entire thickness of the brain wall. [EU]

**Fluoxetine:** The first highly specific serotonin uptake inhibitor. It is used as an antidepressant and often has a more acceptable side-effects profile than traditional antidepressants. [NIH]

**Flush:** Transient, episodic redness of the face and neck caused by certain diseases, ingestion of certain drugs or other substances, heat, emotional factors, or physical exertion. [EU]

**Focus Groups:** A method of data collection and a qualitative research tool in which a small group of individuals are brought together and allowed to interact in a discussion of their opinions about topics, issues, or questions. [NIH]

**Forearm:** The part between the elbow and the wrist. [NIH]

**Forensic Psychiatry:** Psychiatry in its legal aspects. This includes criminology, penology, commitment of mentally ill, the psychiatrist's role in compensation cases, the problems of releasing information to the court, and of expert testimony. [NIH]

**Frontal Lobe:** The anterior part of the cerebral hemisphere. [NIH]

**Gallbladder:** The pear-shaped organ that sits below the liver. Bile is concentrated and stored in the gallbladder. [NIH]

**Gas:** Air that comes from normal breakdown of food. The gases are passed out of the body through the rectum (flatus) or the mouth (burp). [NIH]

**Gastrointestinal:** Refers to the stomach and intestines. [NIH]

**Gastrointestinal tract:** The stomach and intestines. [NIH]

**Gene:** The functional and physical unit of heredity passed from parent to offspring. Genes are pieces of DNA, and most genes contain the information for making a specific protein. [NIH]

**Genetics:** The biological science that deals with the phenomena and mechanisms of heredity. [NIH]

**Glossopharyngeal Nerve:** The 9th cranial nerve. The glossopharyngeal nerve is a mixed motor and sensory nerve; it conveys somatic and autonomic efferents as well as general, special, and visceral afferents. Among the connections are motor fibers to the stylopharyngeus muscle, parasympathetic fibers to the parotid glands, general and taste afferents from the posterior third of the tongue, the nasopharynx, and the palate, and afferents from baroreceptors and chemoreceptors of the carotid sinus. [NIH]

**Glucocorticoid:** A compound that belongs to the family of compounds called corticosteroids (steroids). Glucocorticoids affect metabolism and have anti-inflammatory and immunosuppressive effects. They may be naturally produced (hormones) or synthetic (drugs). [NIH]

**Glucose:** D-Glucose. A primary source of energy for living organisms. It is naturally occurring and is found in fruits and other parts of plants in its free state. It is used therapeutically in fluid and nutrient replacement. [NIH]

**Glucose Intolerance:** A pathological state in which the fasting plasma glucose level is less than 140 mg per deciliter and the 30-, 60-, or 90-minute plasma glucose concentration following a glucose tolerance test exceeds 200 mg per deciliter. This condition is seen frequently in diabetes mellitus but also occurs with other diseases. [NIH]

**Governing Board:** The group in which legal authority is vested for the control of health-related institutions and organizations. [NIH]

**Growth:** The progressive development of a living being or part of an organism from its earliest stage to maturity. [NIH]

**Habitual:** Of the nature of a habit; according to habit; established by or repeated by force of habit, customary. [EU]

**Halogens:** A family of nonmetallic, generally electronegative, elements of group VIIa of the periodic table. They are all multivalent and have oxidation numbers of -1 (the most common), 1, 3, 5, and 7. [NIH]

**Headache:** Pain in the cranial region that may occur as an isolated and benign symptom or as a manifestation of a wide variety of conditions including subarachnoid hemorrhage; craniocerebral trauma; central nervous system infections; intracranial hypertension; and other disorders. In general, recurrent headaches that are not associated with a primary disease process are referred to as headache disorders (e.g., migraine). [NIH]

**Headache Disorders:** Common conditions characterized by persistent or recurrent headaches. Headache syndrome classification systems may be based on etiology (e.g., vascular headache, post-traumatic headaches, etc.), temporal pattern (e.g., cluster headache, paroxysmal hemicrania, etc.), and precipitating factors (e.g., cough headache). [NIH]

**Health Services:** Services for the diagnosis and treatment of disease and the maintenance of health. [NIH]

**Health Status:** The level of health of the individual, group, or population as subjectively assessed by the individual or by more objective measures. [NIH]

**Heart attack:** A seizure of weak or abnormal functioning of the heart. [NIH]

**Hemorrhage:** Bleeding or escape of blood from a vessel. [NIH]

**Hemostasis:** The process which spontaneously arrests the flow of blood from vessels carrying blood under pressure. It is accomplished by contraction of the vessels, adhesion and aggregation of formed blood elements, and the process of blood or plasma coagulation. [NIH]

**Heredity:** 1. The genetic transmission of a particular quality or trait from parent to offspring. 2. The genetic constitution of an individual. [EU]

**Hippocampus:** A curved elevation of gray matter extending the entire length of the floor of the temporal horn of the lateral ventricle (Dorland, 28th ed). The hippocampus, subiculum, and dentate gyrus constitute the hippocampal formation. Sometimes authors include the entorhinal cortex in the hippocampal formation. [NIH]

**Homogeneous:** Consisting of or composed of similar elements or ingredients; of a uniform quality throughout. [EU]

**Hormone:** A substance in the body that regulates certain organs. Hormones such as gastrin help in breaking down food. Some hormones come from cells in the stomach and small intestine. [NIH]

**Hydrogen:** The first chemical element in the periodic table. It has the atomic symbol H, atomic number 1, and atomic weight 1. It exists, under normal conditions, as a colorless, odorless, tasteless, diatomic gas. Hydrogen ions are protons. Besides the common H1 isotope, hydrogen exists as the stable isotope deuterium and the unstable, radioactive isotope tritium. [NIH]

**Hygienic:** Pertaining to hygiene, or conducive to health. [EU]

**Hypertension:** Persistently high arterial blood pressure. Currently accepted threshold levels are 140 mm Hg systolic and 90 mm Hg diastolic pressure. [NIH]

**Hypertrophy:** General increase in bulk of a part or organ, not due to tumor formation, nor to an increase in the number of cells. [NIH]

**Hypnotherapy:** Sleeping-cure. [NIH]

**Hypnotic:** A drug that acts to induce sleep. [EU]

**Hypoglycemia:** Abnormally low blood sugar [NIH]

**Hypothalamic:** Of or involving the hypothalamus. [EU]

**Hypothalamus:** Ventral part of the diencephalon extending from the region of the optic chiasm to the caudal border of the mammillary bodies and forming the inferior and lateral walls of the third ventricle. [NIH]

**Hysteria:** Historical term for a chronic, but fluctuating, disorder beginning in early life and characterized by recurrent and multiple somatic complaints not apparently due to physical illness. This diagnosis is not used in contemporary practice. [NIH]

**Id:** The part of the personality structure which harbors the unconscious instinctive desires and strivings of the individual. [NIH]

**Impairment:** In the context of health experience, an impairment is any loss or abnormality of psychological, physiological, or anatomical structure or function. [NIH]

**Impulse Control Disorders:** Disorders whose essential features are the failure to resist an impulse, drive, or temptation to perform an act that is harmful to the individual or to others. Individuals experience an increased sense of tension prior to the act and pleasure, gratification, or release of tension at the time of committing the act. [NIH]

**In vitro:** In the laboratory (outside the body). The opposite of in vivo (in the body). [NIH]

**In vivo:** In the body. The opposite of in vitro (outside the body or in the laboratory). [NIH]

**Indicative:** That indicates; that points out more or less exactly; that reveals fairly clearly. [EU]

**Infarction:** A pathological process consisting of a sudden insufficient blood supply to an area, which results in necrosis of that area. It is usually caused by a thrombus, an embolus, or a vascular torsion. [NIH]

**Ingestion:** Taking into the body by mouth [NIH]

**Initiation:** Mutation induced by a chemical reactive substance causing cell changes; being a step in a carcinogenic process. [NIH]

**Inotropic:** Affecting the force or energy of muscular contractions. [EU]

**Inpatients:** Persons admitted to health facilities which provide board and room, for the purpose of observation, care, diagnosis or treatment. [NIH]

**Insight:** The capacity to understand one's own motives, to be aware of one's own psychodynamics, to appreciate the meaning of symbolic behavior. [NIH]

**Insomnia:** Difficulty in going to sleep or getting enough sleep. [NIH]

**Interpersonal Relations:** The reciprocal interaction of two or more persons. [NIH]

**Invasive:** 1. Having the quality of invasiveness. 2. Involving puncture or incision of the skin or insertion of an instrument or foreign material into the body; said of diagnostic techniques. [EU]

**Involuntary:** Reaction occurring without intention or volition. [NIH]

**Ions:** An atom or group of atoms that have a positive or negative electric charge due to a gain (negative charge) or loss (positive charge) of one or more electrons. Atoms with a positive charge are known as cations; those with a negative charge are anions. [NIH]

**Kb:** A measure of the length of DNA fragments, 1 Kb = 1000 base pairs. The largest DNA fragments are up to 50 kilobases long. [NIH]

**Large Intestine:** The part of the intestine that goes from the cecum to the rectum. The large intestine absorbs water from stool and changes it from a liquid to a solid form. The large intestine is 5 feet long and includes the appendix, cecum, colon, and rectum. Also called colon. [NIH]

**Larynx:** An irregularly shaped, musculocartilaginous tubular structure, lined with mucous membrane, located at the top of the trachea and below the root of the tongue and the hyoid bone. It is the essential sphincter guarding the entrance into the trachea and functioning secondarily as the organ of voice. [NIH]

**Leptin:** A 16-kD peptide hormone secreted from white adipocytes and implicated in the regulation of food intake and energy balance. Leptin provides the key afferent signal from fat cells in the feedback system that controls body fat stores. [NIH]

**Lesion:** An area of abnormal tissue change. [NIH]

**Lethal:** Deadly, fatal. [EU]

**Library Services:** Services offered to the library user. They include reference and circulation. [NIH]

**Life cycle:** The successive stages through which an organism passes from fertilized ovum or spore to the fertilized ovum or spore of the next generation. [NIH]

**Ligands:** A RNA simulation method developed by the MIT. [NIH]

**Limbic:** Pertaining to a limbus, or margin; forming a border around. [EU]

**Limbic System:** A set of forebrain structures common to all mammals that is defined functionally and anatomically. It is implicated in the higher integration of visceral, olfactory, and somatic information as well as homeostatic responses including fundamental survival behaviors (feeding, mating, emotion). For most authors, it includes the amygdala, epithalamus, gyrus cinguli, hippocampal formation (see hippocampus), hypothalamus, parahippocampal gyrus, septal nuclei, anterior nuclear group of thalamus, and portions of the basal ganglia. (Parent, Carpenter's Human Neuroanatomy, 9th ed, p744; NeuroNames, http://rprcsgi.rprc.washington.edu/neuronames/index.html (September 2, 1998)). [NIH]

**Liver:** A large, glandular organ located in the upper abdomen. The liver cleanses the blood and aids in digestion by secreting bile. [NIH]

**Localized:** Cancer which has not metastasized yet. [NIH]

**Lumbar:** Pertaining to the loins, the part of the back between the thorax and the pelvis. [EU]

**Lumbar puncture:** A procedure in which a needle is put into the lower part of the spinal column to collect cerebrospinal fluid or to give anticancer drugs intrathecally. Also called a spinal tap. [NIH]

**Magnetic Resonance Imaging:** Non-invasive method of demonstrating internal anatomy based on the principle that atomic nuclei in a strong magnetic field absorb pulses of radiofrequency energy and emit them as radiowaves which can be reconstructed into computerized images. The concept includes proton spin tomographic techniques. [NIH]

**Magnetic Resonance Spectroscopy:** Spectroscopic method of measuring the magnetic moment of elementary particles such as atomic nuclei, protons or electrons. It is employed in clinical applications such as NMR Tomography (magnetic resonance imaging). [NIH]

**Manic:** Affected with mania. [EU]

**Manifest:** Being the part or aspect of a phenomenon that is directly observable : concretely expressed in behaviour. [EU]

**Mastication:** The act and process of chewing and grinding food in the mouth. [NIH]

**Meatus:** A canal running from the internal auditory foramen through the petrous portion of the temporal bone. It gives passage to the facial and auditory nerves together with the auditory branch of the basilar artery and the internal auditory veins. [NIH]

**Mediate:** Indirect; accomplished by the aid of an intervening medium. [EU]

**Mediator:** An object or substance by which something is mediated, such as (1) a structure of the nervous system that transmits impulses eliciting a specific response; (2) a chemical substance (transmitter substance) that induces activity in an excitable tissue, such as nerve or muscle; or (3) a substance released from cells as the result of the interaction of antigen with antibody or by the action of antigen with a sensitized lymphocyte. [EU]

**MEDLINE:** An online database of MEDLARS, the computerized bibliographic Medical Literature Analysis and Retrieval System of the National Library of Medicine. [NIH]

**Membrane:** A very thin layer of tissue that covers a surface. [NIH]

**Memory:** Complex mental function having four distinct phases: (1) memorizing or learning, (2) retention, (3) recall, and (4) recognition. Clinically, it is usually subdivided into immediate, recent, and remote memory. [NIH]

**Menstrual Cycle:** The period of the regularly recurring physiologic changes in the endometrium occurring during the reproductive period in human females and some primates and culminating in partial sloughing of the endometrium (menstruation). [NIH]

**Menstruation:** The normal physiologic discharge through the vagina of blood and mucosal tissues from the nonpregnant uterus. [NIH]

**Mental Disorders:** Psychiatric illness or diseases manifested by breakdowns in the adaptational process expressed primarily as abnormalities of thought, feeling, and behavior producing either distress or impairment of function. [NIH]

**Mental Health:** The state wherein the person is well adjusted. [NIH]

**Mental Processes:** Conceptual functions or thinking in all its forms. [NIH]

**Metabolite:** Any substance produced by metabolism or by a metabolic process. [EU]

**Methylphenidate:** A central nervous system stimulant used most commonly in the treatment of attention-deficit disorders in children and for narcolepsy. Its mechanisms appear to be similar to those of dextroamphetamine. [NIH]

**MI:** Myocardial infarction. Gross necrosis of the myocardium as a result of interruption of the blood supply to the area; it is almost always caused by atherosclerosis of the coronary arteries, upon which coronary thrombosis is usually superimposed. [NIH]

**Microbiology:** The study of microorganisms such as fungi, bacteria, algae, archaea, and viruses. [NIH]

**Molecular:** Of, pertaining to, or composed of molecules : a very small mass of matter. [EU]

**Molecule:** A chemical made up of two or more atoms. The atoms in a molecule can be the same (an oxygen molecule has two oxygen atoms) or different (a water molecule has two hydrogen atoms and one oxygen atom). Biological molecules, such as proteins and DNA, can be made up of many thousands of atoms. [NIH]

**Monoamine:** Enzyme that breaks down dopamine in the astrocytes and microglia. [NIH]

**Monoamine Oxidase:** An enzyme that catalyzes the oxidative deamination of naturally occurring monoamines. It is a flavin-containing enzyme that is localized in mitochondrial membranes, whether in nerve terminals, the liver, or other organs. Monoamine oxidase is important in regulating the metabolic degradation of catecholamines and serotonin in neural or target tissues. Hepatic monoamine oxidase has a crucial defensive role in inactivating circulating monoamines or those, such as tyramine, that originate in the gut and are absorbed into the portal circulation. (From Goodman and Gilman's, The Pharmacological Basis of Therapeutics, 8th ed, p415) EC 1.4.3.4. [NIH]

**Mood Disorders:** Those disorders that have a disturbance in mood as their predominant feature. [NIH]

**Morphine:** The principal alkaloid in opium and the prototype opiate analgesic and narcotic. Morphine has widespread effects in the central nervous system and on smooth muscle. [NIH]

**Motility:** The ability to move spontaneously. [EU]

**Motor nerve:** An efferent nerve conveying an impulse that excites muscular contraction. [NIH]

**Multiple Personality Disorder:** A dissociative disorder in which the individual adopts two or more distinct personalities. Each personality is a fully integrated and complex unit with memories, behavior patterns and social friendships. Transition from one personality to another is sudden. [NIH]

**Multivalent:** Pertaining to a group of 5 or more homologous or partly homologous chromosomes during the zygotene stage of prophase to first metaphasis in meiosis. [NIH]

**Mutilation:** Injuries to the body. [NIH]

**Myocardium:** The muscle tissue of the heart composed of striated, involuntary muscle known as cardiac muscle. [NIH]

**Naloxone:** A specific opiate antagonist that has no agonist activity. It is a competitive antagonist at mu, delta, and kappa opioid receptors. [NIH]

**Narcolepsy:** A condition of unknown cause characterized by a periodic uncontrollable tendency to fall asleep. [NIH]

**Nasopharynx:** The nasal part of the pharynx, lying above the level of the soft palate. [NIH]

**Nausea:** An unpleasant sensation in the stomach usually accompanied by the urge to vomit. Common causes are early pregnancy, sea and motion sickness, emotional stress, intense pain, food poisoning, and various enteroviruses. [NIH]

**NCI:** National Cancer Institute. NCI, part of the National Institutes of Health of the United States Department of Health and Human Services, is the federal government's principal agency for cancer research. NCI conducts, coordinates, and funds cancer research, training, health information dissemination, and other programs with respect to the cause, diagnosis, prevention, and treatment of cancer. Access the NCI Web site at http://cancer.gov. [NIH]

**Necrosis:** A pathological process caused by the progressive degradative action of enzymes that is generally associated with severe cellular trauma. It is characterized by mitochondrial swelling, nuclear flocculation, uncontrolled cell lysis, and ultimately cell death. [NIH]

**Need:** A state of tension or dissatisfaction felt by an individual that impels him to action toward a goal he believes will satisfy the impulse. [NIH]

**Nerve:** A cordlike structure of nervous tissue that connects parts of the nervous system with other tissues of the body and conveys nervous impulses to, or away from, these tissues. [NIH]

**Nervous System:** The entire nerve apparatus composed of the brain, spinal cord, nerves and ganglia. [NIH]

**Neural:** 1. Pertaining to a nerve or to the nerves. 2. Situated in the region of the spinal axis, as the neutral arch. [EU]

**Neuroendocrine:** Having to do with the interactions between the nervous system and the endocrine system. Describes certain cells that release hormones into the blood in response to stimulation of the nervous system. [NIH]

**Neuroleptic:** A term coined to refer to the effects on cognition and behaviour of antipsychotic drugs, which produce a state of apathy, lack of initiative, and limited range of emotion and in psychotic patients cause a reduction in confusion and agitation and normalization of psychomotor activity. [EU]

**Neuronal:** Pertaining to a neuron or neurons (= conducting cells of the nervous system). [EU]

**Neurons:** The basic cellular units of nervous tissue. Each neuron consists of a body, an axon, and dendrites. Their purpose is to receive, conduct, and transmit impulses in the nervous system. [NIH]

**Neuropeptide:** A member of a class of protein-like molecules made in the brain. Neuropeptides consist of short chains of amino acids, with some functioning as neurotransmitters and some functioning as hormones. [NIH]

**Neuropharmacology:** The branch of pharmacology dealing especially with the action of drugs upon various parts of the nervous system. [NIH]

**Neurosis:** Functional derangement due to disorders of the nervous system which does not affect the psychic personality of the patient. [NIH]

**Niacin:** Water-soluble vitamin of the B complex occurring in various animal and plant tissues. Required by the body for the formation of coenzymes NAD and NADP. Has pellagra-curative, vasodilating, and antilipemic properties. [NIH]

**Nitrogen:** An element with the atomic symbol N, atomic number 7, and atomic weight 14. Nitrogen exists as a diatomic gas and makes up about 78% of the earth's atmosphere by volume. It is a constituent of proteins and nucleic acids and found in all living cells. [NIH]

**Nonverbal Communication:** Transmission of emotions, ideas, and attitudes between individuals in ways other than the spoken language. [NIH]

**Norepinephrine:** Precursor of epinephrine that is secreted by the adrenal medulla and is a widespread central and autonomic neurotransmitter. Norepinephrine is the principal transmitter of most postganglionic sympathetic fibers and of the diffuse projection system in the brain arising from the locus ceruleus. It is also found in plants and is used pharmacologically as a sympathomimetic. [NIH]

**Nuclei:** A body of specialized protoplasm found in nearly all cells and containing the chromosomes. [NIH]

**Nucleic acid:** Either of two types of macromolecule (DNA or RNA) formed by polymerization of nucleotides. Nucleic acids are found in all living cells and contain the information (genetic code) for the transfer of genetic information from one generation to the next. [NIH]

**Nucleus:** A body of specialized protoplasm found in nearly all cells and containing the chromosomes. [NIH]

**Nursing Care:** Care given to patients by nursing service personnel. [NIH]

**Nursing Staff:** Personnel who provide nursing service to patients in an organized facility, institution, or agency. [NIH]

**Opacity:** Degree of density (area most dense taken for reading). [NIH]

**Orgasm:** The crisis of sexual excitement in either humans or animals. [NIH]

**Outpatient:** A patient who is not an inmate of a hospital but receives diagnosis or treatment in a clinic or dispensary connected with the hospital. [NIH]

**Ovum:** A female germ cell extruded from the ovary at ovulation. [NIH]

**Oxidation:** The act of oxidizing or state of being oxidized. Chemically it consists in the increase of positive charges on an atom or the loss of negative charges. Most biological oxidations are accomplished by the removal of a pair of hydrogen atoms (dehydrogenation) from a molecule. Such oxidations must be accompanied by reduction of an acceptor molecule. Univalent o. indicates loss of one electron; divalent o., the loss of two electrons. [EU]

**Oxygen Consumption:** The oxygen consumption is determined by calculating the difference between the amount of oxygen inhaled and exhaled. [NIH]

**Palate:** The structure that forms the roof of the mouth. It consists of the anterior hard palate and the posterior soft palate. [NIH]

**Palliative:** 1. Affording relief, but not cure. 2. An alleviating medicine. [EU]

**Pancreas:** A mixed exocrine and endocrine gland situated transversely across the posterior abdominal wall in the epigastric and hypochondriac regions. The endocrine portion is comprised of the Islets of Langerhans, while the exocrine portion is a compound acinar gland that secretes digestive enzymes. [NIH]

**Pancreatic:** Having to do with the pancreas. [NIH]

**Parietal:** 1. Of or pertaining to the walls of a cavity. 2. Pertaining to or located near the parietal bone, as the parietal lobe. [EU]

**Parietal Lobe:** Upper central part of the cerebral hemisphere. [NIH]

**Parotid:** The space that contains the parotid gland, the facial nerve, the external carotid artery, and the retromandibular vein. [NIH]

**Paroxetine:** A serotonin uptake inhibitor that is effective in the treatment of depression. [NIH]

**Partial remission:** The shrinking, but not complete disappearance, of a tumor in response to therapy. Also called partial response. [NIH]

**Partnership Practice:** A voluntary contract between two or more doctors who may or may not share responsibility for the care of patients, with proportional sharing of profits and losses. [NIH]

**Penis:** The external reproductive organ of males. It is composed of a mass of erectile tissue enclosed in three cylindrical fibrous compartments. Two of the three compartments, the corpus cavernosa, are placed side-by-side along the upper part of the organ. The third compartment below, the corpus spongiosum, houses the urethra . [NIH]

**Peptide:** Any compound consisting of two or more amino acids, the building blocks of proteins. Peptides are combined to make proteins. [NIH]

**Perception:** The ability quickly and accurately to recognize similarities and differences among presented objects, whether these be pairs of words, pairs of number series, or multiple sets of these or other symbols such as geometric figures. [NIH]

**Personality Disorders:** A major deviation from normal patterns of behavior. [NIH]

**Pharmacologic:** Pertaining to pharmacology or to the properties and reactions of drugs. [EU]

**Pharmacotherapy:** A regimen of using appetite suppressant medications to manage obesity by decreasing appetite or increasing the feeling of satiety. These medications decrease appetite by increasing serotonin or catecholamine—two brain chemicals that affect mood and appetite. [NIH]

**Pharynx:** The hollow tube about 5 inches long that starts behind the nose and ends at the top of the trachea (windpipe) and esophagus (the tube that goes to the stomach). [NIH]

**Phobia:** A persistent, irrational, intense fear of a specific object, activity, or situation (the phobic stimulus), fear that is recognized as being excessive or unreasonable by the individual himself. When a phobia is a significant source of distress or interferes with social functioning, it is considered a mental disorder; phobic disorder (or neurosis). In DSM III phobic disorders are subclassified as agoraphobia, social phobias, and simple phobias. Used as a word termination denoting irrational fear of or aversion to the subject indicated by the stem to which it is affixed. [EU]

**Phobic Disorders:** Anxiety disorders in which the essential feature is persistent and irrational fear of a specific object, activity, or situation that the individual feels compelled to avoid. The individual recognizes the fear as excessive or unreasonable. [NIH]

**Phrenic Nerve:** The motor nerve of the diaphragm. The phrenic nerve fibers originate in the cervical spinal column (mostly C4) and travel through the cervical plexus to the diaphragm. [NIH]

**Physiologic:** Having to do with the functions of the body. When used in the phrase "physiologic age," it refers to an age assigned by general health, as opposed to calendar age. [NIH]

**Physostigmine:** A cholinesterase inhibitor that is rapidly absorbed through membranes. It can be applied topically to the conjunctiva. It also can cross the blood-brain barrier and is used when central nervous system effects are desired, as in the treatment of severe anticholinergic toxicity. [NIH]

**Pilot study:** The initial study examining a new method or treatment. [NIH]

**Pituitary Gland:** A small, unpaired gland situated in the sella turcica tissue. It is connected to the hypothalamus by a short stalk. [NIH]

**Post partum:** After childbirth, or after delivery. [EU]

**Posterior:** Situated in back of, or in the back part of, or affecting the back or dorsal surface of the body. In lower animals, it refers to the caudal end of the body. [EU]

**Post-traumatic:** Occurring as a result of or after injury. [EU]

**Post-traumatic stress disorder:** A psychological disorder that develops in some individuals after a major traumatic experience such as war, rape, domestic violence, or accident. [NIH]

**Practicability:** A non-standard characteristic of an analytical procedure. It is dependent on the scope of the method and is determined by requirements such as sample throughout and costs. [NIH]

**Practice Guidelines:** Directions or principles presenting current or future rules of policy for the health care practitioner to assist him in patient care decisions regarding diagnosis, therapy, or related clinical circumstances. The guidelines may be developed by government agencies at any level, institutions, professional societies, governing boards, or by the convening of expert panels. The guidelines form a basis for the evaluation of all aspects of health care and delivery. [NIH]

**Preceptorship:** Practical experience in medical and health-related services that occurs as part of an educational program wherein the professionally-trained student works outside the academic environment under the supervision of an established professional in the particular field. [NIH]

**Precursor:** Something that precedes. In biological processes, a substance from which another, usually more active or mature substance is formed. In clinical medicine, a sign or symptom that heralds another. [EU]

**Prefrontal Cortex:** The rostral part of the frontal lobe, bounded by the inferior precentral fissure in humans, which receives projection fibers from the mediodorsal nucleus of the thalamus. The prefrontal cortex receives afferent fibers from numerous structures of the diencephalon, mesencephalon, and limbic system as well as cortical afferents of visual, auditory, and somatic origin. [NIH]

**Premenstrual:** Occurring before menstruation. [EU]

**Premenstrual Syndrome:** A syndrome occurring most often during the last week of the menstrual cycle and ending soon after the onset of menses. Some of the symptoms are emotional instability, insomnia, headache, nausea, vomiting, abdominal distension, and painful breasts. [NIH]

**Prevalence:** The total number of cases of a given disease in a specified population at a designated time. It is differentiated from incidence, which refers to the number of new cases in the population at a given time. [NIH]

**Private Practice:** Practice of a health profession by an individual, offering services on a person-to-person basis, as opposed to group or partnership practice. [NIH]

**Prognostic factor:** A situation or condition, or a characteristic of a patient, that can be used to estimate the chance of recovery from a disease, or the chance of the disease recurring (coming back). [NIH]

**Progression:** Increase in the size of a tumor or spread of cancer in the body. [NIH]

**Progressive:** Advancing; going forward; going from bad to worse; increasing in scope or severity. [EU]

**Projection:** A defense mechanism, operating unconsciously, whereby that which is emotionally unacceptable in the self is rejected and attributed (projected) to others. [NIH]

**Prophylaxis:** An attempt to prevent disease. [NIH]

**Prospective study:** An epidemiologic study in which a group of individuals (a cohort), all free of a particular disease and varying in their exposure to a possible risk factor, is followed over a specific amount of time to determine the incidence rates of the disease in the exposed and unexposed groups. [NIH]

**Prosthesis:** An artificial replacement of a part of the body. [NIH]

**Protein S:** The vitamin K-dependent cofactor of activated protein C. Together with protein C, it inhibits the action of factors VIIIa and Va. A deficiency in protein S can lead to recurrent venous and arterial thrombosis. [NIH]

**Proteins:** Polymers of amino acids linked by peptide bonds. The specific sequence of amino acids determines the shape and function of the protein. [NIH]

**Protocol:** The detailed plan for a clinical trial that states the trial's rationale, purpose, drug or vaccine dosages, length of study, routes of administration, who may participate, and other aspects of trial design. [NIH]

**Protons:** Stable elementary particles having the smallest known positive charge, found in the nuclei of all elements. The proton mass is less than that of a neutron. A proton is the nucleus of the light hydrogen atom, i.e., the hydrogen ion. [NIH]

**Proxy:** A person authorized to decide or act for another person, for example, a person having durable power of attorney. [NIH]

**Psychiatric:** Pertaining to or within the purview of psychiatry. [EU]

**Psychiatry:** The medical science that deals with the origin, diagnosis, prevention, and treatment of mental disorders. [NIH]

**Psychic:** Pertaining to the psyche or to the mind; mental. [EU]

**Psychoacoustic:** That branch of psychophysics dealing with acoustic stimuli. [NIH]

**Psychoanalytic Therapy:** A form of psychiatric treatment, based on Freudian principles, which seeks to eliminate or diminish the undesirable effects of unconscious conflicts by making the patient aware of their existence, origin, and inappropriate expression in current emotions and behavior. [NIH]

**Psychology:** The science dealing with the study of mental processes and behavior in man and animals. [NIH]

**Psychomotor:** Pertaining to motor effects of cerebral or psychic activity. [EU]

**Psychopathology:** The study of significant causes and processes in the development of mental illness. [NIH]

**Psychophysics:** The science dealing with the correlation of the physical characteristics of a stimulus, e.g., frequency or intensity, with the response to the stimulus, in order to assess the psychologic factors involved in the relationship. [NIH]

**Psychotherapy:** A generic term for the treatment of mental illness or emotional disturbances primarily by verbal or nonverbal communication. [NIH]

**Psychotropic:** Exerting an effect upon the mind; capable of modifying mental activity; usually applied to drugs that effect the mental state. [EU]

**Public Health:** Branch of medicine concerned with the prevention and control of disease and disability, and the promotion of physical and mental health of the population on the international, national, state, or municipal level. [NIH]

**Public Policy:** A course or method of action selected, usually by a government, from among alternatives to guide and determine present and future decisions. [NIH]

**Pulmonary:** Relating to the lungs. [NIH]

**Pulmonary Artery:** The short wide vessel arising from the conus arteriosus of the right ventricle and conveying unaerated blood to the lungs. [NIH]

**Pulmonary hypertension:** Abnormally high blood pressure in the arteries of the lungs. [NIH]

**Punishment:** The application of an unpleasant stimulus or penalty for the purpose of eliminating or correcting undesirable behavior. [NIH]

**Randomized:** Describes an experiment or clinical trial in which animal or human subjects are assigned by chance to separate groups that compare different treatments. [NIH]

**Randomized clinical trial:** A study in which the participants are assigned by chance to separate groups that compare different treatments; neither the researchers nor the participants can choose which group. Using chance to assign people to groups means that the groups will be similar and that the treatments they receive can be compared objectively. At the time of the trial, it is not known which treatment is best. It is the patient's choice to be in a randomized trial. [NIH]

**Rape:** Unlawful sexual intercourse without consent of the victim. [NIH]

**Receptor:** A molecule inside or on the surface of a cell that binds to a specific substance and causes a specific physiologic effect in the cell. [NIH]

**Receptors, Serotonin:** Cell-surface proteins that bind serotonin and trigger intracellular changes which influence the behavior of cells. Several types of serotonin receptors have been recognized which differ in their pharmacology, molecular biology, and mode of action. [NIH]

**Rectum:** The last 8 to 10 inches of the large intestine. [NIH]

**Recurrence:** The return of a sign, symptom, or disease after a remission. [NIH]

**Refer:** To send or direct for treatment, aid, information, de decision. [NIH]

**Reflective:** Capable of throwing back light, images, sound waves : reflecting. [EU]

**Refraction:** A test to determine the best eyeglasses or contact lenses to correct a refractive error (myopia, hyperopia, or astigmatism). [NIH]

**Regimen:** A treatment plan that specifies the dosage, the schedule, and the duration of treatment. [NIH]

**Remission:** A decrease in or disappearance of signs and symptoms of cancer. In partial remission, some, but not all, signs and symptoms of cancer have disappeared. In complete remission, all signs and symptoms of cancer have disappeared, although there still may be cancer in the body. [NIH]

**Respiration:** The act of breathing with the lungs, consisting of inspiration, or the taking into the lungs of the ambient air, and of expiration, or the expelling of the modified air which contains more carbon dioxide than the air taken in (Blakiston's Gould Medical Dictionary, 4th ed.). This does not include tissue respiration (= oxygen consumption) or cell respiration (= cell respiration). [NIH]

**Retrospective:** Looking back at events that have already taken place. [NIH]

**Risk factor:** A habit, trait, condition, or genetic alteration that increases a person's chance of developing a disease. [NIH]

**Risperidone:** A selective blocker of dopamine D2 and serotonin-5-HT-2 receptors that acts as an atypical antipsychotic agent. It has been shown to improve both positive and negative symptoms in the treatment of schizophrenia. [NIH]

**Rod:** A reception for vision, located in the retina. [NIH]

**Salivary:** The duct that convey saliva to the mouth. [NIH]

**Salivary glands:** Glands in the mouth that produce saliva. [NIH]

**Schizoid:** Having qualities resembling those found in greater degree in schizophrenics; a person of schizoid personality. [NIH]

**Schizophrenia:** A mental disorder characterized by a special type of disintegration of the personality. [NIH]

**Screening:** Checking for disease when there are no symptoms. [NIH]

**Sediment:** A precipitate, especially one that is formed spontaneously. [EU]

**Seizures:** Clinical or subclinical disturbances of cortical function due to a sudden, abnormal, excessive, and disorganized discharge of brain cells. Clinical manifestations include abnormal motor, sensory and psychic phenomena. Recurrent seizures are usually referred to as epilepsy or "seizure disorder." [NIH]

**Self-Injurious Behavior:** Behavior in which persons hurt or harm themselves without the motive of suicide or of sexual deviation. [NIH]

**Semen:** The thick, yellowish-white, viscid fluid secretion of male reproductive organs discharged upon ejaculation. In addition to reproductive organ secretions, it contains spermatozoa and their nutrient plasma. [NIH]

**Serotonin:** A biochemical messenger and regulator, synthesized from the essential amino acid L-tryptophan. In humans it is found primarily in the central nervous system, gastrointestinal tract, and blood platelets. Serotonin mediates several important physiological functions including neurotransmission, gastrointestinal motility, hemostasis, and cardiovascular integrity. Multiple receptor families (receptors, serotonin) explain the broad physiological actions and distribution of this biochemical mediator. [NIH]

**Sex Characteristics:** Those characteristics that distinguish one sex from the other. The primary sex characteristics are the ovaries and testes and their related hormones. Secondary sex characteristics are those which are masculine or feminine but not directly related to reproduction. [NIH]

**Shame:** An emotional attitude excited by realization of a shortcoming or impropriety. [NIH]

**Shock:** The general bodily disturbance following a severe injury; an emotional or moral upset occasioned by some disturbing or unexpected experience; disruption of the circulation, which can upset all body functions: sometimes referred to as circulatory shock. [NIH]

**Side effect:** A consequence other than the one(s) for which an agent or measure is used, as the adverse effects produced by a drug, especially on a tissue or organ system other than the one sought to be benefited by its administration. [EU]

**Signs and Symptoms:** Clinical manifestations that can be either objective when observed by a physician, or subjective when perceived by the patient. [NIH]

**Skeletal:** Having to do with the skeleton (boney part of the body). [NIH]

**Sleep apnea:** A serious, potentially life-threatening breathing disorder characterized by repeated cessation of breathing due to either collapse of the upper airway during sleep or absence of respiratory effort. [NIH]

**Social Behavior:** Any behavior caused by or affecting another individual, usually of the same species. [NIH]

**Social Support:** Support systems that provide assistance and encouragement to individuals with physical or emotional disabilities in order that they may better cope. Informal social support is usually provided by friends, relatives, or peers, while formal assistance is provided by churches, groups, etc. [NIH]

**Sodium:** An element that is a member of the alkali group of metals. It has the atomic symbol Na, atomic number 11, and atomic weight 23. With a valence of 1, it has a strong affinity for oxygen and other nonmetallic elements. Sodium provides the chief cation of the extracellular body fluids. Its salts are the most widely used in medicine. (From Dorland, 27th ed) Physiologically the sodium ion plays a major role in blood pressure regulation, maintenance of fluid volume, and electrolyte balance. [NIH]

**Soma:** The body as distinct from the mind; all the body tissue except the germ cells; all the axial body. [NIH]

**Somatic:** 1. Pertaining to or characteristic of the soma or body. 2. Pertaining to the body wall in contrast to the viscera. [EU]

**Sound wave:** An alteration of properties of an elastic medium, such as pressure, particle displacement, or density, that propagates through the medium, or a superposition of such alterations. [NIH]

**Spasticity:** A state of hypertonicity, or increase over the normal tone of a muscle, with heightened deep tendon reflexes. [EU]

**Specialist:** In medicine, one who concentrates on 1 special branch of medical science. [NIH]

**Species:** A taxonomic category subordinate to a genus (or subgenus) and superior to a subspecies or variety, composed of individuals possessing common characters distinguishing them from other categories of individuals of the same taxonomic level. In taxonomic nomenclature, species are designated by the genus name followed by a Latin or Latinized adjective or noun. [EU]

**Specificity:** Degree of selectivity shown by an antibody with respect to the number and types of antigens with which the antibody combines, as well as with respect to the rates and the extents of these reactions. [NIH]

**Spectrum:** A charted band of wavelengths of electromagnetic vibrations obtained by refraction and diffraction. By extension, a measurable range of activity, such as the range of bacteria affected by an antibiotic (antibacterial s.) or the complete range of manifestations of a disease. [EU]

**Spinal cord:** The main trunk or bundle of nerves running down the spine through holes in the spinal bone (the vertebrae) from the brain to the level of the lower back. [NIH]

**Spinal tap:** A procedure in which a needle is put into the lower part of the spinal column to collect cerebrospinal fluid or to give anticancer drugs intrathecally. Also called a lumbar puncture. [NIH]

**Steel:** A tough, malleable, iron-based alloy containing up to, but no more than, two percent carbon and often other metals. It is used in medicine and dentistry in implants and instrumentation. [NIH]

**Steroid:** A group name for lipids that contain a hydrogenated cyclopentanoperhydrophenanthrene ring system. Some of the substances included in this group are progesterone, adrenocortical hormones, the gonadal hormones, cardiac aglycones, bile acids, sterols (such as cholesterol), toad poisons, saponins, and some of the carcinogenic hydrocarbons. [EU]

**Stimulant:** 1. Producing stimulation; especially producing stimulation by causing tension on muscle fibre through the nervous tissue. 2. An agent or remedy that produces stimulation. [EU]

**Stimulus:** That which can elicit or evoke action (response) in a muscle, nerve, gland or other excitable issue, or cause an augmenting action upon any function or metabolic process. [NIH]

**Stomach:** An organ of digestion situated in the left upper quadrant of the abdomen between the termination of the esophagus and the beginning of the duodenum. [NIH]

**Stress:** Forcibly exerted influence; pressure. Any condition or situation that causes strain or tension. Stress may be either physical or psychologic, or both. [NIH]

**Stroke:** Sudden loss of function of part of the brain because of loss of blood flow. Stroke may be caused by a clot (thrombosis) or rupture (hemorrhage) of a blood vessel to the brain. [NIH]

**Subarachnoid:** Situated or occurring between the arachnoid and the pia mater. [EU]

**Subclinical:** Without clinical manifestations; said of the early stage(s) of an infection or other disease or abnormality before symptoms and signs become apparent or detectable by clinical examination or laboratory tests, or of a very mild form of an infection or other disease or abnormality. [EU]

**Subiculum:** A region of the hippocampus that projects to other areas of the brain. [NIH]

**Subspecies:** A category intermediate in rank between species and variety, based on a smaller number of correlated characters than are used to differentiate species and generally conditioned by geographical and/or ecological occurrence. [NIH]

**Substance P:** An eleven-amino acid neurotransmitter that appears in both the central and peripheral nervous systems. It is involved in transmission of pain, causes rapid contractions of the gastrointestinal smooth muscle, and modulates inflammatory and immune responses. [NIH]

**Superego:** The component of the personality associated with ethics, standards, and self-criticism - the "conscience". It is derived mainly from identification with parents and parent substitutes. [NIH]

**Suppression:** A conscious exclusion of disapproved desire contrary with repression, in which the process of exclusion is not conscious. [NIH]

**Survival Analysis:** A class of statistical procedures for estimating the survival function (function of time, starting with a population 100% well at a given time and providing the percentage of the population still well at later times). The survival analysis is then used for making inferences about the effects of treatments, prognostic factors, exposures, and other covariates on the function. [NIH]

**Sympathomimetic:** 1. Mimicking the effects of impulses conveyed by adrenergic postganglionic fibres of the sympathetic nervous system. 2. An agent that produces effects similar to those of impulses conveyed by adrenergic postganglionic fibres of the sympathetic nervous system. Called also adrenergic. [EU]

**Symptomatic:** Having to do with symptoms, which are signs of a condition or disease. [NIH]

**Symptomatology:** 1. That branch of medicine with treats of symptoms; the systematic discussion of symptoms. 2. The combined symptoms of a disease. [EU]

**Systemic:** Affecting the entire body. [NIH]

**Temperament:** Predisposition to react to one's environment in a certain way; usually refers to mood changes. [NIH]

**Temporal:** One of the two irregular bones forming part of the lateral surfaces and base of the skull, and containing the organs of hearing. [NIH]

**Temporal Lobe:** Lower lateral part of the cerebral hemisphere. [NIH]

**Thalamus:** Paired bodies containing mostly gray substance and forming part of the lateral wall of the third ventricle of the brain. The thalamus represents the major portion of the diencephalon and is commonly divided into cellular aggregates known as nuclear groups. [NIH]

**Therapeutics:** The branch of medicine which is concerned with the treatment of diseases, palliative or curative. [NIH]

**Thermal:** Pertaining to or characterized by heat. [EU]

**Thoracic:** Having to do with the chest. [NIH]

**Thorax:** A part of the trunk between the neck and the abdomen; the chest. [NIH]

**Threshold:** For a specified sensory modality (e. g. light, sound, vibration), the lowest level (absolute threshold) or smallest difference (difference threshold, difference limen) or intensity of the stimulus discernible in prescribed conditions of stimulation. [NIH]

**Thrombosis:** The formation or presence of a blood clot inside a blood vessel. [NIH]

**Tissue:** A group or layer of cells that are alike in type and work together to perform a specific function. [NIH]

**Tolerance:** 1. The ability to endure unusually large doses of a drug or toxin. 2. Acquired drug tolerance; a decreasing response to repeated constant doses of a drug or the need for increasing doses to maintain a constant response. [EU]

**Tomography:** Imaging methods that result in sharp images of objects located on a chosen plane and blurred images located above or below the plane. [NIH]

**Tooth Preparation:** Procedures carried out with regard to the teeth or tooth structures preparatory to specified dental therapeutic and surgical measures. [NIH]

**Toxic:** Having to do with poison or something harmful to the body. Toxic substances usually cause unwanted side effects. [NIH]

**Toxicity:** The quality of being poisonous, especially the degree of virulence of a toxic microbe or of a poison. [EU]

**Toxicology:** The science concerned with the detection, chemical composition, and pharmacologic action of toxic substances or poisons and the treatment and prevention of toxic manifestations. [NIH]

**Traction:** The act of pulling. [NIH]

**Transcription Factors:** Endogenous substances, usually proteins, which are effective in the initiation, stimulation, or termination of the genetic transcription process. [NIH]

**Transfection:** The uptake of naked or purified DNA into cells, usually eukaryotic. It is analogous to bacterial transformation. [NIH]

**Transmitter:** A chemical substance which effects the passage of nerve impulses from one cell to the other at the synapse. [NIH]

**Trauma:** Any injury, wound, or shock, must frequently physical or structural shock, producing a disturbance. [NIH]

**Treatment Outcome:** Evaluation undertaken to assess the results or consequences of management and procedures used in combating disease in order to determine the efficacy, effectiveness, safety, practicability, etc., of these interventions in individual cases or series. [NIH]

**Tricuspid Atresia:** Absence of the orifice between the right atrium and ventricle, with the presence of an atrial defect through which all the systemic venous return reaches the left heart. As a result, there is left ventricular hypertrophy because the right ventricle is absent or not functional. [NIH]

**Trigeminal:** Cranial nerve V. It is sensory for the eyeball, the conjunctiva, the eyebrow, the skin of face and scalp, the teeth, the mucous membranes in the mouth and nose, and is motor to the muscles of mastication. [NIH]

**Tryptophan:** An essential amino acid that is necessary for normal growth in infants and for nitrogen balance in adults. It is a precursor serotonin and niacin. [NIH]

**Tyramine:** An indirect sympathomimetic. Tyramine does not directly activate adrenergic receptors, but it can serve as a substrate for adrenergic uptake systems and monoamine oxidase so it prolongs the actions of adrenergic transmitters. It also provokes transmitter release from adrenergic terminals. Tyramine may be a neurotransmitter in some invertebrate nervous systems. [NIH]

**Tyrosine:** A non-essential amino acid. In animals it is synthesized from phenylalanine. It is also the precursor of epinephrine, thyroid hormones, and melanin. [NIH]

**Unconscious:** Experience which was once conscious, but was subsequently rejected, as the "personal unconscious". [NIH]

**Urethra:** The tube through which urine leaves the body. It empties urine from the bladder. [NIH]

**Urinalysis:** Examination of urine by chemical, physical, or microscopic means. Routine urinalysis usually includes performing chemical screening tests, determining specific gravity, observing any unusual color or odor, screening for bacteriuria, and examining the sediment microscopically. [NIH]

**Urine:** Fluid containing water and waste products. Urine is made by the kidneys, stored in the bladder, and leaves the body through the urethra. [NIH]

**Uterus:** The small, hollow, pear-shaped organ in a woman's pelvis. This is the organ in which a fetus develops. Also called the womb. [NIH]

**Vaccine:** A substance or group of substances meant to cause the immune system to respond to a tumor or to microorganisms, such as bacteria or viruses. [NIH]

**Vagus Nerve:** The 10th cranial nerve. The vagus is a mixed nerve which contains somatic afferents (from skin in back of the ear and the external auditory meatus), visceral afferents (from the pharynx, larynx, thorax, and abdomen), parasympathetic efferents (to the thorax and abdomen), and efferents to striated muscle (of the larynx and pharynx). [NIH]

**Vasodilatation:** A state of increased calibre of the blood vessels. [EU]

**Vasodilator:** An agent that widens blood vessels. [NIH]

**VE:** The total volume of gas either inspired or expired in one minute. [NIH]

**Venous:** Of or pertaining to the veins. [EU]

**Ventral:** 1. Pertaining to the belly or to any venter. 2. Denoting a position more toward the belly surface than some other object of reference; same as anterior in human anatomy. [EU]

**Ventricle:** One of the two pumping chambers of the heart. The right ventricle receives oxygen-poor blood from the right atrium and pumps it to the lungs through the pulmonary artery. The left ventricle receives oxygen-rich blood from the left atrium and pumps it to the body through the aorta. [NIH]

**Ventricular:** Pertaining to a ventricle. [EU]

**Veterinary Medicine:** The medical science concerned with the prevention, diagnosis, and treatment of diseases in animals. [NIH]

**Viscera:** Any of the large interior organs in any one of the three great cavities of the body, especially in the abdomen. [NIH]

**Visceral:** , from viscus a viscus) pertaining to a viscus. [EU]

**Visceral Afferents:** The sensory fibers innervating the viscera. [NIH]

**Vivo:** Outside of or removed from the body of a living organism. [NIH]

**Volition:** Voluntary activity without external compulsion. [NIH]

**War:** Hostile conflict between organized groups of people. [NIH]

**Xenograft:** The cells of one species transplanted to another species. [NIH]

# INDEX

**A**
Abdominal, 119, 128, 137, 139
Aberrant, 17, 119
Acoustic, 119, 140
Adaptation, 5, 119
Adipocytes, 119, 133
Adjustment, 4, 54, 119
Adolescence, 85, 119
Adrenal Cortex, 119, 126
Adrenergic, 66, 119, 121, 128, 129, 144, 145
Adverse Effect, 119, 124, 142
Afferent, 119, 133, 139
Affinity, 119, 120, 121, 124, 142
Age of Onset, 24, 120
Agonist, 120, 123, 128, 135
Agoraphobia, 120, 138
Airway, 120, 142
Algorithms, 120, 122
Alkaloid, 120, 123, 135
Alternative medicine, 94, 120
Amenorrhea, 120
Amygdala, 5, 16, 19, 35, 44, 120, 133
Anal, 5, 24, 33, 61, 88, 120
Analgesic, 120, 123, 135
Anatomical, 5, 120, 121, 132
Animal model, 9, 16, 120
Anorexia, 22, 34, 61, 74, 78, 84, 95, 120
Anorexia Nervosa, 22, 34, 61, 74, 78, 84, 120
Antagonism, 120, 124
Antecedent, 12, 120
Antibacterial, 120, 143
Antibiotic, 120, 143
Antibody, 119, 120, 125, 134, 143
Anticholinergic, 121, 138
Anticonvulsant, 17, 121, 123
Antidepressant, 121, 130
Anti-inflammatory, 121, 127, 131
Antipsychotic, 121, 124, 136, 141
Anus, 120, 121, 123
Anxiety, 7, 8, 15, 16, 19, 46, 54, 72, 79, 85, 86, 121, 138
Anxiety Disorders, 7, 8, 121
Apnea, 121
Aqueous, 121, 122
Arterial, 121, 126, 132, 139
Arteries, 121, 122, 126, 134, 140
Assay, 19, 121
Astrocytes, 121, 135
Atrial, 121, 126, 145
Atrioventricular, 121, 126
Atrium, 121, 126, 145, 146
Atypical, 121, 124, 141
Auditory, 122, 134, 139, 146
Autonomic, 121, 122, 130, 136
**B**
Bacteria, 120, 122, 135, 143, 146
Bacterial Physiology, 119, 122
Bacteriuria, 122, 146
Base, 40, 45, 122, 127, 133, 144
Behavior Therapy, 4, 9, 10, 12, 13, 18, 20, 22, 30, 31, 46, 55, 59, 62, 71, 122
Benign, 122, 131
Binding Sites, 66, 122
Biochemical, 122, 142
Biotechnology, 21, 94, 103, 122
Bipolar Disorder, 17, 61, 108, 122
Bladder, 122, 145, 146
Blood Platelets, 122, 142
Blood pressure, 12, 122, 123, 132, 140, 142
Blood vessel, 122, 123, 124, 126, 143, 144, 146
Blood-Brain Barrier, 122, 138
Body Fluids, 122, 142
Bowel, 120, 122, 123, 128
Bowel Movement, 123, 128
Branch, 66, 115, 123, 134, 136, 140, 143, 144
Bulimia, 27, 42, 61, 84, 86, 95, 123
Buprenorphine, 12, 123
**C**
Carbamazepine, 33, 98, 123
Carbon Dioxide, 123, 124, 141
Cardiac, 123, 126, 129, 130, 135, 143
Cardiovascular, 86, 123, 142
Cardiovascular disease, 86, 123
Carotid Sinus, 84, 123, 131
Catecholamine, 123, 128, 138
Cell, 17, 20, 120, 122, 123, 125, 127, 130, 132, 136, 137, 141, 145
Cell Respiration, 123, 141
Central Nervous System, 123, 124, 127, 131, 134, 135, 138, 142
Central Nervous System Infections, 123, 131
Cerebellum, 123, 126

Cerebral, 71, 84, 122, 123, 124, 126, 129, 130, 137, 140, 144
Cerebral Palsy, 84, 123
Cerebrospinal, 123, 134, 143
Cerebrospinal fluid, 123, 134, 143
Cerebrovascular, 123, 124
Cerebrum, 123, 124, 126
Cervical, 124, 138
Cervical Plexus, 124, 138
Chaos, 45, 124
Character, 25, 59, 124
Chemoreceptors, 124, 131
Cholesterol, 57, 124, 126, 143
Chronic, 5, 12, 16, 17, 25, 28, 84, 86, 123, 124, 132
Clamp, 17, 124
Clinical study, 124, 126
Clinical trial, 3, 6, 31, 81, 82, 103, 124, 126, 139, 140
Cloning, 122, 124
Clozapine, 28, 29, 44, 94, 124
Cofactor, 124, 139
Cognition, 15, 124, 136
Collapse, 124, 142
Commitment of Mentally Ill, 124, 130
Comorbidity, 15, 25, 29, 32, 42, 52, 73, 125
Complement, 125
Complementary and alternative medicine, 69, 75, 125
Complementary medicine, 69, 125
Complete remission, 125, 141
Computational Biology, 103, 125
Conjunctiva, 125, 138, 145
Consciousness, 120, 125, 127, 128
Contraindications, ii, 125
Control group, 22, 34, 126
Controlled clinical trial, 58, 126
Controlled study, 35, 39, 42, 126
Convulsions, 121, 126, 129
Cor, 39, 126
Coronary, 123, 126, 134
Coronary heart disease, 123, 126
Coronary Thrombosis, 126, 134
Cortex, 19, 126, 129, 130, 139
Cortical, 84, 126, 139, 141
Cortices, 5, 126
Corticotropin-Releasing Hormone, 39, 126
Cortisol, 62, 126
Cortisone, 126, 127
Cranial, 84, 123, 126, 127, 130, 131, 145, 146
Craniocerebral Trauma, 127, 131
Criminology, 127, 130
Criterion, 51, 63, 127
Curative, 77, 127, 136, 144

**D**

Data Collection, 5, 127, 130
Databases, Bibliographic, 103, 127
Deamination, 127, 135
Decision Making, 5, 127
Dementia, 84, 121, 127
Dendrites, 127, 136
Density, 37, 127, 137, 142
Dentate Gyrus, 127, 131
Depressive Disorder, 7, 8, 9, 66, 127
Dexamethasone, 33, 39, 127
Dextroamphetamine, 127, 134
Diabetes Mellitus, 84, 128, 131
Diagnostic procedure, 83, 94, 128
Diaphragm, 84, 124, 128, 138
Diathesis, 17, 18, 19, 128
Diencephalon, 128, 132, 139, 144
Digestive system, 82, 128
Direct, iii, 97, 128, 141
Dissociation, 35, 52, 55, 61, 119, 128
Dissociative Disorders, 71, 128
Dopamine, 43, 121, 124, 127, 128, 135, 141
Drive, ii, vi, 10, 65, 128, 132
Drug Interactions, 98, 128
Dysphoric, 127, 128

**E**

Eating Disorders, 22, 54, 70, 84, 95, 128
Efficacy, 4, 5, 10, 12, 13, 16, 18, 20, 49, 50, 80, 128, 145
Ego, 71, 72, 78, 128
Ejaculation, 86, 129, 142
Electroconvulsive Therapy, 42, 129
Electroencephalography, 33, 129
Electrolyte, 129, 142
Electrons, 122, 129, 133, 134, 137
Elementary Particles, 129, 134, 140
Empirical, 11, 40, 88, 91, 129
Endocrine System, 129, 136
Endometrial, 86, 129
Endometrium, 129, 134
Energy balance, 129, 133
Entorhinal Cortex, 129, 132
Environmental Health, 102, 104, 129
Enzyme, 129, 135
Epidemiological, 73, 129
Epinephrine, 119, 128, 129, 136, 145
Esophagus, 128, 129, 138, 143
Estrogen, 86, 129
Ether, 86, 129

Excitability, 16, 130
Expert Testimony, 130
Expiration, 130, 141
Extracellular, 121, 130, 142
Extrapyramidal, 121, 128, 130
**F**
Family Planning, 103, 130
Family Practice, 54, 63, 130
Fat, 119, 126, 130, 133
Fatigue, 86, 130
Fissure, 127, 130, 139
Fluoxetine, 20, 33, 37, 85, 130
Flush, 85, 86, 130
Focus Groups, 10, 130
Forearm, 122, 130
Forensic Psychiatry, 72, 130
Frontal Lobe, 130, 139
**G**
Gallbladder, 119, 128, 130
Gas, 123, 130, 132, 136, 146
Gastrointestinal, 129, 130, 142, 144
Gastrointestinal tract, 130, 142
Gene, 19, 122, 130
Genetics, 6, 38, 130
Glossopharyngeal Nerve, 84, 130
Glucocorticoid, 127, 131
Glucose, 128, 131
Glucose Intolerance, 128, 131
Governing Board, 131, 138
Growth, 5, 119, 120, 131, 145
**H**
Habitual, 124, 131
Halogens, 86, 131
Headache, 25, 131, 139
Headache Disorders, 131
Health Services, 12, 131
Health Status, 60, 131
Heart attack, 123, 131
Hemorrhage, 127, 131, 143
Hemostasis, 131, 142
Heredity, 130, 131
Hippocampus, 44, 127, 131, 133, 143
Homogeneous, 71, 132
Hormone, 126, 129, 132, 133
Hydrogen, 122, 132, 135, 137, 140
Hygienic, 73, 132
Hypertension, 123, 131, 132
Hypertrophy, 126, 132, 145
Hypnotherapy, 73, 132
Hypnotic, 70, 132
Hypoglycemia, 84, 132
Hypothalamic, 15, 39, 132
Hypothalamus, 126, 128, 132, 133, 138
Hysteria, 58, 132
**I**
Id, 67, 74, 108, 109, 114, 116, 129, 132
Impairment, 7, 8, 15, 42, 55, 85, 132, 134
Impulse Control Disorders, 86, 132
In vitro, 132
In vivo, 19, 132
Indicative, 87, 132
Infarction, 126, 132, 134
Ingestion, 130, 132
Initiation, 132, 145
Inotropic, 128, 132
Inpatients, 14, 15, 28, 35, 46, 56, 77, 78, 79, 133
Insight, 17, 133
Insomnia, 84, 133, 139
Interpersonal Relations, 5, 10, 108, 133
Invasive, 133, 134
Involuntary, 84, 133, 135
Ions, 122, 128, 129, 132, 133
**K**
Kb, 102, 133
**L**
Large Intestine, 128, 133, 141
Larynx, 133, 146
Leptin, 57, 133
Lesion, 5, 133
Lethal, 12, 17, 133
Library Services, 114, 133
Life cycle, 56, 133
Ligands, 19, 133
Limbic, 16, 120, 133, 139
Limbic System, 120, 133, 139
Liver, 119, 128, 130, 133, 135
Localized, 133, 135
Lumbar, 9, 133, 134, 143
Lumbar puncture, 9, 134, 143
**M**
Magnetic Resonance Imaging, 37, 134
Magnetic Resonance Spectroscopy, 59, 134
Manic, 121, 122, 134
Manifest, 10, 134
Mastication, 134, 145
Meatus, 134, 146
Mediate, 5, 128, 134
Mediator, 134, 142
MEDLINE, 103, 134
Membrane, 16, 121, 125, 130, 133, 134
Memory, 24, 78, 120, 127, 134
Menstrual Cycle, 134, 139

Menstruation, 120, 134, 139
Mental Disorders, 19, 82, 85, 134, 140
Mental Health, iv, 3, 4, 5, 6, 15, 24, 30, 35, 38, 41, 53, 61, 64, 81, 82, 102, 104, 108, 134, 140
Mental Processes, 128, 134, 140
Metabolite, 19, 134
Methylphenidate, 47, 134
MI, 24, 118, 134
Microbiology, 119, 121, 122, 135
Molecular, 6, 103, 105, 122, 125, 127, 135, 141
Molecule, 122, 125, 128, 135, 137, 141
Monoamine, 44, 127, 135, 145
Monoamine Oxidase, 44, 127, 135, 145
Mood Disorders, 57, 135
Morphine, 123, 135
Motility, 135, 142
Motor nerve, 135, 138
Multiple Personality Disorder, 55, 56, 135
Multivalent, 131, 135
Mutilation, 5, 20, 26, 29, 44, 55, 61, 62, 73, 94, 135
Myocardium, 134, 135

**N**

Naloxone, 13, 135
Narcolepsy, 127, 134, 135
Nasopharynx, 131, 135
Nausea, 121, 135, 139
NCI, 1, 82, 101, 135
Necrosis, 132, 134, 135
Need, 14, 27, 90, 95, 110, 136, 144
Nerve, 84, 119, 124, 127, 130, 134, 135, 136, 137, 138, 143, 145, 146
Nervous System, 119, 123, 124, 134, 136, 144, 145
Neural, 5, 17, 47, 119, 135, 136
Neuroendocrine, 45, 48, 136
Neuroleptic, 121, 124, 136
Neuronal, 16, 136
Neurons, 16, 19, 127, 136
Neuropeptide, 126, 136
Neuropharmacology, 6, 136
Neurosis, 136, 138
Niacin, 136, 145
Nitrogen, 86, 120, 136, 145
Nonverbal Communication, 136, 140
Norepinephrine, 119, 128, 136
Nuclei, 120, 129, 133, 134, 136, 140
Nucleic acid, 136
Nucleus, 129, 137, 139, 140
Nursing Care, 41, 53, 137
Nursing Staff, 39, 137

**O**

Opacity, 127, 137
Orgasm, 129, 137
Outpatient, 6, 23, 78, 137
Ovum, 133, 137
Oxidation, 131, 137
Oxygen Consumption, 137, 141

**P**

Palate, 131, 135, 137
Palliative, 137, 144
Pancreas, 119, 128, 137
Pancreatic, 84, 137
Parietal, 60, 137
Parietal Lobe, 60, 137
Parotid, 131, 137
Paroxetine, 27, 137
Partial remission, 137, 141
Partnership Practice, 137, 139
Penis, 129, 137
Peptide, 133, 137, 139
Perception, 15, 51, 138
Pharmacologic, 138, 145
Pharmacotherapy, 6, 26, 51, 66, 91, 138
Pharynx, 135, 138, 146
Phobia, 86, 138
Phobic Disorders, 138
Phrenic Nerve, 84, 138
Physiologic, 120, 134, 138, 141
Physostigmine, 30, 138
Pilot study, 32, 48, 50, 53, 56, 61, 66, 71, 72, 138
Pituitary Gland, 126, 138
Post partum, 85, 86, 138
Posterior, 120, 123, 131, 137, 138
Post-traumatic, 6, 41, 60, 70, 71, 86, 131, 138
Post-traumatic stress disorder, 41, 70, 86, 138
Practicability, 138, 145
Practice Guidelines, 28, 52, 59, 104, 108, 138
Preceptorship, 6, 139
Precursor, 128, 136, 139, 145
Prefrontal Cortex, 5, 19, 139
Premenstrual, 85, 86, 139
Premenstrual Syndrome, 85, 86, 139
Prevalence, 10, 14, 15, 139
Private Practice, 24, 139
Prognostic factor, 139, 144
Progression, 120, 139
Progressive, 127, 131, 135, 139

Projection, 136, 139
Prophylaxis, 73, 139
Prospective study, 15, 18, 35, 139
Prosthesis, 84, 139
Protein S, 122, 139
Proteins, 125, 135, 136, 137, 139, 141, 145
Protocol, 7, 13, 139
Protons, 132, 134, 140
Proxy, 19, 140
Psychic, 136, 140, 141
Psychoacoustic, 69, 140
Psychoanalytic Therapy, 50, 140
Psychomotor, 123, 136, 140
Psychopathology, 11, 13, 17, 20, 32, 51, 53, 58, 60, 140
Psychophysics, 140
Psychotherapy, 5, 20, 28, 29, 42, 50, 51, 53, 71, 72, 73, 88, 89, 91, 92, 140
Psychotropic, 4, 13, 140
Public Health, 10, 12, 14, 16, 104, 140
Public Policy, 103, 140
Pulmonary, 122, 126, 140, 146
Pulmonary Artery, 122, 140, 146
Pulmonary hypertension, 126, 140
Punishment, 95, 140

**R**

Randomized, 4, 10, 13, 18, 20, 33, 58, 128, 140
Randomized clinical trial, 13, 140
Rape, 138, 141
Receptor, 19, 43, 66, 119, 124, 128, 141, 142
Receptors, Serotonin, 141, 142
Rectum, 121, 123, 128, 130, 133, 141
Recurrence, 15, 17, 122, 141
Refer, 1, 85, 125, 136, 141
Reflective, 5, 141
Refraction, 141, 143
Regimen, 128, 138, 141
Remission, 15, 21, 122, 141
Respiration, 12, 84, 121, 123, 141
Retrospective, 11, 141
Risk factor, 15, 17, 19, 27, 30, 56, 139, 141
Risperidone, 56, 62, 141
Rod, 124, 141

**S**

Salivary, 128, 141
Salivary glands, 128, 141
Schizoid, 63, 141
Schizophrenia, 6, 18, 19, 39, 42, 55, 84, 129, 141
Screening, 124, 141, 145
Sediment, 141, 146
Seizures, 84, 123, 141
Self-Injurious Behavior, 12, 20, 46, 71, 141
Semen, 129, 142
Serotonin, 16, 19, 20, 48, 85, 86, 121, 124, 130, 135, 137, 138, 141, 142, 145
Sex Characteristics, 119, 142
Shame, 13, 142
Shock, 142, 145
Side effect, 97, 119, 121, 142, 145
Signs and Symptoms, 26, 141, 142
Skeletal, 124, 142
Sleep apnea, 84, 142
Social Behavior, 62, 142
Social Support, 17, 142
Sodium, 22, 32, 61, 66, 142
Soma, 142
Somatic, 4, 119, 130, 132, 133, 139, 142, 146
Sound wave, 141, 142
Spasticity, 84, 142
Specialist, 109, 143
Species, 16, 129, 142, 143, 146
Specificity, 26, 119, 143
Spectrum, 32, 58, 143
Spinal cord, 121, 123, 124, 136, 143
Spinal tap, 134, 143
Steel, 124, 143
Steroid, 126, 143
Stimulant, 127, 134, 143
Stimulus, 128, 138, 140, 143, 144
Stomach, 119, 128, 129, 130, 132, 135, 138, 143
Stress, 6, 9, 15, 17, 18, 19, 22, 40, 42, 55, 60, 66, 108, 123, 126, 135, 143
Stroke, 5, 82, 102, 123, 143
Subarachnoid, 131, 143
Subclinical, 141, 143
Subiculum, 131, 143
Subspecies, 143
Substance P, 134, 144
Superego, 129, 144
Suppression, 33, 78, 144
Survival Analysis, 16, 144
Sympathomimetic, 127, 128, 129, 136, 144, 145
Symptomatic, 4, 33, 144
Symptomatology, 25, 144
Systemic, 98, 122, 129, 144, 145

**T**

Temperament, 15, 25, 59, 144
Temporal, 120, 131, 134, 144
Temporal Lobe, 120, 144
Thalamus, 128, 133, 139, 144

Therapeutics, 98, 135, 144
Thermal, 128, 144
Thoracic, 128, 144
Thorax, 133, 144, 146
Threshold, 130, 132, 144
Thrombosis, 139, 143, 144
Tissue, 84, 119, 122, 129, 133, 134, 135, 136, 137, 138, 141, 142, 143, 144
Tolerance, 123, 131, 144
Tomography, 51, 134, 145
Tooth Preparation, 119, 145
Toxic, iv, 145
Toxicity, 128, 138, 145
Toxicology, 104, 145
Traction, 124, 145
Transcription Factors, 19, 145
Transfection, 122, 145
Transmitter, 121, 128, 134, 136, 145
Trauma, 9, 34, 88, 136, 145
Treatment Outcome, 7, 145
Tricuspid Atresia, 126, 145
Trigeminal, 84, 145
Tryptophan, 66, 142, 145
Tyramine, 135, 145
Tyrosine, 128, 145

**U**

Unconscious, 132, 140, 145
Urethra, 137, 145, 146
Urinalysis, 12, 145
Urine, 62, 122, 145, 146
Uterus, 124, 129, 134, 146

**V**

Vaccine, 139, 146
Vagus Nerve, 84, 146
Vasodilatation, 123, 146
Vasodilator, 128, 146
VE, 52, 62, 71, 146
Venous, 139, 145, 146
Ventral, 19, 132, 146
Ventricle, 120, 121, 126, 131, 132, 140, 144, 145, 146
Ventricular, 126, 145, 146
Veterinary Medicine, 103, 146
Viscera, 142, 146
Visceral, 130, 133, 146
Visceral Afferents, 130, 146
Vivo, 20, 146
Volition, 133, 146

**W**

War, 138, 146

**X**

Xenograft, 120, 146

Printed in the United States
58004LVS00005B/16

9 780597 837692